Lurking

# Lurking

## HOW A PERSON BECAME A USER

Joanne McNeil

MCD
Farrar, Straus and Giroux
New York

MCD
Farrar, Straus and Giroux
120 Broadway, New York 10271


Printed in the United States of America
First edition, 2020

Library of Congress Cataloging-in-Publication Data
Names: McNeil, Joanne, author.
Title: Lurking : how a person became a user / Joanne McNeil.
Description: First edition. | New York : MCD, Farrar, Straus and Giroux, 2019. | Includes bibliographical references.
Identifiers: LCCN 2019036423 | ISBN 9780374194338 (hardback)
Subjects: LCSH: McNeil, Joanne. | Internet users—Psychology. | Internet—Social aspects.
Classification: LCC HM851 .M3965 2019 | DDC 004.67/8—dc23
LC record available at https://lccn.loc.gov/2019036423

Designed by Richard Oriolo



1 2 3 4 5 6 7 8 9 10

# CONTENTS


| | | |
|---|---|---|
| | Introduction | 3 |
| 1 | Search | 11 |
| 2 | Anonymity | 39 |
| 3 | Visibility | 81 |
| 4 | Sharing | 113 |
| 5 | Clash | 151 |
| 6 | Community | 187 |
| 7 | Accountability | 223 |
| | Closing: End User | 253 |
| | NOTES | 259 |
| | ACKNOWLEDGMENTS | 291 |

# Lurking

# Introduction

Someone else's boarding pass fluttered out of a book that I picked up secondhand. Printed on the strip of paper was information for an Alaska Airlines frequent flier. I needed a bookmark, so I held on to it. Each time I returned to my reading, I would see the seat number, boarding time at 5:00 a.m., and unfamiliar woman's name. I recognized "SEA" as Seattle, but "PVR" was new to me. So I looked it up. Puerto Vallarta. How nice.

Reading the book, sometimes my mind would wander to the life of this woman leaving before daybreak for what had to be a vacation. Maybe it was the cheapest option on Kayak;

why else would she get up that early? Or maybe she's an early-riser athlete or works a graveyard shift. Eventually my curiosity got the best of me and I looked her up on Twitter. I didn't say hi or scroll her timeline too deep. My own idea of a nightmare is a rando tweeting at me, "Hey, I got that book you traded in. Nice to e-meet ya!" Someone might find such an exchange amusing, but it strikes me as boundary-crossing. Even what I could see, outside her knowing, felt out of bounds. I couldn't bring myself to click through her archive to see how that vacation went. It struck me as privacy I should honor as an internet stranger. It was not for me to riffle through her life online and attempt to construct a narrative. I was contented just to make this odd one-sided connection. I tossed the boarding pass away when I finished the book.

Anyway, now I know the origins of this used paperback. That's lurking.

I don't mean lurking as an act of reconnaissance, eavesdropping, or something sneaky. It is simply that by nature of having this internet, people are so immediate and present—even absolute strangers. Connecting people is one of the things the internet can do. Internet users—like me, probably you—connect to people we like, people we do not like, people we know, people we do not know, friends, family, workmates, any kind of acquaintance, really. We are even connected to non-person human-mimicking human conglomerates, like bots posting in Markov text, mishmashing a corpus of the words of hundreds, even thousands of actual humans. We can engage with people outside the rule-bound linear progression of offline relationships, and discover information about another person, miles and years from the person they were when they posted it. Try responding to a post on a message board dated a while ago, maybe ten years or more. That person might have lived in five cities between then and now, and fallen in and out of love three times, but the person they once were remains a notional snapshot trace, as if it were yesterday, offering thoughts on gardens, allergies, movies, or recipe ingredients.

Lurking can be a waiting room before communication, in brief delay like the brutal clang of an old dial-up modem sound, a moment to pause and prepare oneself for an exchange with others, to get one's feet wet before plunging into the network and its encasement and amplification of identity. Or it could be an act like reading, for work or research or general curiosity. From the beginning, on that guileless but no less thorny internet, lurking was understood as a custom. Perhaps no one ever signed your GeoCities page guestbook, responded to your comment on a BBS, or left a comment on your blog, but you could never be sure the words were for nothing, read by no one—no one could feel totally alone. Perhaps someone was watching: lurkers, warm and indirect, good people, potential friends, even—not creeps, but maybe a little bit weird.

Metaphors get clunky when we talk about the internet because there is much stuff—forms (images, text, videos, audio, maps) and content (advertising, rumors, job listings, advertising, opinions, ideas, facts, advertising, faces, jokes, advertising, lies, pictures of dogs, advertising, pictures of babies, anything)—and it feels like every user inherits a job, an unpaid library science gig, just for having to think about classifications and representation, the epistemic meaning of data and the written word and images. Identity becomes scraps of enterprise, content and dis-content, an unceasing whirl of desiderata and refuse. Anything personally targeted while impersonal is directionless, but those are the results of this exchange. Some data is "shared," some is taken, the harvest is shaken together in a sillage of algorithmic modeling, floating around, predicting and approximating, while never quite defining the user in the middle of it all.

"User" is a particular status, activity, and state of being, but the word is hated by some. Don Norman, who coined "UX"—user experience—said in 2008, "One of the horrible words we use is 'users.' I am on a crusade to get rid of the word 'users.' I would prefer to call them 'people.'" But the word "people," as the artist Olia Lialina responded in her essay, "Turing Complete User," hides the "existence of two classes of people—developers and users." It is not a mellifluous word or elegant, but "user" is, uh, useful. Developers scripted these mazes, these interfaces, which users *use* to communicate and keep in touch. There are humans on the outside and humans on the inside; the platforms created by and used by humans outline and define identities, boxing users in, while tendering new methods of expression.

Despite the obvious power imbalance, users—rather than developers—are often scapegoated as the internet at its worst. Over the relatively short period of time that the internet has existed, users have been cast as narcissists, if not the cause of the downfall of civilization, as the media spotlights bad actors as representative of the internet populace, eliding the quagmire of company policies that foment abuses and calcify hatred. "Engagement" is the inscrutable basis over which these companies present themselves as commonweal rather than mercenary: these companies—the platforms—show commitment to advertisers before users, while expressing otherwise in corporate communications.

"I am a human being, not an algorithm," Kristy Milland, an Amazon Mechanical Turk worker, once wrote in an email to jeff@amazon.com, describing how she relies on MTurk income to keep her "family safe from foreclosure," and wishes to be seen on the platform as a "highly skilled laborer," rather than hidden from requesters like lines of code. She wasn't speaking as a user, but as a laborer. But even users can be conscripted to these platforms just the same, subject to the whims of Silicon Valley mega-corporations as if they were exploited workers or dispirited constituents. Google has its users perform free micro-labor when they solve reCAPTCHA puzzles—ostensibly to keep bots from accessing websites, but in practice, a distributed system of cleaning various machine-learning corpuses. Many of us must maintain online identities with major platforms to stay employed or up-to-date with community functions like church groups and school committees. Consequently, these companies have unassailable leverage over users, to influence and frustrate behaviors, relationships, communities, and identities.

Those who are human beings, not algorithms, have quiet corners, too, the places to lurk or hide somehow, and that's what interests me. The focus of this book is identity, which is why Amazon and Apple, titans in scale and influence, do not figure in as heavily as the other major tech companies. Right now neither plays third wheel in online relationships and neither has much stake in venues of self-presentation. Although it is amusing to read things like Stewart Brand's review of *From Counterculture to Cyberculture* ("As the guy in the subtitle, I might be expected to have all kinds of eye-rolling cavils with [Fred] Turner's book, but I don't") or MacKenzie Bezos's one-star review of *The Everything Store: Jeff Bezos and the Age of Amazon* ("Jeff didn't read Remains of the Day until a year after he started Amazon"), as of now, Amazon is primarily a retailer and not a social site. Its issues of labor exploitation, monopolistic practices, surveillance, and control relate to the domain of private infrastructure and merchandising. Apple, similarly, is a business with customers. The role of consumer or worker has a modern edge, but usership is even less defined—what is traded, and the cost of it, is hard to see.

Like Tron, from the 1982 film, I "fight for the users," but that's not all this book is about. Community on the internet once seemed like the future, and now there is a past. The following chapters cover the shift to contemporary internet communication habits and culture starting with the launch of the World Wide Web. Part of the appeal, in the beginning, was the opportunity to disguise an identity, to hide under usernames—and with no face in photographs, your language was your avatar. Later, the internet transitioned away from anonymity toward online environments that demand authenticity, even if there are just as many lies. I write this as a longtime participant. Over the course of this shift, I grew circumspect. Once I spoke freely and shared my dreams with strangers. Then the real world fastened itself to my digital life. My name is attached to most of my online activity, so my form on the internet is shaped more like a shadow than a vapor. My idle youth online largely—thankfully—evaporated in the sun, but more recent-ish old posts breeze along, colliding with and confusing new images of myself that I try to construct. If I wanted to give up on the internet, or if I even could, I would have to leave the data—the comments, my connections—every single social site holds over me as collateral for my presence.

The story of the internet is not a tale of sanctuary taken for granted and trod on. The internet was never peaceful, never fair, never good, but early on it was benign, and use of it was more imaginative, less common, and less obligatory. Blight always lurked beneath the internet's enchantments, and beside the chaos is wonder. It is an ether that fills the abyss of time and loneliness. It is a venue for curiosity and longing. Life online is powered by traits and conditions in opposition: anonymity and visibility, privacy and transparency, real and fake, centralized and decentralized, physical and digital, friend and stranger, autonomy and constraint, with an operational clash of values between human ambiguity and machine explicitness. Humanity is the spice, the substrate, that machines cannot replicate. At its worst and at its best, the internet extracts humanity from users and serves it back to other users.

# Search

Among my earliest memories is an unknown commercial, some weird, solemn vignette that I watched on TV. I was four years old when I saw it, or not much older. The name of the state where I grew up was tricky to say and it always captured my attention. "Come to Massachusetts," said the woman in the commercial. A little girl repeated the sentence after her. "Now that spring is here," the woman continued. "Now that spring is here," the child echoed again. "Help us celebrate the New Year," the child said alone, with no guidance. The words were inviting, but the voices were chilling and still. The woman and child never appeared on-screen. They were spectral voiceovers layered over footage of a gray river . . . I think. Who were they to each other: Teacher and student? Mother and daughter? Who were they to me? This memory has been corrupted over time and I could be misremembering any or all of it. Each time I revisit it is another laundry cycle with bleach. The other details I remember with even less confidence. Trees, I think. Swans, maybe? As I recall, there was a variegated taupe glare to the picture. It was, after all, a low-budget video production from the 1980s projected on a 1980s TV screen. I think there was a drawing of the swans—or geese—something birdlike and long-necked in a child's scrawl with crayon. I don't know what the commercial was selling. A credit union? A cult? In retrospect, I wonder if it was a state tourism initiative.

Come to Massachusetts . . . for what? I was already there. Now I remember those words and haunting voices when I drive around the state's south shore in the spring. They have been ricocheting around in my head for more than thirty years. That little jingle-like memory comes to mind, like "Up in the air, Junior Birdman" or "Miss Mary Mack" or "Do you like butter?" at the sight of buttercups. I remember that little rhyme to myself, while I have no confidence in it. Maybe I dreamed it up. I have no evidence of it.

I spent last spring in Massachusetts and I heard the lines in my head again. I tried to get to the bottom of this memory again. I turned to Google to deliver either the memory or an origami unicorn in its place. I fed the search engine variations of the words "Come to Massachusetts," as I have done many times before. Every year there is more of what I don't want:

more TripAdvisor posts, more Eventbrite pages, or headlines related to the 2013 marathon bombing or the failed Olympics bid. I zoomed out and searched in more general terms. "Mass tourism commercial 80s" brought me to YouTube clips with kids in polo shirts on old ships, Ted Danson leaving a bar on a soundstage, and a giant plate of lobster served to Marvin Hagler. This was someone else's childhood memory that could be confirmed with a search string.

I want to pin the memory down like a rare moth. File it away and forget. I feel driven to categorize it and give it a name. Maybe one link, someday, will lead me to an archive with specifics about the "Come to Massachusetts" campaign, directed by such-and-such, airing on this broadcast affiliate from launch date through end date. But what use is unquestionableness for something so insignificant? I can't go back there. It is over. It means nothing to my life today. Why does this sensation feel unnatural to me rather than an ordinary longing that humans have experienced through the ages? Most childhood memories have that lens flare of unknowing. The gossamer remoteness of an undefined memory—mine, while totally unfamiliar—exists outside the illusion of order and the vastness of information online. The internet has groomed me to expect that all of culture is indexable and classifiable. In the absence of metadata, I feel a deeper loss and disconnect.

Most other culture I remember from when I was a kid I can instantly retrieve. While my childhood was largely predigital, TV segments and commercials and holiday specials, just as I remembered, have been uploaded to the cloud by other internet users over the past decade. Before it became arcane history, the content would have been enclosed in a plastic black brick with a Polaroid rainbow spine and Sharpie notes on the label lined up on a shelf of equal-size black bricks in someone's den. Now, as files, these clips swim around with the rest of the miscellany on YouTube for users to stumble on in moments of wistfulness and self-reflection. Search, as in turn to a search engine, has become part of my rote process of remembering things. I think of a search string to enter as soon as vague memories come to mind, even if I don't care much to see. I am pinning down moths like a job. Google and YouTube—sometimes eBay, for the old toys, now collectibles—rarely fail me. I don't need to touch what I'm thinking of, but someone else's blurry cell phone snapshot is enough to confirm the reality of it.

Search for something (knowledge, addresses, answers, acceptance, belonging, entertainment, labor, love, whatever) drives the internet. It is why a user opens a laptop or checks a mobile screen. A search string is a key. It unlocks information. The door that opens is a rupture in time. Search is revealing. There is the utter despair, resignation, neediness, and ego that blend together when I google my name at 2:00 a.m. on a Friday night. No one might be surveilling me, per se, in one-to-one Stasi-style peephole intimacy, but *I know* when I do this pathetic thing. And search is affirming. What else offers such minor yet instant and reliable delight as an image search for "afghan hound swimming" or "peacock in flight" or "monica vitti as modesty blaise"? Search is endless because nothing on earth, certainly not Google, contains all the answers. And search is often Google. The company is the intermediary between my ideas and action forward, the glue between my questions and answers, a placeholder for thoughts and a way to sort my desires.

Here is an experiment: type the words "I am 60 and . . ." in a Google search box to see the autocomplete results comprising aggregate previous searches. "I am 60 and alone" is often the first result. "I am 60 and I need a job" is another. "I am 60 and I have no friends" follows that. Now try "I am 65." The first suggested search might be "I am 65 how long will I live." These are people, personal stories, individual lives. They might be reaching out to find others under similar stress and circumstance, looking for compassion—blind and anonymous—or consolation, some odd wisdom, or anything at all. I click on "I am 60 and alone." This search string brings me to several message boards, where people offer advice and commiseration. Try this search experiment for any year. See the wishes people tossed in the well. When I search for my age, I get results on children and marriage. The autocomplete for "I am 15 and" brings up "i have never been kissed" and "i want a job." But even "I am 70 and" delivers unexpected results like "I am 70 and a virgin." It is common to feel stigmatized or ashamed for asking questions or wanting things, but the internet offers an illusion of the eyes and ears of no one, not even a priest behind the curtain, just you and the network. Maybe Google hasn't got the answers, maybe it cannot parse the relevance of your request, but it does something; it has a purpose, it fields your request, it follows commands.

Strange anonymous requests didn't start with Google or the internet. The New York Public Library has an archive of similar questions that librarians have fielded over the years.

“I went to a New Year’s Eve Party and unexpectedly stayed over. I don’t really know the hosts. Ought I to send a thank-you note?” reads one of the cards, noted as a telephone call from a “somewhat uncertain female voice” on New Year’s Day 1967. “How many neurotic people in U.S.?” someone asked in 1946. These anonymous callers knew who they were calling—a librarian—but internet search alienates the questioner from an answerer. This estrangement, coupled with the ease of typing, widens the possibility of make-believe in the form of a question.

Search strings used to be phrased like ingredients:

revolution AND french OR russian NOT american
physics AND aviation NOT aerospace

You don’t need coding experience to recognize that this query language is styled like computational methods. In retrospect, Boolean search strings look like the liberal use of #hashtags #for #emotional #emphasis by today’s social media influencers. When I search for information now, I feel like I should add “please” and “thank you” to every request. There is no way around it, talking to the Google search bar like a human generates more relevant results. To home in on the information sought, a user might type “how do i download a printer driver for mac” rather than “download printer driver mac,” or “why is the capital of ohio columbus” rather than “ohio capital columbus.” Sorry to bother you, but please, Google, tell me, why is the capital of Ohio Columbus? When you’ve got a minute, let me know. Search strings that resemble sentences, with hows and whys and whos and mentions of "I" or "my," muddle how the person typing the information isn't representing their personal experience in each request. Someone who types "I am 70 and a virgin" hasn't necessarily given Google an autobiography in brief. A user searching "stages of pancreatic cancer" might not mean "(I am experiencing) stages of pancreatic cancer" but rather, "(my nephew is experiencing) stages of pancreatic cancer" or "(this fictional character in my screenplay is experiencing) stages of pancreatic cancer" or "(I am researching) stages of pancreatic cancer." This is why I can only side-eye data science researchers who wish to declare one state is more queer than another or more gullible to conspiracy theories than the other, based on unreliable data like Google Trends. Who can say for certain why other people google what they do? A search engine is no truth serum. It is distilled curiosity, which has no borders and is, by definition, undefined. Real people search, but real desire cannot be identified. Words, on a page or screen, should never be interpreted as a perfect Xerox of a person's mind (or else this sentence might have come out as poetic and profound as I intended).

People used to talk about the internet as a place. The information superhighway. A frontier. The internet was something to get on. Even the desktop metaphor was in turn clarifying, then confusing: it helped people understand how a personal computer organizes information, while it invited a user to think of the experience as three-dimensional and spatial. Now people talk about the internet as something to talk to; it is a someone. Even casually, people discuss the internet—insentient, dumb—as living, real. A friend or a foe. Something with eyes. Perhaps you have consulted "Doctor Google" about cold symptoms. Come up with a clever pun and a friend might encourage you to "tell the internet." Bloggers post open letters entitled "Dear internet." Headlines like WHAT THE INTERNET THINKS OF THIS WEEK'S BLOCKBUSTER MOVIE or THE INTERNET LOVES ALPACAS discuss collective reactions on social media platforms as if they were the opinions of an individual person. Kate Bush, as ever, was there first ("I turn to my computer . . . like a friend"). This metaphor reveals how emotionally present and invested people feel when they use the internet. A familiar but mysterious companion, the internet is seductive, idiosyncratic, unreliable, and contradictory, while it is also at your service and by your side. But when anthropomorphized, diverse and divergent communities of users are reduced to a single identity.

The personification of the internet was always there for the taking ("Hello world"), but it took users more than a decade of search and social media to activate it. Over the years, the internet was further populated with archives, texts written by humans in blogs and video clips and essays and other media. People who talk about the internet as a person are not totally wrong. We might think of the personified "Internet" as the macrocosm of all internet users. It is the Voltron of all the family photos, diary entries, jokes, hotel reviews, support group message boards, and VHS-ripped detritus of everyone who ever lived a digital life. We are who we are looking for. A request like "I am 60 and alone . . ." is not to nobody, and it is not to Google, either. The results are ours, that humanity is ours. Google commodified the act of finding it inside one another.

Before Google, I searched with HotBot, and before that, I didn't really use "search." I clicked around. I hopped from lily pad to lily pad. The corpus was limited. A user had to dig for information rather than ask for it, politely ("please, Siri") or not. What we call "search" these days is more of a demand than a struggle to find out what. "Give me this" rather than "where is this?" Perhaps a fruitless search, like that old commercial I'll never confirm, is the only real search. That is why it is especially frustrating when Siri and Alexa retrieve the wrong information. Users of voice-activated services have off-loaded the final decision of any search—is this trash or treasure?—to the machine.

There were only 2,738 websites in 1994 and about ten times as many the following year. By 1996, the number of websites shot up to 257,601, and by 1997 there were more than a million. That number doubled in 1998 (the year that Google launched). Then it ballooned to seventeen million websites in 2000, which was the year of the dot-com crash. The total continued to climb as broadband expanded through the following decade. I got these numbers from the Internet Live Stats project, which charts this growth in comparison to internet users. In 1995, there were 9,297 users for every website. That number plummeted dramatically and then gradually. In 2001, there were seventeen users for every website, and by 2010 there were ten. Now it hovers around three people per page. It is all lily pads now. I wonder who is paying all the hosting fees. Limited content made for common reading, which is why many of the people who were online in 1995 remember the same websites, like *Salon* and *Suck* magazines. A textbook publisher put out a yearly directory called the *The Internet Yellow Pages*, a bright door-stopper of a volume like the phone books for commercial numbers. Users consulted paper to find something on a screen. Most of the first websites I visited, I found out about in alt-weeklies and magazines. The internet was a place back then, not yet a person, so those guides were like AAA TripTiks.

Google created demand for internet search as we now experience it. There were plenty of search engines in 1998—Excite, Lycos, AltaVista, WebCrawler, Yahoo, HotBot, Infoseek, Inktomi, Snap, Direct Hit, Magellan, Ask Jeeves—and none had an obvious revenue stream. The major players, like Lycos and Yahoo, sorted topics in directories with trees of categories (art, sports, news, local), which was helpful for users who logged on and found themselves unsure what to click next. These companies aimed to be "portals," in the hope that users would save their URLs as browser home pages, with sidebars including headlines, weather, email, and other features. The portal strategy was to keep users engaged on one company's website: an attempt to convince users that this lily pad was the circumference of the pond. But Google always sent users back swimming. It was not a portal, but a teleportal, a moving walkway to the rest of the internet. Earlier search engines were a perpetual game: What's behind door number two? Results were often irrelevant, increasingly varied as the total number of websites grew. A search for "Museum of Modern Art," executed through HotBot or Excite, might have recommended content like fan pages for the museum created on GeoCities or a picture of a T-shirt with the MoMA logo. But Google used metadata like the text descriptions in a link to organize search results. MoMA's own home page would be ranked highest in search results because there were so many links to that website that included words like "MoMA" or "Museum of Modern Art." The link would also get a boost if a user searched for "art" or "museum," too. The local knowledge of internet users was Google's winning formula. While other search engines crawled through data as data, Google capitalized on the labor of internet users and the small decisions each made while editing their own pages. Users made Google a more intuitive product. Users made Google.

■

The London Science Museum has a digital art installation called *Listening Post.* Bits of text appear in flashing little lights on two hundred smartphone-size screens, while automated voices pipe out from the speakers, amid other evocative sounds. Mark Hansen and Ben Rubin's 2001 installation is a symphony of an anonymous collective body. The found poetry was scraped from the internet. The snippets of text, mysterious and ruminative in brevity, were compiled from newsgroups, chat rooms, and other internet communications. The fleeting words are presented out of context. The effect is hypnotic. The piece conveys the vastness of the internet, the vastness of experience and emotion shared, and how, in turns ghostly and this-worldly, it is to communicate through it. I thought of *Listening Post* when I saw a video taken by someone walking into the lobby of Google's headquarters in Mountain View. There, back in 2006—Google has since taken it down—a screen would broadcast live search results. It conveyed search strings live as these words were typed around the world, including the profane, the mundane, the esoteric, and the familiar; there was no deliberate presentation to it. *Listening Post* brought out the life and lively wonder of the internet, but the search screen at Mountain View was more like a moose head mounted above a fireplace. Your curiosity is Google's query, and they have plenty of queries; you aren't special. The finite nature of the knowledge you seek is set in contrast with the abundance of desires that route through their servers every second of every day. Wishes, dreams, fears, wonderings—the glimmer of ordinary life—are specks in the sandbox that is its search box. The sand turned to gold because they collected enough.

"Google has single-handedly cut into my ability to bullshit," Owen Wilson's character complains in the 2013 fish-out-of-water comedy *The Internship*, in which he and Vince Vaughn maunder into "Noogler"—new Google hire—positions. The overarching punch line of the film is how Silicon Valley redefined what counts as an alpha guy. Wilson and Vaughn might be the prom kings of the Hollywood Hills, but the sky is the limit to Larry Page and Sergey Brin's privilege. Historians of technology love tales of lone geniuses saving the world, and a lasting collaboration such as Page and Brin's is unusual, while at the same time it explains Google's scope. If Sergey Brin is the colored letters in the Google logo, cofounder Larry Page is the blank white background. Sergey Brin, the extroverted, more politically and culturally minded cofounder, often roller-skated through the office and wore those weird toe sneakers. A modest scandal in his love life was reported in *Vanity Fair*. Meanwhile Page tends to let the company speak for him, an unusually subdued public profile in a region full of big personalities and eccentrics. They were Ph.D. students when they started the company, a counterpoint to the stereotype that Silicon Valley is run by college dropouts (there's little stigma about that in the tech industry, where the youth of an entrepreneur is taken as testament that the person wastes no time). Brin and Page were an improvement on virtually every sort of megacorp executive before them. They seem genuinely concerned with climate change, education, and "democracy," but there's a difference between individuals, structures, and collective action. How is it possible to operate a private company at this size ethically?

Company culture is to a company what motivation is to character. It is the personality and drive that come through in products. Google's culture of laid-back efficacy was influential and boundary-breaking. A stereotypical Google employee has perfect SATs, but loves April Fool's Day humor and a weekend with nature. Not all of its engineers are triathletes—some enjoy snowkiting and kayaking, too. There were office ski trips from the very beginning. Google is the summit of the Montessori-to-MIT pipeline, for a person bright and logical who does not think Sergey Brin's toe sneakers are weird. The headquarters in Mountain View has mini-golf and a *T. rex* fossil mold, snacks and Ping-Pong, scooters and climbing walls. Teams can reserve a "conference bike," an octopus-like contraption that seats seven (yes, they conduct meetings on it). There's free food—very good food—with many varieties of cuisine. It is a dream come true to a certain type of worker, and even those who aren't fully on board with these trappings might prefer the decent lunches and refined indoor air quality to anything else out there in officeland. Until recently, this public-facing corporate quirkiness served as cover for a company-wide problem of sexual harassment, bolstered by how lax—even encouraging—it had always been about workplace relationships (Brin, Page, and Eric Schmidt all have, at one time or another, reportedly dated their subordinates). Tens of thousands of employees participated in a walkout in November 2018, following a *New York Times* investigation that revealed numerous abuses of power (among the damning findings: a ninety-million-dollar exit package awarded to an executive who left after an accusation of sexual misconduct by a subordinate). The problem is a thicket, of course, but unlike with some of Google's other ethical impairments, the company has a definite goal: to rid itself of sexual harassment. Actions it has taken in the wake of this scandal, including an end to forced arbitration for sexual harassment claims, appear to serve that goal. But the gumball machine façade that insulated Google from public scrutiny for as long as it has continues to be hard to crack.

The word that almost always comes up when people talk about Google's staff is "brilliance," a specific and subjective interpretation of that word. There's nothing romantic or out of the ordinary about Google "brilliance." There's no poetry to it, nothing tender or exuberant. Valorizing "brilliance" is how Google disguises its employees who come from less privileged backgrounds, economically and educationally. Google has an internal class system legible by the color of worker badges: full-time employees wear white badges, contractors wear red, and interns wear green. Red-badge workers are internally known as TVCs ("temps, vendors, and contractors"), and many of them found work through temp agencies. In 2007, the artist Andrew Norman Wilson, a contractor in the video department at the time, noticed workers wearing yellow badges. They were ScanOps, the division hired for the Google Books project. These workers were there to scan every book, page by page. Every book in existence, or so Google wished the world might think. The employees were visible for reasons other than the yellow badges. They were predominantly "black and Latino, on a campus of mostly white and Asian employees," Wilson wrote in an essay about the ScanOps workers. He also made a short film called *Workers Leaving the Googleplex*. The ScanOps employees began work at four in the morning, and left in the early afternoon so they wouldn't mingle with white-badge employees in the parking lot.

In Silicon Valley, hiring humans (other than triathlete-mathletes) is always less preferable than programming machines to do something. Google cannot eradicate its demand for yellow-badge-tier labor, but it can make these workers invisible. "As long as the data gets collected, that's all that matters," a Google Street View driver once told me. I appreciated his stories about what music he would play in the car, driving around and photographing his surroundings for the map. Once he met up with some of the other drivers at the New York International Auto Show. But all his human experience is erased from how Google Street View presents the images he created. A user browsing Google Street View might assume, very reasonably, that a machine created them. It is photography without a human perspective, but humans, indeed, are the ones who have photographed these panoramas.

Sometimes Street View is an accidental paparazzo: Jean-Luc Godard and Anne-Marie Miéville were stitched in the fabric of Google's panoramas of Rolle, Switzerland. Leonard Cohen, on a lawn chair outside his home, became a frozen landmark in Street View documentation of Los Angeles. The picture was taken shortly before he passed away. There's no way to tell if the driver recognized these public figures. A driver is expected to perform as a robot would under these circumstances. Only rare glimpses, like the reflection of a car in a mirrored skyscraper, remind the user that you are observing another person's experience.

■

A user of Google products might be put off by its chipperness, sympathize with the colored-badge underclass, and believe that its old byword, "Don't Be Evil," was always bunk; but the company's steady dominance over internet infrastructure leaves skeptics with few alternatives. In this bind, Google releases its boggling new ventures. Users, at its launch, complained about ads in Gmail—*it's creepy and feels like a robot is reading my email!*—and Google Street View appeared, at first, as an obvious invasion of privacy, not to mention an act of hubris with an undercurrent of colonization. But a person—a user—can hardly rail against technology forever, when it is widely deployed. It isn't normalization, exactly, but the nature of priorities in a busy life. Public discomfort with Google Glass was enough for the company to jettison its development; but an example like that is rare, not to mention never so extreme that users, en masse, boycotted Google for its missteps. Not that it is easy to give up searching. Because above all, Google is easy. Use became second nature so easily. All you had to do was wonder about something.

In the recent past, Google articulated its purpose, fundamentally, as providing inroads and access to all possible digital representation. It seemed as though the company was at work to make instances like my "Come to Massachusetts" example hover near zero. Google even assumed responsibility for the absence of digital representation. "We're trying to build a virtual mirror of the world at all times," Marissa Mayer, then Google's VP of geographic and local services, said at a conference in 2010. Later that year, Eric Schmidt told Stephen Colbert that we were entering an age in which "everything is available, knowable, and recorded by everyone all the time" (and findable, through his company, of course). These comments were made at a time when internet companies were thought to be quicksilver entities rather than institutions building legacies. "Mirroring the world," while impossible, was coherent with the company's story and execution. After all, Google's most immediate scandals back then related to how well—how invasively well—PageRank worked. Predictive search—the words that appear in autocomplete when a user enters a query—can snitch on someone's past. Because of it, I have turned up the names of people's spouses and ex-spouses and estranged children, which I never intended to find out—these autocompletes indicate what other users googled in sessions before me. What it calls "relevancy" might seem, to an individual, like a personal invasion, with secrets spilled to other users who never even asked to know—information for the sake of providing information.

From 2004 until 2012, Google seemed determined to

create a digital copy of everything. It was scanning all the streets and all the books in the world, or so they wished for you to believe. Google's commitment to information abundance carried over in its resistance to deletion. Gmail had no delete option when it launched in 2004. The button was introduced later. It was a blustery decision, demonstrating at once that Google's spam filters were superior and that the Gmail storage capacity was so generous that users would never have to delete anything. But there was an outlier in Google's "mirror" stage, and in retrospect it signals where Google was always heading: the company launched a service called GOOG-411, "Google Voice Local Search," in 2007, back when most phones in people's pockets were dumb ones. If a user dialed 1-800-GOOG-411 and provided their city and requested business ("Miami," "Thai food delivery"), the service would connect users or send a text, like a more personalized Yellow Pages. It shut down three years later. The point all along was to collect audio samples of many accents and pitches and kinds of voices for artificial intelligence research. The writing was never on the wall for GOOG-411; instead, its true purpose was buried in a lengthy interview *InfoWorld* conducted with Mayer in 2007, around the time of the product launch. "We need to build a great speech-to-text model," she explained. "So we need a lot of people talking, saying things so that we can ultimately train off of that." All the data it indexed and represented, and all the potential for matchmaking, could and would be thrown in the bin when it wasn't necessary. The following decade involved quieter procedures of deactivating services and deleting some of the same archives Google once boasted about acquiring.

Jessamyn West, a librarian and writer in Vermont, told

me that part of the problem is that Google has nothing like a support line. Even Comcast lets you call in—that's not anyone's idea of fun, but you can call and ask a human a question. Comcast has customers. Google has users. If Google users have questions about Google, well, Google wants you *to google*. Google's approach is to give a user tools to find things, which is, as West puts it, the "opposite of what I do." There's no such thing as a library with no librarians. "One of the things that is really important to libraries is the concept of institutional memory," she explained. "It's not just that you've got this building full of information in whatever form it is in, but that you've got human beings who understand the corpus of what's in your buildings, or what's in your collections." Libraries are designed to serve their communities. Someone's ability to use the library is a "factor in whether you are doing a good job as a librarian," West said. "That's not true with Google. They're not answerable to people."

Google, early in its ambition to mirror the world, tried to ingratiate itself to the librarian community, with mixed results. Representatives went to library conferences like the annual gathering of the American Library Association (ALA) with great enthusiasm, eager to partner with groups, and especially to find librarians who might help scan books. In 2006, Google started a blog called *Librarian Center*, complete with the URL google.com/librariancenter. They hired a "Library Partnership Manager," who sent out the "Google Librarian Newsletter," which included a mix of links to news on libraries and its own products like Google Earth. The newsletters were sent less frequently in 2007, and they finally came to a stop in 2009. Later, the Librarian Center page was taken offline, although it is still available to view on the Internet Archive's Wayback Machine. After abandoning the community, Google returned to the ALA Conference in 2012 with convenient corporate amnesia. Google claimed it was a first-time exhibitor. A number of librarians were confused and insulted. "Librarians remember," West said. But so much had changed in the years between Google's ALA debuts, and part of that was the company's influence elsewhere. Google was deliberate about attaching itself to the culture of books and libraries in the aughts, with a fetish for books that "made more sense as a 2004 metaphor," West explained. Now there is more knowledge spread digitally over different formats and platforms, in addition to the information contained in books. An individual might turn to the web before visiting a library to research a subject. With this shift, Google no longer has to associate with "books" and "libraries" to articulate its company mission.

If Google had ever been sincere in its desire to mirror the world, the company's carelessness and lack of standards hindered its execution. In 2014, I was part of a panel discussion organized by the Institute of Contemporary Arts (ICA) in London and hosted remotely over Google Hangouts, as a collaboration between the museum and the Google Art Project. While I was assembling notes for this book, I went back to the video to recall something another panelist had said. I found the video on the website for the ICA, with the familiar black embed rectangle. But when I pressed play, there was a notice on a blank screen that read, "This video is unavailable." I contacted the museum first. A developer, who was new to the position, answered that it was a direct-to-YouTube recording and no separate file was created. The ICA could not access the account, and for whatever reason, someone at Google decided to make this video private. The developer added in his email to me, "I'm sure some internet-savvy guru has said something along the lines of 'the price of instant convenience is perpetual ephemerality'—you definitely need to ask for copies as soon as something is made available, because you can't trust that any given platform will be there tomorrow!" I wrote to a few contacts at the Google Art Project but no one could help. It could be that someone switched jobs and has a new email account, and now there is no one who can log in to update the settings so the YouTube video might be made public once again. I point to this example not just because it is a reminder to back up files (advice we all know, if we don't always have the time to practice it), but also to demonstrate what comes from rapid growth: Google prioritized scaling over the maintenance and continuity of its archive and products.

It can be harder for an individual to "pivot," as they say in Silicon Valley, than a multibillion-dollar company. Here was the hidden implication of the "mirroring the world" stage: Google could replicate information on its own terms, and with no further commitment to maintaining data, any information erased or lost could be interpreted as something the world itself was missing. The company coasted for a while, fostering user trust from its appearance of robustness. Why use products other than Google Docs or Gmail if a start-up's competing offerings are more likely to break down, get hacked, go bankrupt? Why bother uploading videos to any service other than YouTube, where it will be stored on Google servers, which are reasonably secure? Yet Google could make a mistake or shutter one of its products without alerting you.

You—a user—or a school, or an institution, or another body smaller than Google now have habits shaped by Google's influence. The ICA is a museum, which has standards and practices of archiving, collecting, and preserving objects and information. If Google had never had a hand in the event, the video probably would be available today. The consequence of Google's "mirror" stage was that public institutions relaxed certain functions and services that Google tools appeared to provide—and for free.

When Google Street View launched in 2007, I thought of it in terms of Google's ambition to "mirror the world." The audacity of the experiment is what excited me. Street View was beautiful—it wasn't art, but it was wistful, strange, and compelling, similar to the way art stirs the heart of an individual. It made the faraway seem close and the familiar defamiliarized. All the world was piled up as images in this expansive and yet stationary website. A few years later, the project moved indoors, recording the insides of buildings, not just the façades. Google Street View interiors launched with no fanfare. I noticed it myself only by accident, in 2012, when I was looking up a restaurant on Street View. The chevron pointed at its door, and so I clicked on it. Then I could see the bar and the booths, and a crowd of people with blurred faces. The faces troubled me. Street View, on the street, was there to grab data like curbs and landmarks, but when the camera scans inside an establishment, the people are the point. Users might judge what race the clientele tend to be and how they dress (Yuppies? Poor?) and decide if the atmosphere is conducive to their taste. Like Google Books, Street View interiors refused to concede to the adage of judging a book by its cover.

It grabbed the content of the work, and the metadata, with no methodology to parse anything more. These people with the smudged orbs for heads are regarded in these images as no different from doors or furniture. The images are presented to a user as a machine-learning algorithm would interpret them: as categorical, no value differential between a table in the picture or a waitress.

Nowadays, I try to avoid using Street View—inside or out—because it strikes me as created memories for some impossible AI experiment. I already do enough labor for its driverless vehicle research team by clicking on all CAPTCHAs it forces on me. It is a private company with a bottom line to make money off of users, not a public service accountable to constituents. I wonder how often Google strips its archives for parts—like GOOG-411—to use as machine-learning corpuses before burying the data. How about search itself? Are your queries nothing more than raw material to assemble into something else? There are reports that Google will eventually do away with search—do away with "googling." Already, certain functions, like the link search operator (a method to search for websites that link directly to another), are unreliable, if not totally unavailable. The company hopes that you will talk to it like a maid in the kitchen, rather than search with searching instincts. It would like to predict what you want to know with the data it has collected from you and about you.

We have more reason for concern when Google is the standard bearer of navigation systems, the way we sort through information, a common tool in education ("Be Internet Awesome" is the name of one of its programs teaching the "fundamentals of internet citizenship"), and the dominant guide and directions to information we seek. But Google's standards and lens on the world can never perfectly square with user values—it has too many users, too many people. In 2016, the writer Dennis Cooper found that his blog of ten years had disappeared. Blogger, a Google product, posted the default message "Blog has been removed" in its place. Cooper is a queer writer, and he often tagged items on his blog as "adult content." He received no warning or explanation for why his work was gone. Later, he found out that someone inexplicably flagged content on the blog as child abuse. It took over a month to finally recover Cooper's archive, with help from a lawyer, contacts at Google, and public advocacy from organizations like PEN America. This happened to a public figure. A user without Cooper's connections and profile probably would be out of luck. So what about those of us who can't rally similar support? What if our memories and lifework disappear, too? We can back up our files, but this is a time-consuming task that isn't exactly fail-proof. While backing up files is an individual solution, Google's deletion of information is a break in shared knowledge: blog readers looking to reread an old post that has been lost are left with only their faulty memories of it.

Steven Levy's 2011 book *In the Plex* details a baffling exchange with Sergey Brin, who couldn't understand why he was writing a book about the company in the first place. "Why don't you just write some articles?" Brin asked Levy. "Or release this a chapter at a time?" (Mark Zuckerberg had similar antipathy. On his own social network, in its early years, he responded to the profile topic "Favorite Books" with "I don't read.") Brin made similar comments to Ken Auletta, who relayed these quotes in his book *Googled*, published in 2009. "People don't buy books," Brin said to Auletta. "You might make more money if you put it online." Brin must have felt strongly about the uselessness of books, or why would he say this to the two journalists who received extensive access to his company—to write books? Why write books? Why go outside? Why have a family? Love of books isn't something I can argue for on merit, any more than I can find words that come close to capturing the experience of love or how food is delicious. I am similarly bereft of language when it comes to making a case for privacy. I think of books as vessels for conditions, emotions, senses, preferences, history, analysis, and values that cannot come alive in representation alone. This is everything Google never had a handle on, even if the company ever wanted to mirror the world.

Google releases an annual video in December called "The Year in Search." It is a compelling and emotional summary of world events in images, captioned with a search box and representative queries like "how many refugees in the world." But something is always missing from this annual recap, year after year—Google itself. For example, the 2017 "Year in Search" has no mention of the EU's General Data Protection Regulation or James Damore, the former Google employee fired for writing a hostile anti-diversity memo. The video is Google positioning itself as the through line of humanity rather than an acting body and influence. The company desires universally entrenched power and invisibility at once.

Disappearing information is consistent with Google's

mirror metaphor: a mirror reflects only what is within its frame. When he was CEO, Eric Schmidt called multiple search results a "bug." Google "should be able to give you the right answer just once. We should know what you meant." When a YouTube video ends and autoplay selects another, that's Google's attempt at a "right answer." Right now YouTube autoplay is notorious for pushing users toward men's rights and conspiracy theory videos, as the consequence of the trolls who are prominent there and how the platform's predictive algorithms are written. What lies within the mirror frame is itself a distortion. The UCLA professor Safiya Umoja Noble has researched how Google algorithms—written and edited by humans, but presented as a black box—cook in biases, such as how a search term like "black girls" until recently suggested pornography in first-page results. The results may have reflected the search habits of Google users, but the company will modify its algorithms in certain cases, especially following public outcry (as it did after Noble raised this issue). Google also has the power to invent what it does not know. Typos on Google Maps have resulted in new names of neighborhoods. Fiskhorn in Detroit is now known as "Fishkorn." Years ago, Google made this error; now local businesses and published advertising and other services have codified it. Google harvests inquisitiveness: something so fundamental to being human, the act of having a question. It has so firmly embedded itself inside the experience of learning new things that "search"—once a word that meant quest, yearning—is now synonymous with "googling." Google has colonized the act of asking a question as it whittles possible answers and influences which is the "right" one.

The common archive is no stable archive; more than "search" or connection, or even artificial intelligence, Google should be defined by its ceaseless practices of secret deletion and careless disorderliness. In the end, the fun-loving, ski-bum-in-a-ball-pit campus is a fitting image: Google is a burnout, a flake, a layabout. It bails on people.

## 2

# Anonymity

It used to be that all a user had was their words. The most important word was your name. A username assumed the apprehension and ballast of a first impression; it was the skeleton that others on the internet had to start with to assemble a notion of your identity. This name was a term of endearment that you christened yourself. Selected well, a single word might conjure up your humor, interests, spirituality, originality, solitude, beauty, apathy, and dreams. Even someone easygoing and indifferent about it, selecting their given name as a username—LaylaRose, Julian78—communicated something on the information superhighway, amid fellow travelers, self-named in puns and references or the oblique, those who answered to Knocktillucent, Ellen-Ripley85, or ViolaString.

Back then, the term for the internet was earnest and atmospheric: "cyberspace." Now the word is received as a joke—a coinage with limitations, yes, but I find it helpful to differentiate the internet past from what happened next. When William Gibson came up with "cyberspace," as a word and concept for the virtual worlds in his fiction, he wasn't just thinking about the destination through the screen, but the surface where a user's feet touched the ground. The idea came to him as he watched kids in an arcade, "so physically involved," he told *The Paris Review*, that it seemed that "what they wanted was to be inside the games, within the notional space of the machine." Every time I read that Gibson quote, I am transported back to the physical space that was obliterated when I entered cyberspace: the white walls, the tan carpet under my feet, and the cumbersome beige box of a personal computer in front of me. The keys, a sierra of peaks and slopes, felt heavy and pressurized at every click; nothing like the uniform flat buttons I'm tapping as I write this. I shared that computer with the rest of my family. That is where I grew up: immobile and hunched over while resplendent in release, my feet there and my head elsewhere. I arrived in cyberspace in the mid-nineties, a decade after Gibson gave it a name but the perfect time for me. I would enter the password (not challenging—my dog's name, probably, or the name of my elementary school typed backward) and wait patiently through the duration of my electrifying commute. The ding ding bong bong wooosh-woosh dinggg sound trembled through my skin, in discord with my heartbeat, like the rattling of rails and wind against a train cabin. Then I was ready at the landing page to dive in and hide.

■

The first internet message was sent over a packet-switching network in 1969. Two decades later, the launch of the World Wide Web added another gust of excitement. This development was more accessible and customizable than previous online functions. Tim Berners-Lee humbly announced his new "hypertext browser/editor" in several posts to Usenet newsgroups in 1991. "This project is experimental and of course comes without any warranty whatsoever. However, it could start a revolution in information access," he offered. The web is now core to the online experience, and many users mistake it for the internet itself, but the web is *web*sites or *web* pages that a user accesses with a browser (like Chrome or Firefox, or Netscape or Mosaic before). By the way, the word "online" is always a good hedge whenever you are unsure about how a computer is talking to another computer, because it refers to a network, any network—a network can be two computers linked, or a campus network, or the internet broadly. (The "information superhighway" is just as all-encompassing, even if the term is out of fashion these days.) If the internet was a house, the web was a trapdoor opening up to limitless rooms. The web was all that endless potential, but there was potential in the tight quarters of online services and internet products that came before it, too.

Commercial online services, which began in the late seventies, were compartmentalized in the first decade: Quantum

Link users could play games only with other Quantum Link users, and CompuServe users alone could use the CompuServe forums. These companies sold the originality of their content—a sensible enough business model in an era of magazine subscriptions—even if it wasn't always clear to new internet users what GEnie had over The Source, or what made Prodigy any different from PlayNET. A few of the early online services never even connected to the actual internet. There is a material difference between dial-up online services until the late nineties and the internet service providers (ISPs) today, besides the prodigious uptick in speed. The content unique to these companies, like the custom-built forums, chats, and games, was a user's primary destination. Nowadays, if there is any unique content an ISP provides (say, the Comcast home page), a user probably bypasses it, without a second of delay, to connect to the rest of the internet.

Advertising for these online services told a story with a common theme: that of psychic teleportation, the power to travel beyond the borders of the physical world. The invention of the telephone celebrated sound over distance (the magic *was* the distance, two people connected through wires). But online services, early on, conceived of their products as more than objects or communication tools. The language used in these ads seemed to borrow from Emily Dickinson's lyricism about books (a "Frigate . . . To take us Lands away"). The internet was a way to "connect," to meet user-to-user in an abstract territory and transcend physical boundaries, even the boundaries of physical bodies. The metaphor was underscored in company branding, like this slogan for The Source: "It's not hardware. It's not software. But it can take your personal computer anywhere in the world."

Bulletin board systems (BBSs) were another innovation beginning in the late seventies. These services were partitioned and predominantly regional (access to a BBS out of state was possible, if a user could swing the costly long-distance charges). On a BBS there were forums, similar to contemporary online forums, but the emphasis on location shaped the discussion. General community activity on a BBS might be compared to a corkboard in the back of a café, with notices about local matters, even people looking for roommates or trying to sell a bike. Usenet also had a "public broadcasting sensibility," as journalist Katie Hafner put it. Usenet ("users network"), where Berners-Lee posted the now legendary announcement, was established in 1980. The simple interface and nature of community participation was similar to BBS, but Usenet was for the internet public rather than a specific demographic or location. All it took was the right software client to download messages. A user would subscribe to a "newsgroup," categorized with a distinctive naming hierarchy (e.g., alt.gothic.fashion or rec.audio.pro). It was comparable to the World Wide Web as a distribution network, in that there was no rival to Usenet; however, it was moderated at the top level. Anyone can reserve a domain name to set up a website, but newsgroups were created on request, often vetted on Usenet itself through groups like news.groups.proposals and news.announce.newgroups.

America Online launched in 1991, the same year that the World Wide Web opened up to the public. It sprang from the ashes of Quantum Link (Q-Link) in an attempt to mainstream online services. The web and AOL expressed two tendencies at the time: some developers were drawn to the grassroots creative freedom of the internet, while others, like AOL and Prodigy executives, believed that their products could balloon into media empires like Viacom. This is not to say there was an overt rivalry between two factions. It was a period of castle-building rather than competing over scarce territories. The open web offered a diversity of viewpoints, because it was easy to build websites; companies like GeoCities and Tripod made it even easier. But there was some diversity of entertainment and information options inside the walled gardens too, as AOL looked to cable television and magazines for ideas on how to atomize cultures into demographics. AOL offered channels like Netnoir ("the community room for the Afrocentric fellowship"), iGOLF, Health Zone, and Hecklers Online ("It goes the extra mile to be politically incorrect"). The inspirations were MTV, BET, and other cable stations, which sold their specific audiences as target markets for advertisers. Meanwhile, there were outliers that didn't fall neatly inside either camp. Among the most compelling online services to blend creative and commercial service was Echo ("East Coast Hang Out"), which debuted in New York City in 1990.

Echo users, in a daily poll, once answered the question "Why Do You Lurk?" Almost a quarter of them selected "I have nothing to say." Another 16 percent said they were shy, or intimidated, or felt like an outsider. Other responses included "to get the lay of the land," or because they were voyeurs. It is easy to see why some "Echoids," as they called themselves, felt the digital equivalent of tongue-tied. Echo was cool.

In a 1993 *Wired* profile, Echo's founder, Stacy Horn, with her sheer black top and blunt-cut dark bangs, looked ethereal and smart, like the lead singer of a shoegaze band just signed to 4AD. For $19.95 a month, a user had up to thirty hours of access to a community of New Yorkers, many of them artists and writers, and other wits about town. Echo situated the internet within arts and culture rather than the other way around. *The Village Voice* and the Whitney Museum were among its institutional affiliates. The Sci-Fi Channel invited the community to post in a chat superimposed over *The Prisoner*, Patrick McGoohan's cult classic spy series, when it aired at 4:00 a.m. The online service was covered in *The New Yorker* and in the culture section of *The New York Times*, attracting readers of these publications. Echo bartered online service for advertising with the arts quarterly *Bomb*. One of the Echo web ads had the tag line, "When the voices in your head are not enough."

John F. Kennedy, Jr., once carried his bike up five floors to Horn's one-bedroom apartment in the West Village for an in-person computer lesson. He chose the username "flash," which Horn assumed was in reference to cycling. She was too starstruck to ask why he picked it. That day, he browsed Echo discussions on culture and politics while sitting beside her. Horn tried to play it cool, despite a flurry of private messages. Her computer was beeping like a "nest of baby birds" ("That's not really John F. Kennedy, Jr., is it?!" "Tell him he should be studying"). He participated for a short while afterward. Perhaps some users clicked on the profile for "flash," which read, "John Kennedy. I'M an Assistant D A in New YORK city and am also learning to type." Other Echoids might have assumed "flash" was just another user in the city. They were an intergenerational group, with ages ranging from teens to people in their sixties. Contrary to prevalent stereotypes about online users at the time, 40 percent of its subscribers were women (granted, it was, to the dismay of Horn, very white). While conversations were broadly cultural, about all kinds of film, books, and music, community favorites tended to skew toward the cyber-introspective and science fictional, like *Blade Runner* and Neal Stephenson. "Everybody in the early days had at least some part geek to them," Horn told me.

■

Echo was clever and communal in threads, where users were constantly joking, but conversations also accessed a depth of intimacy that Horn compares to "group therapy." Someone might have created a "conference" with a subject like "Tell me about your mother," and scores of responses would accumulate, in great detail, expressing trauma and pain; users would share their stories and sympathy throughout the week. In retrospect, Horn feels that as the founder and key admin, she missed out on a lot. She felt her presence was "like a teacher attending a party the students were having." Plus she had a team to lead: not just staff, but volunteer moderators, called "hosts." Two hosts were assigned to each conference, and in exchange, they received free Echo subscriptions.

Users couldn't explore all of Echo—there were private conferences, too, like the women's conference, which a user could access after requesting an invitation from the host. But the partition between content found on public and private Echo conferences wasn't as strict as an outsider might expect.

Once there was a public conference under the topic "the Menstruation item." There, women on Echo began sharing stories, sometimes graphic stories—commentary on types of tampons and pads, stories about first periods, and recent hassles. Only women contributed, but they weren't alone in the forum. Horn checked to see who was reading it and noticed there were a number of men, just lurking there. Eventually men started—gently, respectfully—asking questions, which the women happily answered. Her description of this exchange reminded me of quietly salutary moments I've witnessed on private listservs and other private online communities. Sometimes the moment is right, and people will talk about awkward matters, because the friction is lifted. A question that could come off as nosy in person might be welcome and even sensitive in text. The remote nature of exchange dissolves typical barriers between people, such as needless stigma or overcorrections in decorum.

Echo was a place for a shared experience, a venue to check in and vent. Members experienced breaking news together, like O. J. Simpson's white Bronco chase. They were simultaneously glued to the conversation on their computer and what unfolded on their televisions; as separate screens, not yet intertwined. People often speculate what 9/11 might have been like if Twitter had been around, but Echoids experienced an approximation of that. It was a New York online service and this was an attack on their turf, in some cases just a short walk from their homes. Stacy Horn could see the fire engorge the sky from her window. Meanwhile, she conversed with other users, who in that moment shared their shock and fear in collective comfort. It is tremendously affecting to read the transcript today, with time stamps, as users parse what little information they have, a mix of what they see outside and hear on TV ("There is a huge fucking hole in the side of the WTC!" posted by just charlene, 11-SEP-01 8:56). Some of the users were worried about friends and family, and others, in that instant, broke down lucidly what the attack meant for that moment and the future: "I had the mistaken idea that it was still early morning (I'm oblivious) but I now realize there must be thousands of people at work in there right now. I can't believe this," wrote an Echoid who went by the username Pez. The exchange went on for hours in a post titled, "Item 245: Breaking News." They were stunned and shaken, but together for one another in that moment.

"Cyberspace," Horn wrote in her book *Cyberville*, is "just a place like any other place. As we realize this, as we become more sophisticated users, it won't be such a big deal anymore. People born in the eighties are probably reading this book and saying: duh." Reading this book, published in 1998, I was struck by her grounded pragmatism about the internet. She was careful to avoid utopian language, and never claimed that computers would democratize anything. The book, with its down-to-earth perspective, offers great insight on what drew people in to Echo. "Being online does satisfy an almost universal homesickness," Horn wrote. "Everybody has a trace of an ache, some eternal disappointment, or longing, that is satisfied, at least for a minute each day, by a familiar group and by a place that will always be there." A number of the stories in *Cyberville* foreshadow online community matters that continue to cause strife; for example, a section on banning users for racist remarks in the forums. "Cyberspace does not have the power to make us anything other than what we already are," she elaborated. "Information doesn't necessarily lead to understanding or change. It is a revealing, not a transforming, medium."

Reading *Cyberville*, I felt envious of Echo's blissful internet experience and engaged community. After all, it was New York City in the nineties, with nineties rent, alt-weeklies in print, a robust independent music scene, and a city only on the cusp of gentrifying. They were hanging out in an era with optimism about global politics: the Iron Curtain had fallen, apartheid ended. Then again, to look at the past with envy and borrowed nostalgia always means discounting the grit of reality. I don't envy those who lost countless loved ones in the AIDS crisis or anyone who lived through the dog-whistle racism of the era and other bigotries. I guess all that outweighs how much I wish I could have been there to comment on *The Prisoner* and see my username on the Sci-Fi Channel at that ungodly hour.

I was curious to learn what kind of person would found a company as idiosyncratic as Echo. So I reached out to Horn with the technology available today. In the spring of 2017, about halfway through reading *Cyberville*, I clicked the follow button on her Twitter profile. She followed me back. I sent her a direct message and we made plans to meet for coffee when I was in New York the following month. She talked about Echo as a natural fusion of her two passions: technology and words. Growing up in the sixties, she remembers being the first on the block with whatever gadget was new, like color television. Her father was an engineer who designed cameras, and her mother helped out with his business. She loved books and wanted to be a writer, a dream she realized after founding Echo (she's published several books, most recently *Damnation Island*, a well-received page-turner history about the bleak origins of Roosevelt Island).

Horn built what she wanted from the internet and held on to it. "Many hundreds" of users still keep in touch, although most of the Echoids chat on Facebook instead of Echo, which, while operational, requires the same computer commands as it did in the beginning. Horn and a few hard-core Echoids jump between Facebook and the conferences, with the same interface that they used in the nineties.

"How would you categorize the community now?" I asked. "Like extended family? Like an alumni network?"

"Like people in a small town who never left," she answered, laughing.

The Echoids, who were once teens to sixty-somethings, are now forty years old to very old. There have been funerals. There have been weddings and children, too. Two people who met on Echo married and had a kid. That kid is now in his twenties. The New-York Historical Society is currently working to archive all public conferences and make the text accessible. Then anyone can lurk on Echo, not because we are shy or intimidated, but because decades divide us in time.

That the Echo community remains close-knit and resilient through decades and platforms owes something to the face-to-face meetings that were vital to the user experience. There were thousands of members on the service in its prime, and almost all of them lived somewhere in the five boroughs. They had regular Monday night get-togethers at Art Bar—moving it to Tuesday temporarily so no one missed *Twin Peaks*—

and they hosted an open mic series called "READ ONLY" at KGB Bar. When it was nice out, the Echoids played softball in Central Park and gathered in Bryant Park for summer film screenings. Or they would stay at home and read about those who did, knowing there was always next time, and the next Echo meetup was only a subway ride away. The forums were anchored in the eventual likelihood of connecting a face to a username—unlike the partially hallucinatory fleeting encounters that made up so much of the rest of cyberspace. Echo's community existed in the friction between the screen and the street, and kindling with its spark was friendship that endured.

After publishing her book, which refers to users only by their usernames, a handful of Echoids accused Horn of "publicly embarrassing" someone in the community. But public to whom? She told a story about how this user acted out, which everyone on Echo already knew. His name wasn't in the book. "I'm not embarrassing him to the greater world," she told them. His identity on Echo was locked inside a system you would need a password and telnet to access, and Echo-specific commands to navigate. There was no Google then, so there was no way to google it. Only Echo users knew who he was, because their usernames had no purchase over the wider world. Echoids were not anonymous, at least in the 1990s sense of the word, as they had to use their real names to sign up for the service, but Echoids had anonymity as a collective, and that was part of their bond.

Echo users were not anonymous to one another, but they had contextual privacy in the community and in the moments they shared. It was possible to get a person's real name on their profile page, connecting the goofball in the comments with a name—the identity of a person who was three-dimensional and real, even if users hadn't met at Art Bar yet. But there were aspects of anonymity even within the community. A name in an Echo profile said only so much. Nowadays, entered in a search engine, names become a through line, the spine between everything a person has said or done that the network can index. A "real name," after Facebook, is emblematic of "one identity," but back when Echo was queen, a name was just a name. There was no way to dig into the internet and find out who a person was, because that data was largely unavailable. There was nothing privacy-slaughtering like Spokeo, which lists a person's address, let alone extortion directories, like mug shot databases. Even the idea of using a search engine to learn more about a random acquaintance, rather than a celebrity, was unlikely to occur to anyone. What would anyone find? Echo users, with their real names accessible to others on the service, had no volley between their online experiences and offline lives, apart from their meetups—meetups they voluntarily attended, which were known only to the Echo community. The friendships and personal connections existed on- and offline, and knowledge of one another remained contextual.

Anonymity is not privacy, although the concepts overlap. The lone figures in a crowd depicted in Edward Hopper paintings are anonymous, because no one knows their names and they are private, because no one notices them. Anonymity is the state of being public but unacknowledged, while privacy refers to protection from intrusion from the public. To write a book anonymously is to avail oneself of the spotlight without impacting the book's distribution. The easiest way to achieve that is writing under a nom de plume. Or, since anonymity is contextual, too, one might use their real name but provide no bio, maintain no social media accounts, and exist as an unknown while hiding nothing. A private book, in contrast, might have an author's name on it, but the audience for it is controlled. That could be a diary, or a text shared with a select group of people in confidence.

Early internet users made a choice to present themselves somewhere on three spectrums: private or public, anonymous or named, factual or make-believe. The extent to which one's identity mimicked real life did not have much bearing on the depth of one's online experience (someone with a username like BradGSmithSeattle79 might have logged in every other week, bored with everything on the screen, while ZuccoThe-Parakeet, who said nothing in chat rooms but "chirp chirp chirp," lived for the internet). Fantasy coupled with a search for belonging meant that online communities opened up new ways for people to be cruel to one another, too. The pain of online harassment was frustrating, leaving users with inchoate torment, because the internet was thought of as a playground noosphere and not real life. Julian Dibbell's classic essay "A Rape in Cyberspace," first published in *The Village Voice* in 1993, told the story of a sexual assault animated in a LambdaMOO game. A user ran a subprogram that attributed text—sort of like stage direction—to other characters in gameplay, including lines that detailed sexual assault. "Posttraumatic tears" were streaming down the face of one of the victims as she called for the community to punish the instigator afterward. These tears were "real-life fact," Dibbell wrote, "that should suffice to prove that the words' emotional content was no mere fiction."

Central to the cyberspace experience was the fleeting nature of content; ephemerality engendered both privacy and anonymity. Users infrequently saved emails and few took screenshots. Information online was treated as if it would wilt and die, eventually. Users changed usernames and deleted posts and pages unconcerned, because cyberspace, in addition to its chimerical possibility, was its own ecstatic surround with no bolts and no belay. There was little culture of continuity, or notion of making history. The conversations people had in forums, chats, and multi-user dungeon games on Q-Link or CompuServe went down the drain with those companies.

The deliquescence of the early internet put a cap on mechanisms for accountability—such as the virtual rapist Dibbell profiled—but it wasn't always a drawback. Truly rotten racist trolls online were free to ruin communities for the rest of the users (we'll get to them in later chapters). However, the scope of their abuse was curtailed by the limits of the services and data available: communicating username to username, your real life remained private—a troll couldn't send nasty emails to your boss or threaten your parents, let alone have a SWAT team dispatched to your front door. If someone knew a user's real name, as they would on Echo, they might check a telephone directory to find a phone number and address (although the phone company allowed people to go "unlisted," a layer of privacy that seems like centuries rather than decades past as a difference in standards and norms). Anonymity, through the fleeting nature of the internet, for users—evil, neutral, and good—was a perpetual freedom to reinvent oneself online. A user could wake up one morning, delete a newsgroup subscription from their Usenet client, and go about the rest of their life never talking to that community again. You couldn't look up old ghosts on Instagram or find them through search engines. These anonymous users walked back into the ether where they came from. And who were the lurkers—the people who never showed up at Art Bar, but were sufficiently entertained just reading about the antics in the forums? They were the ether.

Cyberspace was collectives and communities, like Echo's quirky pockets of activity and inside jokes. That might be why Echo, and the New York art and tech scene more broadly, isn't more widely remembered or honored for its cultural contributions, apart from those who kept the candle burning. Silicon Alley had a thriving downtown subculture, but there was no Jean-Michel Basquiat or Fran Lebowitz or Lou Reed—no legends or legendary work emerged from it. The chat rooms and forums were constant after-parties to an after-party. Parties are merely the atmosphere of a culture, which lifts and fades away. To remember, a culture needs substance: something as a memento, something that can be contained.

Art in cyberspace was nebulous at the edges rather than framed. Institutional recognition wouldn't come for another decade, and with no criteria in place to assess the work, it was a free-form period to develop new standards and customs. Art-ish stuff online existed on a continuum from aesthetic to idle experimentation, like the camgirl/"lifecaster" phenomenon, which was performance art and proto-oversharing all at once. Jennifer Ringley, the most famous among lifecasters, was a nineteen-year-old student in central Pennsylvania when she installed a webcam in her dorm room. This was 1996, only two years after Connectix webcams hit the market. What could you even do with a webcam back then? Take it out and record a few things as an experiment, then stuff it back in a box and forget it until the technology is too antiquated to revisit? Ringley did something different: she left the camera running. She made it part of her everyday life, creating a backup of her very existence. Black-and-white still images updated to her website every three minutes, nonstop.

Ringley once sat on a couch beside late-night talk show host David Letterman and joked, "Now what you can see is my empty apartment." Stacy Horn appeared on *Charlie Rose* explaining Echo. On television, they were ambassadors from the internet, because the internet wasn't a mass shared experience yet. The internet, and those who used it, was still a subculture interest. On television, they presented screen-based activity as novelty. They were akin to zookeeper guests with animals doing tricks, rather than a signal that cyberculture was becoming culture.

"I keep JenniCam alive not because I want to be watched, but because I simply don't mind being watched. It is more than a bit fascinating to me as an experiment," she explained on her website, five years into the project. Her justification was as curious as the project itself. In 1998, Ringley claimed that JenniCam received 100 million page views a week. What was she doing? What did this audience get out of it? Terri Senft, in her book *Camgirls: Celebrity & Community in the Age of So-*

*cial Networks*, details how she got hooked on watching something that to anyone else must have sounded dull:

> I typed the URL and watched a webcammed image of a living room refreshing every few minutes. Jennifer wasn't even home. The whole thing came across as an exercise in deferred gratification, with an endless expectation that something might happen. Waiting for the webcam to display something besides her empty couch, I browsed the JenniCam's archived photos and online journals. The moment I figured out that I could match the date and time stamps on the photos to the journal entries, I was hooked. In viewing the images as a narrative, I was getting an inkling of who Jennifer was, and why she might find it useful to share her life with the world. When she finally did appear, I found myself jumping back and forth between her new webcammed images and the archived images and journals.

JenniCam, both Ringley and the people watching her, were alone in company. Hundreds of similar cam-sites emerged, most of them run by young women. On these sites, the camgirl would act as a host, inviting guests to communicate on forums and in chat rooms. Their interaction made it less of a peepshow than a fan site with a community and a moderator. She wasn't an internet TV host; her online persona doesn't translate into today's understanding of "personal branding." There was something almost wholesome underpinning the curiosity of these audiences. They weren't merely "voyeurs"; far more explicit content was readily available elsewhere on the web. There might have been some teasing, and the chance to see a lifecaster undressed or with a partner was always in the air as bait. But in most accounts, just as fascinating, was the possibility to observe the monotony of another person's day. It was a look inside a space that is ordinarily private and sacred: a person's home—where they rest, where they dwell, where they recharge and hide from the world. Lifecasting cracked through to an experience more vulnerable than desire: the longing to feel like one is not alone in the world. Spectators were in the room while not physically in the room. They formed a one-way intimacy with the person on the screen, witnessing them in a domestic setting, while at the same time remaining strangers—remaining anonymous. The audience tuned in from their homes, likely alone, to watch someone alone in a room at the same time. They shared a moment but not a location, together but not. After the internet, being alone meant something else. The state of solitude, once plain and obvious, was newly abstracted: Was it the empty room you sit inside, or the absence of human connection, whether virtual or in person?

Ana Voog was another prominent camgirl of the era. While Ringley presented her broadcast as an unadorned documentary transmission, Voog's screen image was a virtual vitrine. Her project—Anacam—broadcast to the web twenty-four hours a day, just like JenniCam, was visually rich, with evocative colors and primitive special effects. She posed before the camera and often staged her room like a set. One of Voog's projects was called the "Universal Sleep Station." A group, with sometimes as many as twenty users, would gather online and film themselves sleeping on camera simultaneously. They appeared together on a split screen. This private, solitary act—sleeping—became a shared experience, innocent and fanciful. Recently Voog has talked about the webcam as a solution to her personal circumstances; because of it, she could balance her agoraphobia with her desire to share performance art with an audience. In a 2018 essay for *Vice*, revisiting the project that broadcast every day for thirteen years from 1997, she explained that it was a "long-chain event I constructed in order to help me make sense of the world. I have an eccentric and resilient way of dealing with my suffering, for the most part. I turn it into art."

Looking over the Anacam archive now, I am struck by how her work captured the defining cyberspace aesthetics. It was the design persuasion of self-taught hobbyists, those who made their own zines or built their own web pages, and had an intuitive notion of how to work around the limitations of Kinko's copiers or create an eye-catching layout with basic HTML skills. Videos on MTV and indie magazines like *Mondo 2000* sometimes channeled this style, but it was always cyberspace-aware and cyberspace-native; the signature of the first years of pages on the World Wide Web.

Archives reveal only so much. The camgirl documentation that exists is incomplete and perplexing to a visitor from its future. "I turned my cam off for good in 2003, and when Flickr launched in 2004, my archives were the first images I thought to post," wrote Melissa Gira Grant in an essay reflecting on her time in the lifecasting community. But Flickr lost the "silence and stillness we created in the gutters and in the seconds between images." Without the shared moment, and live, these images failed to resonate. Someone watching television is an audience, but someone watching Ana Voog was a coconspirator—still unknown, an anonymous coconspirator. The relationship between camgirl and fan had no traction outside the confines of cyberspace and its interruption of time and place. In 2007, this style of performance was weaponized in the artist Wafaa Bilal's exhibition *Domestic Tension* (also known as *Shoot an Iraqi*). Bilal set himself up as the target of a paintball gun controlled by an internet public, with a chat room and livestream to document it all. When the website appeared on the social link aggregator Digg, internet users flooded his chat rooms and livestream. Users began to shoot the paintball gun at Bilal nonstop. When he checked the threads about his project on Digg, he found comments spouting rage, racism, and bile. Another cohort of anonymous users wrote a script to keep the paintball gun directed left, which prevented the trolls from shooting him. The artist wiped away tears in gratitude. In recent years, Twitch, ostensibly a video game livestreaming site, has popularized this phenomenon. People talk about Twitch like it is weird, even though it is only a new sheen on one of the internet's oldest styles of connecting. There's nothing like Anacam's Universal Sleep Station on there, as far as I can tell, but a few Twitch streams are "gentle," as a 2019 Gizmodo piece characterized them, with hosts who knit before their viewers or read stories aloud to them.

■

"Information Superhighway" had a valence of provocative optimism, sort of like "Green New Deal" does today. It was an idealistic term, glamorizing the "highway," an American romance, the physical expression of ambition—the texture, plotting, and substance extending to the near future. ("What is more beautiful than a road?" George Sand wrote. "It is the symbol and the image of an active, varied life.") Forget the gridlock; online was endless on-ramps. Information superhighway or cyberspace, I remember it like an intense dream; my feelings come before the details, tone and emotions before coherence. It can be easier for me to recall the concrete and tactile elements—carpet, mouse pad—than the fragile memories of friendships and my lives and lies on the early internet. That's where the "information superhighway" metaphor fails. What I remember best of the road trips is my seat in the car, not what I saw out the window. But I remember how I felt along the way.

The cacophony of a 2400-baud modem announced my passage to a secret world. It felt like my spirit traveled through the wires, dialing, dinging, convulsing, and thrashing its way to a mind-meld connection with my invisible friends. The internet was an alternate vector for expression, at a time when I felt I had no connection to the physical world, just a body in space with little to say. I was shy, and in any previous era I might have spent my teen years as a shut-in, totally bored and completely lonely. Maybe I wasted the years just the same, but the internet was more than civilization had ever offered youth with my privilege and spare time and disposition. It was an escape hatch from the trials of my adolescence: uncertain identity, no autonomy, nowhere to go, nowhere to be. (The car-versus-computer evaluation in 1986's *Ferris Bueller's Day Off* seemed less settled ten years later.) I wasn't even in with a cool exclusive BBS or Internet Relay Chat (IRC); my internet experience up until college was plain old AOL. It wasn't much, but it was enough for me.

The dial-up sound seemed timed to a span of hesitation I took for granted, as much as the delay of online gratification. I preferred message boards over chat rooms, and I wished everyday conversation could be similarly asynchronous. I liked that I could pass off a witty response that took me an hour to craft, as if it casually, instantly came to me. I like to be alone with an objective, and writing on the internet provided a pretext (like writing in general would, as I'd discover later). Offline, I might prepare for a confrontation in the mirror in the minutes before it bursts, but writing online, under a pseudonym, the emotional pressure landed differently, with the calculation and temporal padding of revision. It wasn't entirely lack of confidence, although that was a factor. Rather, it was that rewriting was part of the framework of my identity as a user. Lurking was another internet superpower—it was a real-life invisible cloak. No one could judge me for what my body said about me. When I tried to talk to other students in class, I would stammer and blush with anxiety that was limited to the physical world. Then I logged on and found community of another sort. There, I could join conversations in my own time and without awkward silences. I had control over my identity and I could choose what aspects of it I revealed to others; the intensely confessional and honest encounters spiraled out from there.

Despite a world of other options, what I chose to reveal of myself online was often not very far from myself. I spent most of my time in forums with teenage girls like me, like the AOL message boards for *Seventeen* and *Spin* magazines. Our communities were our shared secrets, forged between strangers, surface details unknown, but an intense understanding came to pass through all the interiority spilled. It was a lacuna of kinship. We comforted one another while confessing to self-harm like cutting or mental breakdowns, and we shared stories about our first sexual encounters and drug experimentation. Through those communities, I could see the universality of my fears and insecurities. There were others out in the world as wounded and alienated as me. These stories tumbled out in bits, pointed and pleading, like the time in a thread about Tori Amos when someone said, unprovoked, that she carved T-O-R-I into her inner thigh. There was no reason to treat another sad girl unkindly. My internet friends were an amorphous collective, echoing and validating in the dark. It was different exploring the web: alone and reading things on my own. Some online friends kept up pages on GeoCities and Tripod, and I would click around there. The pages looked a certain way, with design choices like pixelated purple toile wallpaper against lines from an Anne Sexton poem in vulgar cursive. But on occasion, the look of some of these pages was cover for a darkness: dangerous, unspeakable things were communicated there, like how to live on seven grapes a day and a teaspoon of cottage cheese. A website proprietor's inner brutality laid bare through a graphic interface felt too real, more real than the text of forums, and I couldn't talk back to a website. I would press the "go back" key—it was not for me.

I came to these bewildering online adventures through my family's shared computer station. The absence of privacy in physical space had little influence over the material I accessed in cyberspace. I was sitting at a computer, so my parents assumed I was doing something educational. It was like reading *Story of the Eye* with the cover swapped out with *The Wind in the Willows*.

I lived in the suburbs and I had a home in the suburbs of the internet, too. AOL, the internet's first suburb, had its headquarters in Tysons Corner—a clustered shopping mall in Northern Virginia disguised as a bedroom community. The AOL interface was a series of grids and right angles of options, from the white text boxes to communicate in emails and instant messages, to the long rectangular buttons that opened up to channels; it was boxed and specific like the kiosk maps inside the Tysons mall. Maybe I can't remember what was out the window, but I will never forget the robo-voice of the man announcing "You've got mail," or its ominous sound effects, like the creak of a door opening or slamming shut to represent whenever a Buddy List contact signed on or logged off. It was unsophisticated and trifling, but like the suburbs of the physical world, the weird, uncanny, and perverse also thrived there in secret.

If I wanted to know more about the invisible people I thought of as my friends, I could look up their profiles, and what they answered in the AOL questionnaires about age and where they lived, hobbies, and "personal quote," which was usually a quote from someone else. But we rarely took the

AOL profile questions seriously. Once I filled out my profile in the voice of an overeager Conway Twitty fan. I barely knew who Conway Twitty was, but it was funny to me for reasons I can't explain. I still barely know who Conway Twitty is, or why I wrote the profile this way, but still it strikes me as hilarious, for reasons I couldn't try to articulate. I guess it tickled the absurdity of having to be someone online, having to be someone at all. Why on earth would I be myself online—a person I hated?

Sometimes my online friends and I would loiter in general chat rooms and annoy the other users—the lonely adults—with our inside jokes and indecipherable references. We went exploring together, following internal hyperlinks to desolate corners of AOL, to squat there, and use the chat and forum setups as our own semiprivate group communication tools. I could even get lost there. On one excursion, I found an old AOL menu bar that included phased-out channels and internal content that hadn't been updated in months or even years. AOL hadn't deleted this content detritus; it only delinked and delisted these channels that were no longer in operation—but somehow I clicked my way over to it.

There was a dead channel in that expired menu, which was called "DeadOnline," too on the nose in name, but it was a real thing. Most of the posts in its inactive forums were from 1995, and it had to be a year or two later when I discovered it. There were a few recent posts, which sounded like graffiti tags; sentences like "LazySusan was here" or simply "Hi!" It wasn't a community, it was an excavation site. The other recent users must have found it, as I had, through an AOL back alley—a rectangle that wasn't supposed to be there, which they clicked on anyway. I posted something myself: "hi. Is anyone here?" The note was as conversational as marginalia in a library book. There were no notifications. The only way I might have seen if anyone answered my message was if I returned to the DeadOnline forum, either through the bookmark or the outdated menu I'd found. It could have been months or years until another person accessed it. I don't know if they did, because I never remembered to check back. Only now, more than twenty years later, with the power of Google, did I look up the name of this channel and learn that indeed it was called "DeadOnline" or "Deadline," after the old British comics magazine. The AOL channel was created to promote the upcoming *Tank Girl* movie. That's what I mean about how hazy my cyberspace memories are: I remember my excitement when I stumbled on this digital ghost town, but it wasn't until this very minute, and with the assistance of a modern search engine to connect me to someone else's reminiscences, that I could recall all that *Tank Girl* branding on that dead community, DeadOnline.

AOL was a closed platform, a "walled garden," a term that always makes me think of Frances Hodgson Burnett, but it was full of weeds. AOL's own executives talked about their product as tacky, and their users as dupes. "We have the opportunity to become the Carnival Cruise Lines of this environment," Ted Leonsis, the company president in 1995, told *Wired*. He was shepherding an environment to compete with the astronomical two-hundred-thousand-odd sites on the World Wide Web. The company strategy was to build accessible, attention-grabbing content so new users wouldn't feel overwhelmed. The company's target audience, Leonsis said, was the kind of person who might "run to the Hard Rock Cafe" once they arrived in a foreign country. The CEO's comments confirmed all the suspicions of longtime internet users. "Eternal September"—a term that fittingly outlived Usenet—was coined in the fall of 1993, when AOL offered Usenet access to its users, disrupting countless communities; the influx never ceased, but continued to wreak havoc on various rec and alt groups. To them, AOL users were the fanny-pack masses, an invasion of the squares. AOL users poked around Usenet with unsophisticated usernames, posted in ALL CAPS, left tacky newbie questions, and suburbanized cyberspace and its atmosphere.

AOL wanted America . . . online. Just what it said on the tin—well, polycarbonate plastic. It tried to onboard the country with ubiquitous setup disks and CDs that seemed to erupt from every magazine or cereal box. "When we launched AOL 4.0 in 1998, AOL used ALL of the world-wide CD production for several weeks. Think of that. Not a single music CD or Microsoft CD was produced during those weeks," a former AOL employee reminisced on Quora. AOL was as much training wheels for the internet as it was a gateway drug to full-on internet addiction. Before the service allowed unlimited use, its cap at twenty hours a month was excruciatingly stingy. Bills could run more than a hundred dollars in overage fees (and, yes, I got in trouble for that more than once). People who might have only just learned what the internet was a few months before were soon cooking up schemes to cheat these limits. I always wondered why some of my friends on AOL cycled through so many usernames. I thought it was just teen angst and identity stress, like a new shade of Manic Panic hair color. Later, I learned they were phishing. Someone might create an official-looking username like "JanetAOL" and pretend to be an admin and request a password. Then they'd create a fresh new username on that user's account (every AOL subscriber could maintain five usernames). They would log in with the phished account on their home computers, and the time they spent on AOL would be counted as the phishee's outlay. Evidently not everyone was maxing out their fifteen to twenty hours, because the person who told me—ten years after our last AOL chat, in a conversation face-to-face—never got caught.

Now AOL is little more than an email service and home page on the web for boomers and seniors who never moved on. After social media, broadband rollout, routine service outages ("America on hold"), and a disastrous merger with Time Warner, it floundered, but not entirely. As recently as 2015, the company reported two million dial-up subscribers, and—in accord with the times—ad sales was its major source of revenue. More recently, it entered a dinosaur internet supergroup along with Yahoo under the banner "Verizon Media" (formerly "Oath"). America Online is easy to mock. It was pedestrian, hypercapitalist, and a failure—as we see now; but some criticism of it was tinged with classism. What was wrong with reaching out to communities outside hipsters and hackers? What's so bad about using the internet to exchange recipes or read about gardening—or, yes, recommend cruise vacations—instead of creating mailing lists for Pavement fans or developing multi-user dungeon games? AOL's lasting influence is that it disentangled the identity of a general internet user from any kind of subculture or aesthetic. But I am biased, because while AOL zeroed in on customers in the suburbs, it collected another audience common there: the children of cruise-goers, those who are dragged to the Hard Rock Cafes unwillingly—the alienated and over-it teens, like I was then.

I left AOL behind once I got to college and experienced the euphoria of a dorm room Ethernet connection. The web, which I only dallied with as an AOL user, became the centerpiece of my internet life. All the energy I had once put into appropriating various AOL spaces for my own purposes, I later applied to exploring what seemed like infinite web pages. A few months into the first semester, I began to miss my AOL friends. I wondered what was happening back in my favorite forums and chat rooms. Then I discovered I could download the AOL software and check my account over the Ethernet. "You've got mail," said the disembodied robo-guy. It was just as I remembered, except that all my old haunts had turned to ghost towns. Many of my online friends had also left AOL when they went off to college. In our absence we created new dead sites, new DeadOnlines. All our conversations and confessions could be turned over and pored through by some intrepid lurker, as the community was no longer living, but the posts were there, for a few years after we had moved on. Later, when AOL transitioned into a web-only ISP, all those channels and forums and chats were purged. But it is okay. We weren't recording ourselves. We were just living on it.

There is no way for me to verify this, but there is little doubt in my mind that my closest online friends were as I imagined: other teenage girls. There may have been impostors who showed up in our forums and chats out of curiosity. But anyone who participated in our conversations regularly would have been filtered out, because their references wouldn't have sounded right. We trusted one another to be alike in a certain way—American teenage girls, sometimes the odd Londoner or Kiwi—and any other details were spared. Maybe some of these young women did not appear to be women to the outside world, at least not yet. But how did we know the vast majority of our community weren't, say, old men pretending, like so many internet stranger-danger magazine cover stories? Because we knew. Some things can't be faked. Interiority can't be faked. Still, the aspects of anonymity that forged our trust also let us off the hook and prevented us from recognizing where our community was deficient. I cannot confirm the identities of any of these young women, except for a handful who are my friends now and whom I have met in person, but thinking back, these were message boards for indie music and zine culture, late riot grrrl interests (predominantly white). The internet offloaded the burden of us having to recognize our whiteness—our privilege; whereas at a concert, an art exhibition, or any other physical-world gathering, our homogeneousness would be visible to us, substantiating our collective failure and the tacit segregation we upheld. To my shame, I can recall only a single interaction with a person of color when I used AOL. One of the users in the message boards complained about racism in Weezer lyrics and said that as a half-Japanese girl, she found the album *Pinkerton* offensive. I would not have known she was a person of color if she hadn't said it. Because I bought into the branding of cyberspace as post-race, I failed to thread the needle that "post-race" was another way of assuming whiteness.

The internet, like many new communication technologies

before it, sold itself as a social-change agent—a public good, a free education, something that promoted a broader "discourse." Radio, television, and more recently, virtual reality have all rolled out with similar lofty promises, only to fail, typically due to the privileged homogeneousness of clueless early adopters. The claim is tempting at first, until you realize that technology in this equation is meant to do the work that white people are unwilling to do themselves. There's a classic example of this in Thomas Berger's 1970 novel about cryonics hustlers, *Vital Parts*, in which a white salesman tries to pitch a black man on the frozen quasi-burial service, with the appeal, "I hope when you return to the world the people of all races will be living like brothers." Then the son of his potential client howls with laughter, and says to his family, "I knew he'd get around to saying that sooner or later."

Cyberspace did not submerge our identities under a universal oneness of "user." Rather, the internet heightened our awareness of identity, similar to how sound is even more thunderous underwater. A sociologist once told me that before the internet, *The Presentation of Self in Everyday Life* by Erving Goffman was a difficult text to teach. Now students get it. They perform a self in one app or website, while other aspects of their identity are on full blast in different internet channels. When interests and talents are isolated and limited before projected, that is privacy in action: control over how information is distributed. This compartmentalization is never strict, and parts of one self will bleed into another, across many platforms and friendships, but it is fair to say that no one has the same conversation with their boyfriend that they do with their grandmother. In the past decade, on scaled-up mixed platforms where keeping identities pristinely separate is next to impossible, the resulting drama is known as "context collapse." So let's zoom out a bit. Rather than "end racism," the internet does—however modestly—inspire people to think differently about race. Racism didn't end in cyberspace because there was no talk of justice and decolonization or accountability underpinning these utopian scenarios of a future that looks like "all brothers." This is something the black man hearing the pitch in *Vital Parts* understood, and the huckster all-lives-mattering him with a vision of a "post-race" future world didn't.

Lisa Nakamura expands on these ideas in her 2002 book *Cybertypes*, one of the best and earliest books to explain the contradictions in how cyberspace dictated expression of race. She contrasts the "fantasy of a race-free society" assembled online, and propagated in Benetton-style advertisements for various online services, with the reality that amorphous cyberspace usually amounted to a white male monoculture. Fluidity of identity online, due to anonymous communication, may have offered respite to marginalized groups. However, in online communities where majorities of users were white men, their own identities set the standard. There was never an opportunity to be a faceless, genderless, raceless internet user, because the public imagination of online identity has always defaulted to standards that white men had constructed.

Much thornier is a situation Nakamura calls "identity tourism," in which privileged people represent themselves online in appropriation of the identities of others. It might seem like a harmless act of fantasy, but to use the example Nakamura gives, a white man pretending to be an Asian person online, employing stereotypical references like samurais and geishas, has reinforced racist caricatures. Another white user who mistakes the impostor as an authentic Asian person is perpetuating this stereotype, sealing it in with an extra brushstroke. "Identity tourism" is the product of ignorance, sometimes grossly disguised empathy, but there are examples of playing across identity in constructive ways. Trans internet users often talk about creating online identities that match their gender identity long before they have come out to the physical world. Numerous cis people have benefited from pretending to be another gender online, if only because the experience is eye-opening. The difference is when an "identity tourist" sets the agenda for the identity of characters they pantomime online, due to the perceptions of other users, when internet forums are anonymous.

The best cyberspace entities for diverse communities were created and maintained for and by those same communities. Lavonne Luquis founded LatinoLink with credit cards and all of her savings, telling reporters that she was frustrated when she searched the internet for "Latino" and uncovered few results other than Latino Studies departments at universities. Skawennati, a Mohawk digital artist, and other aboriginal artists created CyberPowWow, a series of interconnected chat rooms for their community. Then there was Cafe los Negroes (CLN), a subscriber-based website and forum founded in 1995 by McLean Greaves, providing "futurism from a practical perspective that speaks to Generation Xfro (the wired segment of diasporic peeps of color)." CLN chat rooms included the poetry-oriented "Dread Poets Society" and "Q-Tip" for queer users. The content site included regular features profiling young fashion designers and filmmakers of color ("Hood Couture" and "Cine Noir") as well as columns—blogs, essentially, before they were called "blogs"—by Greaves and other CLN regulars. The website received upward of a million views a month. Greaves showed an early concern for digital privacy and included a notice on one of his pages informing the user of how cookies work ("Find out what else does the Net know about you [or better yet, what should you know about the Net]"). Bedford-Stuyvesant was the spiritual and physical hub of the CLN community (Greaves ran operations from his apartment). Cafe los Negroes even advertised locally, with posters up on phone booths around the neighborhood reading, "Not tall enough for the N.B.A.? Too 'unique' to get signed to a record deal? Don't worry; there's another way to get outta the ghetto: the Internet . . . Representin' Bed-Stuy in Cyberspace."

As with Echo, there was an emphasis on in-person meetups (including joint meetups with the Echo community). Greaves's web design company Virtual Melanin Inc. (VMI) primarily served black and Latino culture creators, and it even led to a collaboration with HBO called *Cybersoul City*. His company was featured in a number of articles in *Wired* and *The New York Times*, yet many of these reports also revealed the trouble he had finding investors. CLN eventually shut down in 1998 after a membership drive failed to meet its fund-raising goal.

■

While major internet companies tried to pander to these communities (like AOL's attempt at a BET-style channel to capture the black commercial market), the founders of Cafe los Negroes, LatinoLink, and similar ventures created their own online spaces for their own communities. They set the rules and the agenda. These founders were pioneers, and they were right—after all—that internet users of color would continue to rise in number. How unfortunate, then, that they did not reap the benefits of a more diverse internet. As of yet, these companies are rarely mentioned in internet history books. That could change, and I hope it will, but Greaves won't ever see his legacy take off, because, sadly, he passed away in 2016.

"The appeal to, or marketing to an assumed white world is a function of whiteness, not a unique function of the internet," Mendi and Keith Obadike explained to me over email. The artist duo came to public attention with their 2001 work *Blackness for Sale*, in which they listed Keith's "blackness" on eBay. The online auction site removed the listing despite numerous other auctions selling "African exotica and Nazi paraphernalia," as Keith told Coco Fusco in an interview shortly after the project ended. "I really wanted to comment on this odd Euro colonialist narrative that exists on the web and black people's position within that narrative. I mean, there are browsers called Explorer and Navigator that take you to explore the Amazon or trade in the eBay," he said, back in 2001. The piece went viral, and Black Planet—another early social network for black internet users—conducted a poll. About a quarter of the respondents thought it was brilliant, 29 percent found it offensive, and 45 percent believed the artist had "too much time on his hands."

While cyberspace was no post-racial sanctuary, at best

it allowed communities to find one another, and for that reason it provided special relief to queer users. It may have even served as a progressive step toward wider LGBTQ acceptance. A number of my queer and trans friends talk about the internet as one of the doors they passed through to exit the closet. Someone questioning their sexuality could find information in secret and with stigma diffused—resources that might be unsafe to look for in their hometown. Members of the trans community speak of the internet more viscerally, because as a user, with options for anonymity and pseudonymity, it is possible to express an identity more "real" and factual than what the physical world can see yet. One reason I hesitate to attribute too much of the internet's influence in the acceleration of mainstream acceptance of queerness is that the timing overlaps with another major culture shift. In 1990, as the World Wide Web, Echo, and AOL took off, 24,835 people died of AIDS complications in New York alone. Meanwhile activists—making sure no one ignored this and no one would forget—were out on the streets in protest. Since there's no way to do this accurately, it can only be stated theoretically, so I write this, opening myself up to the risk of sounding glib: the web took off in the nineties, absent a community who might have taken to it. I don't know how to count the spaces where queer people are missing in internet history because they were not there. Many of the people who might have been mentors, elders to young queers, had died before they could impart their wisdom. I see the gaps, sometimes. What would the internet be like today if they had lived? It would be better. But I don't know how. It is our collective loss.

Not that the internet was deserving of the creativity it transmitted. Phil Agre, an academic who researched internet policy and development in the 1990s, once explained online communication as a trade-off: a computer "can only compute with what it captures; so the less a system captures, the less functionality it can provide to its users." Cyberspace, which some imagined as a fluid, free-floating mesh of information, was, in practice, engaging its resources of data—data that could be aggregated, mined, and surveilled. The internet is, after all, a technology built for and by the military; every social exchange through it is enabled and occasioned in a system designed for tracking, monitoring, and analytics. The façade of weightless expression of identity against the mechanics of data capture and surveillance created ideological fractures among the internet's most involved netizens. Fred Turner, in his classic *From Counterculture to Cyberculture*, recounts a revealing exchange that happened in an online conference on The WELL in 1989, in collaboration with *2600* and *Harper's* magazines. One of the panelists, John Perry Barlow—a founding member of the Electronic Frontier Foundation (EFF) and, before that, a lyricist for the Grateful Dead—had the best intentions but a hopelessly optimistic idea of the internet. It was a communal town square, the Wild West, a democratizing change agent, notions that he would synthesize in his influential text from 1996, "A Declaration of the Independence of Cyberspace," which claims freedom as a central and untrammeled tenet of the internet experience. ("We are creating a world where anyone, anywhere may express his or her beliefs, no matter how singular, without fear of being coerced into silence or conformity. Your legal concepts of property, expression, identity, movement, and context do not apply to us. They are all based on matter, and there is no matter here.") But conferencing on The WELL, back in 1989, there were already detractors. As Turner recounts, "Acid Phreak lost patience with Barlow and in a classic bit of realpolitik, used Barlow's Pinedale address information to download and publish Barlow's personal credit history."

Neither side won, exactly; there was still plenty of hippie libertarianism about the internet through the next decade, but the dream of cyberspace—strangers, strangeness, anonymity, and spontaneity—lost out to order, advertising, surveillance, and cutthroat corporatism as the internet grew more commonplace—and faster. Independent companies run for and by marginalized communities were among the casualties of the dot-com collapse. Neighborhood-oriented services, like BBSs, could not compete with the speed and price points of corporate broadband. Broadband also meant that users could begin an internet experience on the web, rather than inside the chat rooms and forums housed in online services like AOL and CompuServe.

Usenet was searchable on the web, too, through a website called DejaNews. Then Google acquired DejaNews's Usenet archive and nested it under its own Google Groups. Unsurprisingly, Google has not done a great job at keeping the archive searchable or usable for internet historians. Even before Google took over the archive, Usenet fizzled out, due to a combination of increase in internet users, no tactics for moderation at scale, and opportunities to cluster elsewhere on the bustling web. “Everybody’s given up on sci.physics,” a system administrator told *The New York Times* in 1999. “It used to consist of serious discussions among physicists; then the U.F.O. people took it over.” They moved to sci.physics .research, but “then the lunatics took it over.”

3

# Visibility

"Zoe has invited you to join Zoe's personal and private community at Friendster, where you and Zoe can network with each other's friends," read the default invite that appeared in my inbox. It was the night before Valentine's Day in 2003. The folding-chair-thick laptop on the kitchen table was my only companion. I didn't know what Friendster was, but I didn't question it; she was my friend, it had to be something fun or funny. I clicked the link and scrolled and added people—mostly Zoe's housemates—lurked on other people's profiles, and filed out a profile of my own.

When I saw her in person next, Zoe told me that two local DJs had a bet going over who could add the most friends. That was why the community, as far as I could see it, skewed toward twenty-something scenesters gussied up in avatar images with asymmetric fringe, black-rimmed glasses, and tattoos. By the end of the bet, the DJs had successfully added so many friends that they kept on using it as a group chat. The people they added went on to add other friends. That's how Zoe got looped in, and then me, and then my friends, who would receive an email, "Joanne has invited you to join Joanne's personal and private community at Friendster . . ."

■

Before long, Friendster routed and overpowered my social life. I had only recently upgraded to the speed and silence of broadband from the chugging inconsistency of dial-up. The speed was multiplied with dislocation through social websites, where I traded in a cyberspace disguise for a mask shaped like my face. Those of us who were once xSonicYouthx and Marathon83 were recast as John S and Katie L (but not yet John Smith and Katie Lee). Identity online had solidified from a rippling essence. Communicating over the internet was newly blundering and revealing, in the same way that stress in the summer is especially aggravating: you can't hide under a dozen blankets.

It isn't difficult for me to imagine why someone decided to ride in a car for the first time, or call someone on the telephone or watch TV, when such inventions were new and shiny. But I get the feeling that generations to come might wonder why it was that anyone voluntarily signed up to be on the first social networks. We already had email. We had websites. Did the companies pay us? Did the government force this on us? Did our schools or jobs make us? Why did we skim the surface of our identities and post it to the internet? Who benefited? Speaking for myself, and the Friendster users I knew: we joined because it didn't matter. What I remember about Friendster now is laughing at it while I wanted exactly what it offered.

Friendster was the cutting edge of nothing, a utopia for no one. Users let their guards down on it because it was a novelty and nothing more. It arrived with no grand message about democratizing society. There was no lofty claim that the platform conjured up a magic world post-race or post-gender. It was a stupid website from a stupid company, nothing more than a boredom antidote and gossip fodder, with a name that sounded like a belabored Rob Schneider punch line. It was dorky, crass, oddly designed, unsophisticated, unspecific, and it never could have worked without these aspects commingling. Friendster's corniness was an instant icebreaker: everyone could laugh at how ridiculous it was, while participating inside the network and inside the terms of the network. This ironic acceptance of Friendster reminds me of how Mark Hamill once categorized Harrison Ford's character in *Star Wars*: "When Han Solo is cynical, it takes away that weapon from all the cynics in the audience and allows them to enjoy [the movie] the way it should be enjoyed." Every single person who signed up for Friendster was too good for Friendster, a Han Solo of Friendster. The social network didn't demand respect—just use. That levity and lack of commitment canceled out any conceptual dilemma over loss of privacy or identity crisis. It was not an obligation or a bind; it was a lark. But a user doesn't have to respect a social network to get sucked into it.

There wasn't much to do on Friendster, but what you could do was more than enough at the time. Among its limited functions, a user could add friends, search for and click through the profiles of strangers in their network, message people, post to a bulletin board, leave "testimonials," and compose answers to the questionnaire that was the user's own profile. That's it. Friendster's inscrutable purpose—for dating, but not really—was fulfilled in the ways users would window-shop people and hold on to people as inventory. Plus, the inventory was an acquisition in itself—without those friends of DJs, and the allure they offered one another, who else would have stuck around to play? The users were people I wanted to be like, to be friends with, to date, to know, to be. Someone at a party might ask me if I was on it and I would roll my eyes; we'd laugh—and add each other as friends once we got home. Meeting people at parties resulted in more friends on Friendster. Meeting people on Friendster resulted in more friends on Friendster. I felt pleased with myself when I had a neat one hundred people in my "friends" box—collect 'em all! The word "friend" meant nothing to me; I realized it would be too awkward to reject the friend requests of people in my social circles that I didn't like or know very well. Soon, it was more than an eye roll. It became a ritual. We were still unserious, but our use of the service wasn't temporary. We were hooked, and we were creating behaviors and tendencies that would last.

The Friendster interface revealed how strangers weren't

so strange; strangers might be a mutual friend or two away. I could see all the people my age within three connections. It represented the puzzle of my fate: the Friendster users a connection away were people I expected I'd meet eventually. Among the people two connections away were some of the sort of people—cute people—I always hoped to bump into at a record shop or café, but never did, because talking to complete strangers is forward and strange on the street. But sending a message—that's what the silly website was for, right?—required less confidence; the risk of rejection was less to bear. Inevitably, every opening line to a beguiling stranger was something about what a tawdry mess Friendster was, but hey, we're both here, right? What are you reading? I have an extra ticket to the show tomorrow—care to join me?

If the dream of cyberspace was expanding interiority, the dream of visibility on social networks was something more like fame. I was, on the screen, a hazy approximation, rather than a partial figment of my imagination. I had a part to play, like a semi-fictionalized sitcom character, like Jerry Seinfeld in *Seinfeld* or Lucille Ball in *I Love Lucy.* All my friends on Friendster played themselves, too. I found my world of relationships and cliques and their pecking orders and power struggles reduced to the legible order of trading cards. As more people joined, it felt like a high-concept exercise in what a person's life even means to another person, how close to or how far from one another everyone is, as I could observe which friends overlapped in which communities, or who knew someone from my past. The platform rotated friendships from my previous online existence into the light. I had exchanged mix tapes and postcards with some friends on AOL, so I knew their full names. After Friendster came along, we looked each other up and added each other as friends. Years after we first communicated, cloaked in usernames no longer, we could connect names with faces (at least, in the pixelated photographs we uploaded to Friendster). I met two of my AOL friends in person this way, ten years after we first started chatting online, and after a break of several years. Meeting up with friends from high school after years of silence is not uncommon. But the step remove here—never seeing each other, imaginary pen pals—created a rare dynamic. We had a bond, but it was undefined. For as little as I knew about them—what they looked like, how they moved through the world, their voices—I found that my understanding of who they were matched up with my impressions in our offline meetups. Their essence came through, even if we never went to concerts together or hugged before, let alone saw each other. We are still friends; in fact, they are my oldest friends, but I know them as ciphers, just barely, like novels I once loved reading but scarcely remember now (this is a compliment, by the way).

Friendster wasn't direct about how the service facilitated dating, as were websites that were specifically called "dating sites," like Nerve or Match, but from the jump, people were using it as that, and offline dates continued the ambiguity. Like the ironic way we joined these networks, the dates were abstracted from an agenda. At face value, an offline meetup was hanging out with a potential new friend. But new "friends" tended to be attractive, and the interface further blurred the lines. There were boxes to click, indicating a user was "looking for women" or in an "open relationship," but people could search for all people in their area, looking or not, and since so few women clicked these boxes, they were all regarded as potential conquests. I went on many dates that were not dates and not-dates that were dates. This fractured way of meeting initiated departures just as fractured. "Ghosting" is what such an incompletely resolved circumstance is called now, but until that coinage came to prominence, there was only the sensation of loss and unsureness about it. Friendster provided an easy and context-free way into someone's life and out of it. Thinking back to this period of time, there are dozens of people that I remember like I do a dead-end street: I drove in by mistake, and reversed back out, to return to the main road, in the direction I was heading. There was an abrupt ending, but no story that came before. However, if any rules or binary logic had been applied to these interactions, if intentions had been made concrete, I would have been too embarrassed to continue to keep meeting people through that silly website. I could protect myself, even trick myself, into thinking I was not emotionally invested and that anything connected to the social network had no mission or integrity. Through Friendster, the real world and the real people in it adapted to the pliant and ephemeral ways of the internet.

Some of the sweetest words ever published online were the gracious and concise testimonials users left for one another on their Friendster pages. A testimonial was individual to individual, but available for the public to see. These encapsulations combined the spirit of a yearbook signature and a wedding toast. This brief message, no more than a sentence or three, had to capture someone's spirit and put them in the best light (potential hook-ups would be reading, after all). A touch of humor had to come through so the sincerity of the endeavor didn't get too treacly. A testimonial was always a one-off, and there was no space for someone to respond to another person's testimonial. And if it was no good, the recipient would delete it (mortifying). Unlike email (private) or forums (within a community), the testimonial widened online communication within set parameters: user to user in public, or user to an audience (friends and onlookers). A testimonial was written with the expectation that lurkers would see it.

In recent years, Jonathan Abrams, the founder of Friendster, has tried to retcon his legacy as an early pioneer of authenticity and trust on the internet and all the other bullet-point terms that come up in contemporary discourse about the "digital age." But, as one of his investors told *The New York Times*, Abrams created the platform as a "way to surf through his friends' address books for good-looking girls," although he later denied this in an interview with Mashable. However, an *SF Weekly* journalist also reported that Abrams had asked her if she had "cute single friends" in an interview. Whatever he intended with Friendster, Abrams had great timing. Websites like Six Degrees and Classmates had tried something like it earlier—too early. By the time Friendster came along, scanning a photo of oneself and sharing it with friends wasn't that uncommon. It had the formula that every successful social network has required since: people post on it only if someone they want to impress is there (or people might just look, if someone they want to watch is there).

Messages sent user to user and public testimonials were how people communicated, but the promise of the social network was realized in the observable and intuited. There were no alerts when changes were made; a person had to look over the same profiles again and again to see their latest updates. Even if someone changed their profile picture, a user had to look at all the friends in their friends box to notice it. I found myself lurking on the same several people, day after day: glancing at the bands, the movies, the summary they gave to see if there were any changes. It was like engaging with a cardboard cutout, but then sometimes—once a week, a month—there would be something different. A user was "in a relationship," received a new testimonial, or decided *The Conversation*, rather than *The Godfather*, was their favorite movie. These changes were incremental. Friendster was monotonous, with irregular stimulation, but rather than boring its users, the combination of dullness and occasional surprise made it addicting.

I spent the most time on my own profile. It was a looking glass time-shifted and askew. The profile was a space to dwell on my own wavering self-esteem and statuses (*I am a genius! I am a receptionist. I am a receptionist AND a genius, goddamnit!*). As I edited my favorite books and films, and swapped one photo for another, I felt as though I had control over my image and could project the illusion of a better me. What was my profile *for*? Meeting others, yes, and also dwelling on myself. Friendster arrived at a time in my life when I wore anxiety like a baggy scarf. Set starkly, in images and neurotic lists of favorite things, my identity was malleable, fixable. I could clean up in questionnaire responses; reckon with what I wanted, who I thought I was, and the person I was in relation to everyone else in the set terms—a little box on the internet, the same size as every other box and containing the same questions. At the time, I could count every flaw on my body to the magnitude of eyelashes and pores. I wanted to be Logan Tom, the fawnlike, scowling volleyball powerhouse at the Athens Olympics, innocent and angry at once. Her face casually telegraphed murder, and an acquittal for it. In posey pictures I took just for Friendster—bathroom mirror, elbow out and up—I tried to channel her: eyes open wide in a blank stare, with the right measure of impatience and hostility. I looked better in other photographs, but these were the pictures that fit the story of who I was trying to be.

What happened between <form> and </form> was self-portraiture. A user had to trim branches of contradiction in order to fit the tight quarters of narrative performed on platforms. The terrestrial and unsexy—direct statements like "I hate hugging and I'm allergic to mushrooms," things that are actually useful to know about a person one might encounter, scarcely ever appeared in these profiles. It was a performance in the ether for the ether, where two-dimensional better selves were situated among other two-dimensional better selves. So what if a user didn't watch Criterion films as often as they said? What was the harm in uploading an unrealistically comely photograph with dark circles under the eyes blurred out? Listing art and music, reducing one's personality to obsessions and tastes, was a way to hint at inner darkness or light, without revealing any lusterless specifics. Taste might indicate a person's politics and standards, but a favorite movie says nothing about whether someone is grieving the death of a loved one, struggling financially, suffering addiction, or experiencing any other matter of misery and hardship that rounds out a life. Similar to how sketch artists make decisions about what to abstract or emphasize as a focal point, the ordinary drudgery of the lives of users could be swatted away in the construction of an online profile. Such is the nature of social media profiles and self-editing, even today, when images shared are more plentiful and in finer resolution. Sometimes what looks like narcissism online is more a matter of privacy-keeping.

Then again, people fulfilled with their lives generally do not waste time on social media. A friend of mine explained this to me when he deleted his Friendster account after using it constantly for a few months. The self-presentation and need for something—approval of some kind, or a sense of belonging—was so distilled on the platform that after a while he couldn't stand a minute more of it. It was more than searching for something, it was a privilege of discontentment that Friendster users all seemed to broadcast. "Everyone on it wants something," he told me. That was in 2004. I was sad that the very well-written testimonial he posted on my page disappeared along with his profile. Now, I think of this conversation often. We didn't call that desperation "thirst" at the time, but that was the element he was sensing and dreading.

■

Blogging was a similarly flippant pastime that turned sticky. There were always a handful of bloggers determined to find pretentious and ahistorical intellectual antecedents ("Proust was the first blogger!"), but a self-deprecating sense of humor was the real prerequisite. Blogging was voicey—sarcastic, fully aware of its constraints as a microscopic bully pulpit. And it was another silly name for a product. "Blog" sounded like a fast-food-chain breakfast hot dog no one wanted. "You should blog that," someone might say after a quip. "Must be a blogger," they might say after a nosy acquaintance left the room. Bloggers themselves would be the first to laugh.

There were many bloglike things before blogs, like online diaries, web pages of notes and links marked with time stamps, zines printed at Kinko's, and the novel-length walls of text posts that people published on forums and Usenet. There are about as many claims that something or other was the "first social network." Generally speaking, blog and social network trends were concurrent in scope and mass adoption, emerging in the collective rage, alienation, and yearning for community following 9/11. The practice ramped up through the Iraq war, where the internet became an ideal valve to release opinions. Who didn't have an opinion on the Iraq war? A blog was a little patch of land in the internet's community garden to harvest these opinions.

Earlier websites like LiveJournal, Indymedia, and MetaFilter, all founded in 1999, had blurred what would become a distinction between online publishing and social networks. On LiveJournal—and similar online diaries of that era, like Pitas and Melodramatic—a user was the star of their own URL, but friendships could form in comments and community groups. Indymedia, a collectively authored platform that spun out from the 1999 "Battle of Seattle" WTO protests, operated as a major online hub for activism for a decade, prioritizing information on local events and on-the-ground reporting. Contributors often uploaded video footage or reports about a protest while it was under way, bypassing the approval process and time delays that slowed down traditional publications. The Indymedia interface resembled other collective publishing platforms like Slashdot, where users could submit stories and comment on them. MetaFilter, also known as the "blue," for its deep cerulean background (HEX color #006699, to be exact), did not look like the other collectively authored blogs. Its emphasis on brief setups to provide context for the links shared, followed by sarcasm and banter from the community, predated the kind of collective joshing that happens on Twitter nowadays. These websites usually ran on bespoke software, what would later be known as "content management systems," or CMSs (an example of which now would be something like Drupal or WordPress).

By 2003, blogs and social networks were not only distinct but complementary, additive rather than rivalrous. A user could compartmentalize their ideas and politics on Blogspot or Movable Type, while Friendster remained a domain of cultural interests, potential face-to-face connections, and dating-or-not-dating. But the practice of blogging was about building relationships between bloggers. The blog community—the blogosphere—was self-reinforcing and cleared away initial user shyness. Doubts like "Who am I to just write things?" or "How will I find someone to listen?" were less inhibiting when scores of ordinary people who wanted to share their thoughts were already doing it and supporting one another. The community of bloggers had a DIY spirit, and fostered connections between an author and an audience, outside the approval of traditional publishing gatekeepers.

Blogging was a departure from the sanctitude and solitude of writing. Readers and feedback were part of the endeavor rather than the light at the end of a tunnel. A blogger was accessible, like a neighbor someone observed but hadn't met yet. Early- and mid-aughts blog communities were porous. Cities had blogger meetups. Blogs had "blog rolls," a list of friends, online or off, or just a collection of randos who happened to leave a nice comment every once in a while. Those blog rolls operated like a Friendster user's list of friends: a way to scope out a scene and find like minds. In 2003, I entered my blog URL in a directory that was organized on a picture of a transit map. Clicking on various subway stops would reveal as many as a dozen different blogs, each authored by someone who lived by the locations, but there were still so few examples, it was possible to visit all of the blogs in a single evening.

Even if a blog was precise and elegantly composed, the text was a meal, not a diamond. You could bite into it. It was efficient: *Look at this—quip, block quote, link to something in the media, kicker* . . . Aggregation and commentary are faster than writing a new piece from scratch. Plus, the sociality of blogging introduced a layer of welcome and informality. A blogger's voice was different from an op-ed columnist's or an essayist's, because readers were friends or future friends or friendly lurkers. No editor meddled with the content or struck bits with a red pen for failing to adhere to the institutional voice or purview of a publication. Personal detail blended with specialized commentary. I learned about the families and hobbies of these writers between their posts on the Digital Millennium Copyright Act or a bombing in Kabul. Some established journalists took to blogging as a way to be more confessional in writing, as well as a way to create deeper connections with readers. Likewise, readers trusted bloggers because they appeared to be open about their personal lives, casual and accessible. There seemed to be something honest about a blog's informality, and one might trust in the mess. The first-draftish quality of most blogs—often rambling and scattered with "kinda" and "sorta" colloquialisms and interruptive "likes"—seemed like a brain dump: infused with more interiority and marked with less self-censoring. These were casual words authored by a person with something to say. What did they get out of it, if they weren't being honest—being themselves?

In time, blogs sorted into micro-genres, but without the strategy of a corporation like AOL cutting communities into segments to better serve up ads to them. There was an architecture blogger community, film bloggers, food bloggers, bike bloggers. "Warbloggers" (pedants, all of them) could be readily identified by their aggressive, self-aggrandizing usernames, like GinAndPundit, BlogHawk, and FreedomSnark. Blogs devoted to social justice or education were not always as integrated with the political blog scene, often for reasons that proved their point. Businesses used blogs as another layer of a company's media arm, rewriting and quoting from the press releases. Linkblogs dished up links. The compiled art and culture ephemera *Wunderkammer* format of blogs like *Robot Wisdom* seemed to come from a collecting impulse. Bloggers interested in art, style, architecture, and design used the format like proto-Pinterest, as well as a place for criticism and commentary. There were local blogs with updates on communities, and specialists in all sorts of subjects, who either got into the nitty-gritty of their field or offered up industry gossip. Personal blogs tended to read like status updates, with information about a person's life. Another common format was using a blog to relate a personal journey, including matters of health, like cancer diaries or experiences with IVF, major life events (divorce, caring for aging parents), or training for goals like running a marathon or reading every book in a canon. The taxonomy was never rigid; blogs were flexible, above all, and, thus, could speak to multiple communities.

Bloggers were moonlighters, probably. A fiver here and there might show up in a blogger's PayPal "tip jar," but few could dream of making a living off it. Bloggers had lives—workplaces and relationships that could be at odds with the image they presented on their blogs. Blogging happened in the transition from a widely anonymous web to visibility online, and one of the growing pains was the number of people who were fired for their blogs. Now, anyone with experience temping forty hours a week can understand how a personality spicier than a lukewarm washcloth might register as a threat in a corporate setting. An individual—by day an office manager, by night a snark goddess blogger—might be interpreted in the context of the former as insubordinate in practice through the latter. There were no clean boundaries between an employee acting as an individual online and speaking for themselves in real life. Naturally, it was assistants—the office pawns, rooks at best—who were the quickest to get sacked, especially if they blogged about their office life. Bosses and the managerial class didn't have to worry as much. One counterexample I could find was an exaggerated affair: a Google associate product manager launched his blog on his first day and was fired eleven days later, foreshadowing a number of Google's privacy-for-me-and-not-for-thee institutional policies to come later. Recently I searched for the username of a blogger who was fired in 2004 for blogging, in a high-profile instance. I was unsurprised to find her tweeting up a storm of opinionated commentary on current events. For all the opining these days about how we live in echo chambers and can't talk to one another or, conversely, how the First Amendment is dead, it feels like a milestone that so many of us might speak out through social media now—not without some self-censoring, but with freedom that was unthinkable then.

The outing of anonymous bloggers was another painful and involved process, because a user might have taken their privacy for granted at the time. Someone blogging under a pseudonym would have reason to expect privacy, but even a blogger using their real name might have assumed that no one was going to care to find out what they were doing online. This is a self-defeating but sometimes totally accurate way of thinking about privacy: no one actually cares what you are doing in public. Surveillance is attention. Attention is caring. No one keeps an eye on you—as an individual—if they have better things to do. This construct fails where power imbalances exist. Users had come to the internet expecting a personalized view and communities of their choosing. Almost 60 percent of all adults in America experienced the internet in 2002, and yet many of us old-timer users—that is, anyone who had any email account for more than five years in 2002—still thought of it in cyberspace rubric: that it was a generational thing, a subcultural interest for artists and nerds and artist-nerds only (or people on AOL, who stuck to their own cruise-like quarters). This blind spot happened because users flocked toward subcultures and communities with people similar to themselves. Users were less private, revealing their names and faces on blogs and social networks, but there were no customs around screening for online mischief. It wasn't naïve to expect contextual privacy then, just as one might expect that the people at the table next to yours in a restaurant aren't hanging on your every word. But bloggers were fired, and soon a sense that one must act with decorum online crept in.

As blogs took shape, Craigslist, a platform that traded in face-to-face meeting—prospective roommates, bikes for sale—maintained a text-based, simple interface with blue and purple default links. Like blogs, it chipped away at the news business, but as a direct hit, it dematerialized newspaper classifieds, rendering a business model for newspapers obsolete. It looks the same now as it did when it launched in 1995, and in the early aughts, the anonymous bile (and occasional "rave") found in "Rants and Raves," and the array of "Missed Connections," creepy or poignant, seemed like a throwback to the nineties web. Second Life was another proto-platform with one foot in the old ways of the internet and another in the near future. It launched in 2003 with cyberspace-like methods of engagement, but instead of text, visible faces and bodies were animated in virtual avatars. At its peak, the average age of a Second Life user was thirty-seven, suggesting that those who spent their twenties and early thirties in cyberspace were not ready yet to give up their masks. Likewise, not every Friendster user wanted to be Jerry on *Seinfeld* on a social network platform or blog. Those who preferred the cautious, cloaked way of interacting before, or were ambivalent about this deliberate method of self-presentation, still had options on social media. To fray the cord between person and user, they used avatar images of people and things that were not their own faces—old Hollywood celebrities were common, as were tropical fish and stars in the sky. A user with an abstract expressionist painting as an avatar image was defining themselves not unlike "JacksonPollockFan74" might have done a few years earlier.

Some users were ideological about their preference to use Friendster for experiences more gamelike and aesthetic than literal. These users—fakesters—brought the platform into a crisis. Their identities were in character as culture icons, fictional characters, even concepts ("War"), locations ("Broadway"), and things to eat. Friendster, despite minimal community involvement, routinely pruned these accounts. "Roy Batty," a user who presented himself as the persona of the replicant in *Blade Runner*, posted a manifesto to his bulletin board, urging the Friendster founder to see it differently. "Identity is provisional," he explained:

> Who we are is whom we choose to be at any given moment, depending on personality, whim, temperament, or subjective need. No other person or organization can abridge that right, as shape-shifting is inherent to human consciousness, and allows us to thrive and survive under greatly differing circumstances by becoming different people as need or desire arises. By assuming the mantle of the Other, it allows us, paradoxically, to complete ourselves. Every day is Halloween.

Half call to arms, half B-minus philosophy term paper, the manifesto's next item, "All Character Is Archetypal, Thus Public," referencing Jung and Joseph Campbell, and the third, "Copyright Is Irrelevant in the Digital Age," muddled its initial provocation. But the text elucidated how Friendster's agenda was at odds with what its own users wanted. After all, there never would have been fakesters if no one friended them. A Friendster account, "Elvis P," with an avatar image of the King, and profile information like a Memphis address and interest in peanut butter and banana sandwiches, would have been like a proverbial tree falling in the forest without users approving the friend request. The fakesters were another way for non-fakester users to author their identities online. Adding a fake "Stanley K" account as a friend might feel more authentic as an act of fandom than listing Kubrick among one's favorite films. Most of these fakester accounts were silent, like landmarks on the highway. Perhaps they were alt-accounts, and their hosts normally used Friendster in their own image. Or maybe, as any kid who has been to Disneyland knows, when one person is in costume, and the other is a fan, there just isn't much to talk about after the initial greeting.

As fake people on social networks go, these fakesters were among the most authentic. Once I was sitting with a group of guys around a lampshade iMac with the Safari browser open to Friendster's new user login screen. They carefully constructed a character with found images of a Brazilian model and goth-tinted interests like Bauhaus and *Don't Look Now*. Then they used this marionette account to exchange flirty messages with men and women on Friendster, out of curiosity rather than malice. It was a chance for them to see what a day was like—well, a day online—for a beautiful woman. They weren't the only ones populating Friendster with fake people. A social network was a social experiment, and a prompt to experiment.

But Friendster developers were unbudging about its purpose. Rather than capitalizing on emerging user behavior, they banked on their product as a sorta-kinda dating space that mapped how various people were connected to one another. Fakesters were an innocuous presence, but the company believed they contaminated the data the platform collected and provided as a hook. Imagine that a user named Luis sees he's connected to Asher through Sarah and Marcus. If both he and Asher were friends with Elvis P, the fakester account, rather than a mutual friend, would connect them. The Supermarket Sweep approach to friending on Friendster meant that even a "real" person couldn't always vouch for a "friend" any better than fake Elvis, but Friendster prioritized friendship maps over what users wanted from the platform—a wider range of new people to message and meet. Friendster users outside three degrees of separation were invisible to other users, and that created an unfortunate disadvantage to those who signed up for Friendster *because they didn't have many friends.* A woman interviewed in *SF Weekly* in 2003 said she created a Friendster account for the dyke bar Lexington Club because there were so few queer women in her connected network. Abrams, however, responded in the alt-weekly that the "whole point of Friendster is that you're connected to somebody through mutual friends, not by virtue of the fact that you both like Reese's Peanut Butter Cups." Regardless of whether a Friendster participant had any interest in user cosplay, the platform's oversize hostility to the fakesters looked like misallocated time and resources. After all, they did not extend this energy to the neo-Nazis and white supremacists who were becoming an increasingly visible and hostile presence on the platform. Those very real users represented real hate group affiliations. Too real. Friendster had no online abuse support or community management team to speak of, yet the platform spared no expense purging fan-made peanut butter cup accounts and fake Elvises.

What the fakesters knew, and Friendster struggled to understand, is that visibility isn't the same as being verified and vetted. There were enough gaps in these networks—friends who you met in person who couldn't see the point of social media, co-workers who had no idea it existed—to reinvent oneself or fib a bit with little consequence. These profiles were assembled over shifting plates rather than rooted to the core. Plenty of profiles were fake. It wasn't good or bad, just part of the deal. Tethering an identity to the internet meant a user could only travel so far.

Roy Batty was part of the "Borg Collective," a fakester cohort that coordinated trolling and tactics on a Yahoo listserv called "friendsterrevolution." Their antics included fakester parodies of Abrams, with "about me" statements like "I'm a fucking wanker who has such a hard time meeting women that I invented my own dating service. For some reason no one used it for that purpose though. Instead people made up characters and started having fun being creative." The Borg Collective began flagging "realster" accounts, especially those with too predictable taste and interests. But it was no use.

They weren't welcome. When a platform is at odds with its own users, it creates a business opportunity for a copycat. And before long, an alternative presented itself in Myspace, a roundabout shelter for all social network outcasts. It was the social network on the wrong side of the tracks. Myspace wanted users—any users at all. It welcomed those who were kicked off Friendster for faking or adding too many friends, or a number of other situations that sound incredibly tame by today's standards of trolling and online harassment.

Expansive and unstructured, inconsonant and haphazard, Myspace seemed like a more logical transition from cyberspace to visibility online than Friendster, with its prescribed user behavior. Even the name was an accident. It wasn't "my space" as in a custom little corner on the internet, but "space" as in online storage. Cofounder Chris DeWolfe bought the domain from an early cloud company in its liquidation process, at the time unsure about what he would make with it. A lot of Myspace—maybe most of it—didn't make sense. There were features like journals and games that, despite limited use, cluttered up the interface. The profile questionnaire was more detailed and some questions cut right to the chase: religion, height, have/want children? It was brazen and messy, but the fakesters, with their chimerical inclinations, could find a home there. Any weirdo could. You didn't even need friends. "Myspace Tom," Tom Anderson, one of the founders, would automatically friend someone whenever a user opened an account.

"Don't you think dreams and the internet are similar?" a character asks in the 2006 anime film *Paprika*. "They are both areas where the repressed conscious mind vents." Myspace was air in the vents. Its incremental differences exposed the barren pointlessness of Friendster's commitment to "authenticity," as that company interpreted it. Who cared if you met someone in person, or if they were a real person; what is this, a government-run database? The GMAT? A court of law? It's just the internet. Go ahead and friend away. As Myspace gained traction, Friendster's place in its users' digital lives began to feel replaceable and unnecessary. Myspace never quite shed its Island of Misfit Toys beginning, and that was part of its appeal to users, while it also roused latent classism from tech and design writers. One critic, in comments representative of Myspace's reception in the media, called it a den of "trailer-park aesthetics . . . and borderline personality types." The design might have been eyesore-ish, but Myspace—like GeoCities and LiveJournal before it—let its users customize their pages in code, and consequently, it was there that many users learned to code in HTML and CSS. The users themselves might have called Myspace the home of the Myspace angle—avatar images from the perspective of a camera looking down from above, eyes enormous, forehead vast, chin chiseled to a no. 2 pencil point—"trashy," but self-parodying. It was possible to develop a kind of platform microcelebrity just by promiscuously friending people, a practice that propelled Jeffree Star and Tila Tequila into dubious fame. Even those who preferred Friendster's clean presentation eventually made the switch like the fakesters before them. Friendster had endless technical problems. It was often down, and a disorienting bug would revert recent updates like messages and testimonials, which would disappear and reappear hours later. By 2005, Friendster was a digital ghost town, and the one generalization that could be made about the Myspace user base was that they tended to be young. Soldiers in Iraq used it at internet cafés. Suburban honor roll kids used it. Musicians loved that they could promote their music through it.

Myspace was another social network built to look at others and build an image to be looked at, but for a few savvy users, the mirror looked back. There was an app called Spyspace. I came across it in an appropriately Myspace-ish fashion, when I was scoping out the Myspace profile of the girlfriend of someone I had recently come to know (who did not tell me he had a girlfriend). One of the people leaving a testimonial for her made a joke about "Spyspace." At first, I thought it was simple wordplay, some inside joke between them, but then I googled, and there it was: Spyspace, a Myspace spying service. After the sting of humiliation, I downloaded the app myself.

Spyspace was a Myspace tracker that recorded the profiles of people who clicked on your page. All a user had to do was add simple JavaScript code to their profile. There was no indication to the viewers that it was active. The log included the time of visit, IP address, and Myspace avatar of each viewer. On the website, there was a note encouraging users to take it all in stride; "remember: just because someone looks at your profile doesn't mean they are stalking you. some people just like clickin' around. that one guy is totally stalking you though." It took social networking to new self-referential heights. People were curious about who looked at them, which is why Spyspace adoption didn't travel well by word of mouth. You certainly wouldn't tell someone you were interested in about the tracker because then he'd stop clicking on your page. Maybe. A user could figure out so much about the social landscape just looking at their analytics. Who was thinking of you, who was looking at or looking for you. Then again, the Spyspace "about" section had already put the app in a proper context. It wasn't mind reading. "Some people just like clickin' around." That's the modus operandi of internet users as concisely as it has ever been described.

Before long, another social network that begins with *F* put an end to all the fun. But instead of hipsters, Facebook offered proximity to Harvard students. Its interface aesthetics seemed corporate to longtime internet users, while it comforted those new to social networks or skittish about the internet, similar to AOL a decade before it. In 2006, danah boyd observed, "Subculturally identified teens appeared more frequently drawn to MySpace while more mainstream teens tended towards Facebook. Teens from less-privileged backgrounds seemed likely to be drawn to MySpace while those headed towards elite universities appeared [to] head towards Facebook." She also noticed a race and ethnic division between platforms—black and Latino teens tended to use Myspace, and white and Asian teens flocked to Facebook. Among the factors for this switch was the number of moral panic stories about child predators on Myspace. People who didn't worry about their kids meeting older men in hotel rooms in the nineties—either because their kids weren't old enough then, or they weren't online—had new fears over Myspace riffraff. Facebook, associated with the university where every helicopter parent dreams of sending their kids, had none of that stigma.

Myspace was transparently scuzzy and unabashedly vulgar, but that was preferable to covert slime. The industry-standard social media origin story is that a young white man wanted to look at women online and had a eureka moment about how to make money off the prototype. Many are loath to admit it now, but the "Hot or Not" web page for ranking attractiveness is at least as much of an influence in Silicon Valley as *The Whole Earth Catalog* or the Homebrew Computer Club. Mark Zuckerberg's creation started as "Facemash," in which he compiled all the photos of students in Harvard dorms and built a website for users to rank which of two people presented at random was "hotter." Max Levchin, of Yelp and PayPal, created something similar in 2005 that he called a "babe ticker," before rebranding the product as the general photo-sharing widget Slide. Then again, Jared Kushner once ordered *The New York Observer* to create a ranking website called "Socialite Slapdown," after he bought the newspaper at the age of twenty-five, so perhaps this is the inclination of status-obsessed youth, rather than fodder for the debate over old media versus new.

Myspace Tom cashed out for $580 million in 2005, when the social network was acquired by Rupert Murdoch's News Corporation. Now Tom Anderson travels the world, which he documents in glistening photographs that look somewhat like Trapper Keeper covers or images you might find as the nature options in a folder of default screen savers. He's living his best life. Most surprising is how fondness for Myspace has grown as time passes. It has come to represent a particular moment of freedom and drama online, especially to those too young to remember it. "Some people say, 'I wish I could have gone to Woodstock!' And Myspace is the new Woodstock," the electronic pop musician Kyunchi told *Paper* magazine in 2019.

But there isn't quite the same nostalgia for Friendster, and part of that could be attributed to Jonathan Abrams's recent attempts to retrofit the history of his company so it neatly appears first in a lineage leading up to Facebook's "authenticity" and oppressive real-names policy. Friendster failed when it tried to classify its users as real or fake, or visible or anonymous, before users were ready. Even if the desire for "real identity" had been present back then, it meant very little in the mid-aughts, without status updates, notifications, feeds, and an omnipresence of information buttressing a name as a through line of information about a person, rather than just another detail like favorite film or height.

A number of decades-old companies never quite came to an end, but continue on in a locked-in syndrome of content paralysis: scraping-the-barrel ad revenue with lack of upkeep. LiveJournal is "active," in that the site—which became unusually popular in Russia—was sold to a Russian media company. When its terms of service changed to conform to Russian law in 2017, a number of users worried about their data canceled their accounts. Even George R. R. Martin, the "last holdout," migrated his LiveJournal and data from the platform to his personal website. Indymedia has also collapsed without a clear finish. Its participation steeply declined in 2010 due to factors including commercial platforms siphoning off activity, dependence on volunteer labor, conflict over the best practices to defend users from state surveillance, and issues of hierarchies within its nonhierarchical organization that will sound familiar to anyone who has read Jo Freeman's "Tyranny of Structurelessness." In contrast, MetaFilter is another online equivalent of "people in a small town who never left," as Stacy

Horn said of Echo. It has struggled in recent years, especially since 2012, when Google's updated search algorithms impacted its traffic, and consequently its ad revenue; but the tight community, and consistency of that community, transitioned into a subscriber-style funding model. As of 2018, almost half of MetaFilter's operating budget is supported by its users. They don't want to give up their home away from home online.

In 2005, a Pew study said that eight million internet users had created blogs. By 2009, Pew blogged about another study, under the title, "Blasé about Blogs." It was death by fatigue and assimilation. "Sorry I Haven't Posted" became the most common blog-post subject. Contemplating the demise of blogging, I am reminded of Art Spiegelman's comment that comics, like any mass media, had to make a deal, "become art or die." Blogging did not become art, nor was it ever experimental beyond its structure and community. There was never a blogging avant-garde, because implied in every post was "this is what I think" and "here is something I like or dislike and I think you should notice," which left little room for subversion of the form; and thus, no "graphic novel"–equivalent highbrow endpoint of it. Eventually the format merged and dissolved with the rise of the clickbait economy. Publications like *The New Yorker* and *The New Republic* began to publish web-exclusive content, less formal than the pieces that made it into the magazines; other publications like *The Washington Post* and *The Atlantic* hired bloggers to blog on their websites—ideal content to capture page views, and thus generate ad revenue. At best, these publications finally noticed how their gatekeeping practices left so much talent on the table. Blogging itself became indistinguishable from the contemporary news climate of hot takes and think pieces, while platforms like Twitter, Facebook, and Instagram absorbed the community aspects of the blogosphere.

The early social networks never quite made the leap from defining identity to commodifying it. Online advertising on Friendster and Myspace was basic rather than targeted. But modern advertisers might even target a user's past. Enter "Friendster" in the browser bar now, and a user is redirected to the home page of a corporation in Southeast Asia, while Myspace is a zombie advertising trap. Ownership of it changed hands (it is currently the property of the Meredith Corporation). New investors saw value in the old user data, which could be used to combine with more recent information mined by data brokers such as Experian.

Now visibility is demanded from social media users: without a Facebook profile, you might be deemed untrustworthy and lose out on professional opportunities. Back in the time of Friendster and Myspace, however, the distance between a person's identity and what they wrote in the white boxes in their profile was part of the fun. To be visible online is not an act of total transparency. The condition can be another tool of privacy—a way of controlling one's image as others regarded it. Privacy was inferred, with the expectation of ephemerality: profiles were edited constantly, blog posts might be deleted, content was in flux and subject to a user's whims. For that reason, I feel as though I commit a temporal trespass when I inspect old Myspace profiles and blogs. This information wasn't created for me, a person from the future. It was written for a moment that is now long gone. Users might have assumed this content would drain naturally, like when Prodigy or The Source shut down. Social networks that have turned to digital ghost towns are more uncanny than inactive AOL forums were when I trawled them. Like a stranger's yearbook left in the rain, there are faces, names, and interests expressed broadly, but no connective tissue to make sense of what is there. There are clues, but no stories.

4

# Sharing

The country star Brad Paisley released a song in 2007 with lyrics unusual for the genre. Absent of clichéd imagery like deserted highways, loyal canines, shotgun weddings, or empty whiskey glasses, instead "Online" told the story of an "overweight" internet user, who lived with "Mom and Dad."

*I'm a sci-fi fanatic*
*Mild asthmatic*
*Never been to second base*
*But there's a whole 'nother me*

*That you need to see*
*Go check out Myspace*

Backup singers, including the then unknown Taylor Swift, chimed in at the chorus, "I'm cooler online." Ten years later, Paisley updated these themes with "Selfie (#Theinternet-isforever)." "You oughta be ashamed of your selfie," he sings in the newer song, with lyrics considering the public images of internet users, and how picture-sharing apps like Instagram and Snapchat distort user identities and expectations of one another:

*Posing in the bathroom mirror*
*in a skimpy little two-piece*
*In the background there's a toddler*
*cryin' on the toilet seat*

According to Paisley, internet users were reclusive losers, and later, irresponsible narcissists. What happened in between? The iPhone. It launched the same year as the first of his internet songs. "Online" and "Selfie" serve as bookends to the years in which smartphones ascended from covetable accessory to the primary device to share digital content and keep in touch with others. These tunes sound unmarked by time to my steel guitar indifferent ears, but his lyrics castigate two different generations of users: indoors and stationary in the aughts, and those out in the world, sharing their lives through mobile technology, ten years later. Even the presumed gender of Paisley's target changed. While "Online" is about a sad sack who claims to be handsomer and more popular than he is, "Selfie" skewers the vanity of women flexing for the 'gram. The stereotypes in Paisley's internet polemics echo the wider media portrayals of users: from hermits to strumpets, nothing digital is authentic and everyone on the internet is lying.

In this period of time, "user" became a general identity, nonspecific and available for most Americans to claim. Conflating a demographic—white, male, age twenty-five to thirty-four, college-educated, say—with "internet user" always distorted the diverse reality; and after mass adoption of smartphones, this misconception became obvious. A few hucksters ("social media experts") in the late aughts charged exorbitant fees to set up Facebook pages for clueless small businesses, but by the time Paisley released that second song, no one could mistake the commonplace act of creating a social media page for a specialized talent. Even the idea of "digital natives"—those who grew up online—became less useful as a distinction. Someone who first encountered the internet as a child might have an online routine, governed by social media, that is not much different from a senior who first typed on a computer at the library only a year ago. By 2016, 42 percent of American seniors used smartphones, four times as many as five years prior. About a third of that group, age sixty-five or older, have tablets and social media profiles. While Myspace users had been predominantly under the age of thirty-five, the platforms that grew to dominate in the decade that followed were catchalls, absorbing all sorts of communities of new users as the internet became a living infrastructure and a basis of everyday life. Instead of a variety of communities congregating on a variety of specialized platforms, a vast number of internet users, both veterans and new, flocked to Facebook, Twitter, Instagram, and YouTube.

What happened is what would happen if you stuffed all the people in the world in an elevator: people blamed one another for their discomfort, instead of the elevator itself or proprietors who insisted it was safe. Focus on personal responsibility, and thinly veiled misanthropy, resulted in a vacuum of pointed tech criticism about surveillance, data mining, online harassment, and corporate power. Instead the media talked about the internet in broad generalities—is the internet good, or is the internet bad? Is the internet making us smart, or is it making us stupid? The supposed answer to any user's problem was less internet rather than a better internet. Or, as the techno-optimists would have it, the answer was more internet, rather than purposeful use of the internet. Internet companies were rarely held accountable for their deceit, exploitation, and naked power grabs. According to the broader media narratives, it was up to us, the users, to shape our own experiences online, even when the choice to opt out became itself a fantasy.

While Echo, Cafe los Negroes, and other nineties online communities were discussed in arts magazines and style sections, coverage of the internet in the late aughts was largely conducted in business sections, or addressed in product reviews, in which the criterion was whether or not features worked, rather than a product's impact on society, culture, and human behavior. General interest stories that were published tended to follow two scripts: the Paisley accusation—that users are narcissists—or concern-twaddle that the internet was making us lonely, as a 2012 cover story in *The Atlantic* declared. In other examples, critics zeroed in on the personal deficiencies of various founders and let that stand for critique of the power of their companies and abuse of that power. David Fincher's 2010 film, *The Social Network*, followed this line of attack, as it characterized Mark Zuckerberg as a spiteful backstabber and Facebook as a product in his image (auteur theory, but for Silicon Valley). This correlation without basis—bad man equals bad company—offered an easy gambit to neutralize the diatribe. Indeed, several months after the film was released, its message was subject to reappraisal. Aaron Sorkin apologized to Mark Zuckerberg at the Golden Globes, where he received an award for best screenplay. He was "wrong," he said onstage at the Beverly Hilton Hotel. Clutching the gold trophy, Sorkin wondered aloud if the Facebook founder was watching, and said, "You turned out to be a great entrepreneur, a visionary, and an incredible altruist." Who knows why he backpedaled? Maybe they had a tennis buddy in common who intervened, or maybe he understood the inevitability of Facebook's growing influence and hoped to get on the founder's good side. Whatever his motivation, Sorkin, on that stage and with that trophy, might as well have shouted out: *Don't worry, world. It's just a movie. Facebook is good after all!*

A 2013 *XKCD* comic satirizes the flip side of misfires in tech criticism. One character in the drawing says to another, "Maybe before we rush to adopt <Google Glass> we should stop to consider the consequences of blithely giving this technology such a central position in our lives." The caption below the panel reads, "Don't have any insights about a new technology? Just use this sentence! It makes you sound wise and you can say it about virtually anything." The hover-text drives the point home: "The great thing is, the sentence is really just a reminder to the listener to worry about whatever aspects of the technology they're already feeling alarmist about, which in their mind gives you credit for addressing their biggest anxieties." I'm as guilty as anyone of worrying about "consequences" of technology (obviously). Many times I have a bad feeling about a new product or tech concept and I don't know why. Such a feeling motivates me to ask questions, to pinpoint what is troublesome. "Stop to consider the consequences" is a sensible call for further pointed inquiry, but as a command—"Stop!"—it is no different from a desire to halt the passage of time or change in general.

There was much to "stop to consider" from 2007 to 2017, but anyone calling "stop" would have been trampled. The most dramatic shift was how smartphones shredded the boundary between online and offline experience. Before I got an iPhone, the internet and the street came together for me only when I would wander about looking for a blue USPS mailbox to stuff my red Netflix envelopes in, because the postal service rarely fetched my outgoing mail, and I was impatient for the next DVD in my queue. Sometimes I took my laptop to a coffee shop to work, and I always received texts on my old (dumb) phone, but the internet—email, search engines, and the like—was contained in my cubicle at work and in my home. The internet had a station before, like a shoebox full of recipes on a countertop, like the kitchen itself. As smartphones blurred organizational boundaries of online and offline worlds, spatial metaphors lost favor. How could we talk about the internet as a place when we're checking it on the go, with mobile hardware offering turn-by-turn directions from a car cup holder or stuffed in a jacket pocket? IRL—"in real life," a common acronym—revealed itself as a spurious notion, because life through the internet was very clearly, very purposefully real. Both were real, but only one could be touched. The internet realm and the world outside your phone were—while not quite one and the same—interleaved, entwined, mutually dependent.

■

Around the time of its first smartphone launch in 2007, it was possible, if unwise, to talk about Apple as an underdog, and adopt the corporation's own narrative, a holdover since its famous *1984*-inspired Super Bowl commercial, directed by Ridley Scott, featuring a spry bleached blonde racing to attack "Big Brother" with a sledgehammer. In 2007, Apple was ranked 367 on *Fortune*'s Global 500. Ten years later, it was ninth on the list (between Berkshire Hathaway and Exxon Mobil). With the iPhone, Apple was off to the races: in 2010, Apple sold almost forty million devices, and by 2014, sales were just shy of 170 million. Now the figure is north of two hundred million new Apple phones each year.

The company, unique for its fastidious design-first approach to product, developed a near universally acclaimed gadget, both in function and appearance—a totem, a scrying mirror for the twenty-first century. The iPhone was gorgeous, "intuitive," and it was built to be handled like an intimate acquaintance. In time, people would learn more about Foxconn and the loss of human lives associated with the iPhone's creation. It was too expensive, certainly. But from the stage at Macworld, on January 9, 2007, Steve Jobs announced the future betimes.

The iPhone's first decade nearly parallels Barack Obama's years in the White House. Elected in 2008, Obama left office in January of 2017, ten years after Jobs's presentation. Barack Obama was the first president to have a Twitter account and the first to use Instagram. The founders of both Airbnb and Uber were in Washington, D.C., for Obama's inauguration (crashing in very different accommodations—friends' couches and an upscale hotel room, respectively), and independently, they have talked about the experience as a eureka moment—the spark that crystalized into an idea for a company. The corresponding timelines of Obama and the iPhone are abundant pasturage for future historians, but let's not forget that meanwhile there was the Great Recession. A lot of broke people carried fabulous magic phones, too. In 2010 or 2011, it seemed like all the ads on the subway were for apps. Then all the straphangers had iPhones (some Android phones, too). Maybe it was the other way around. "There's an app for that" was an iPhone slogan, and there was, very often. The iPhone became common and everyday like eyeglasses, but it felt new, for a long while—past the point of actually being new. Apple's crowning achievement conjured up a curious atemporality. Ten years after the phone hit shelves, people still talked about it like a new creation. The changes occurred in little icon boxes on little iPhone screens, and the changes happened inside the people tapping away at them. Users changed while the hardware—for the most part—did not.

There are moments when I will pause and reflect on how

powerful and world-changing the iPhone has been, like the time I happened to observe someone at a grocery store using FaceTime to talk to a friend in American Sign Language. Before the iPhone, people texted from "clamshells" and chocolate bar approximations, slipshod contraptions that got the job done. In 2005, I picked the slickest device from the T-Mobile online store, which came free with a two-year commitment, but now I remember that silver Samsung flip about as well as an old toaster oven. It had a throaty shutter click like a power tool. My hand trembled a little when I pressed a button to take a photo. The badly compressed images looked like maroon finger paints on a postage-stamp-size screen. I don't think I ever bothered to upload any of the pictures to my computer. But the phone seemed good enough, because I didn't think it had to be any better. The iPhone came around just as that contract ended. I wanted one, of course, but I wanted it like a shinier paperweight. It would cost five hundred dollars, and still another two-year commitment, to send email and place calls and keep papers from blowing off my desk—what? I thought the difference between a clamshell and an iPhone was like the difference between economy or first class, not the difference between two destinations. That autumn, I signed up for a focus group through Craigslist that was organized by a local start-up. I walked away with a tiny check and an iPhone as a parting gift. Through several models, and multiple contract renewals, it has been in my hand or pocket or tote bag ever since. The tactile quality conjured up feelings of intimacy and trust. I held the iPhone so gently at first, like applying eyeshadow with my fingertips—the lightest touch. What else do people handle with such care? Bodies. I started to go to bed with it. It became a paperweight to rest on a pillow. Then it seamlessly integrated with my daily life, so that now I scarcely think of it, the same way I don't think of my fork but of what's on my plate. The world, as in elsewhere and far away, became more immediate through the iPhone; but the world surrounding me, my periphery, meanwhile, was less present, less urgent than what, in the moment, I wondered about. I found myself bumping into strangers more frequently. I grew less likely to notice landmarks on a walk in a new city. I never got bored waiting for a train. I no longer dreaded sitting alone with a drink when a friend was running late—I always had something to do; my focus on the screen could keep bar vultures at bay. I was never alone, even when I wasn't using the phone to talk. Never alone. There was always this one little window in between my thumbs.

The iPhone latched onto my thought process and memory habits. It became part of the assemblage of my day, a companion to my quotidian routine. The stray observations that barreled around my head had a vessel now. Random thoughts that would blanche and desiccate out of mind before now had propulsion and contrails. Only a faint nudge of effort was needed to capture and hold these thoughts; the burden was what to do with the inventory. The iPhone had a storage limit, but it was prodigious—virtually limitless, in contrast with thirty-six exposures per roll of film. I can type faster than I can pull out a pen. Suddenly I was writing about vast swaths of my life and sharing photographs widely. The increase of information about myself that I documented through the internet did not correspond with an increase in moments that were significant to me. Writing and photographing grew less precious and deliberate. I spun my existence into digital content in an act that was a way to preserve memories as much as it was a way to communicate with others and extinguish loneliness.

It is either that there are no feelings of *l'esprit de l'escalier* on the internet or that the internet is all staircase wit. Social media on mobile had a different tempo and friction as users documented in the moment, rather than retrospectively. Posts to Instagram and Twitter were on the go, rather than composed with a moment of reflection. The formality of communication online went away; posting was no longer deliberate, like essay-writing, but casual, even when it wasn't temporary. Expectation that internet content was ephemeral was itself ephemeral—posts on social media turned into archives to be viewed again, but still this digital communication had the signature of fleeting temporality. A number of scholars study online communication as part of the tradition of oral culture. They argue that cat memes and hashtags and the like aren't evidence of the decline of the written word. These exchanges are more like chitchat and hanging out than modern-day belles lettres. Once I spent days trying to come up with testimonials for Friendster friends; now my typical friend-to-friend exchanges online are typo-laden and typed out as fast as I can think. To differentiate this activity from communication online before smartphones, in this chapter I refer to this casual writing as sharing.

"Sharing," a word we learn as small children—the opposite of hogging all the toys—is now the go-to verb to describe being an active and vocal entity online, or having an online identity at all. Like the saying about open-source software—it's free as in speech, rather than free beer—sharing on the internet is sharing thoughts, rather than sharing resources. Sharing politicized visibility. And opinions defy the law of scarcity. "Share" buttons are slingshots for these opinions, propelling the thoughts of users, both considered and glib, to ricochet and reverb through the perpetual, cross-extended speaker's corner that is the internet. Sharing made the internet in the same way editing made cinema.

While participation on early social networks was never required of anyone, in the following decade, users had a digital shadow, like it or not. Engaging with various platforms—updating a Facebook profile, leaving reviews on Yelp, tweeting, and posting photos to Instagram—gave users an opportunity to make the digital representation of themselves look more like themselves, their taste, their values, their interests. Crucially, instead of answering questionnaires ("What are your favorite movies?"), the contrail of status updates became a user's identity; the archive was more of a zoetrope than a photograph.

Public assumptions about shared content shifted from a belief that posts were temporary and ephemeral to an expectation that even casual updates were enduring and entrenched. Online content wasn't "forever," as Brad Paisley insisted, but there was resilience due to the network effect of more users connected, while anchored with the coercive stability of mega-companies like Facebook and Google. The social memory of someone's post can feel like forever, even if a user deletes it—and especially when content travels beyond intended immediate circles. Platforms for the masses, rather than specific groups, meant a user could share with broader audiences, by accident or intention. For example, a tweet someone assumed only their friends would see could, due to the amplifying function of a "retweet" button, volley beyond friends and family to a broader public—while these distinctions eroded amid the frenzy of the internet's takeover of everything. Friendster users found themselves liberally adopting the word "friend" to describe various relationships. Instagram and Twitter used language that accounted for the potential of a mass of strangers watching another user's activity. Instead of friends, users "followed" users and were "followers." Lurkers weren't just a possibility now, but an expectation; users could attain online a small-scale celebrity—akin to the most popular kid at school—or even real celebrity. These platforms introduced greater asymmetry of attention. Every public online activity in social media was posted in the possibility that somewhere, someone was a fly on the wall for it. A famous and innocuous example of context collapse at scale happened when a woman texting photos of a dress to her daughter initiated a global debate over whether it was white and gold or black and blue. But other examples are less whimsical. Someone tweeting an inside joke, thrust before a wider audience—even the world stage—that doesn't get it, could be subject to harassment, or, at the very least, an unpleasant measure of attention.

If the iPhone was a sharing trade route, Twitter was a shipping container: a transportive enclosure for those barreling thoughts, to disperse and release them. While Twitter predates the iPhone by a year—it had a 140-character constraint because that was just shy of the limit imposed by SMS—the product found its purpose at their conjuncture. It was an invitation to comment on one's surroundings and make it quippy. Social conventions and mores spread quickly;

behaviors like "mansplaining," basic etiquette like "don't ask strangers about their scars," and complex issues like the egregiousness of cultural appropriation came to prominence on Twitter as individuals who thought they were alone with their concerns found sympathy, expressed in retweets and likes, among a wider body of internet users. Viral content can be amusing and eye-opening, like an old tweet I saw from someone asking, "What age were you when you first saw the 8 in the middle of the 8 of diamonds?" It was shared with a picture of an eight of diamonds Bicycle card showing the eight, right there, in the white space. (First reply: "Cripes! I just saw it right now. And in 3 months and 2 days I'll be 67.")

Twitter is a marketing tool and a hangout spot all mixed up, and on Twitter "user" is an identity that applies to people, corporations, institutions, and bots. On this platform a person might perform as a company or bot, or corporations might act like individuals. It can be jarring to observe a user swivel from one type of sharing to the next. You might be laughing together with someone in @ replies and the next minute see they tweeted, "Download my PDF guide: 'Real Data Solutions Your Company Needs to Master' #bigdata #martech #strategy." Likewise, the more aggressively despicable a company's enterprise, the more likely it seems to employ an innocent twenty-two-year-old social media assistant to joke with users in affected slang like "spill the tea" and "lit."

Jangly and feral, a crisscross of communities and contexts, information feels chaotic and urgent on Twitter, and it jerks users to attention. This wild urgency might be why absurdity is the humor of choice—it is distancing on a platform that trades in presence and immediacy. Ironic content, trolling, and "shitposting," the practice of estranging the intention of shared content from meaning or posting in an outlandish way, were common in tweets wedged between news and personal news updates. In 2012, this humor was aligned in a niche community of emerging comedians and poets known, reluctantly, as "Weird Twitter." A classic tweet from that time comes from Twitter's bard @dril, "who the fuck is screaming 'LOG OFF' at my house. show yourself, coward. i will never log off," with its purposeful misspelling, was like a cartoon caricature of road-rage-like online peacocking and aggression—the kind of behavior we might call being "extremely online." After Weird Twitter, the world became weird, with a Verhoeven-movie subtle villain of a president, and that disillusioned humor was no longer an in-joke—it was the joke. I never would have guessed the jaded, obscurantist humor I remember from AOL days could become something accessible to most; but it was internet humor—not specific to us or our time and place. Our jokes—like Dril's, some twenty years later—were the gallows humor of young people with a screen and no future.

Now that the world is weird, Twitter—at its weirdest—makes sense: even when it's unpleasant and chaotic, art, poetry, and spectacle are baked into the experience. My favorite tweet, if it is possible to even award this distinction, is by @stefschwartz: "someone stole my credit card and made a $30 donation to the american red cross." Some of my other favorite tweets come from the author Jeff Noon, who began a project of tiny, tweet-size fictions on the platform that he called "spores." Collective humor made use of the character constraint through format jokes ("*Record scratch* *Freeze frame* Yup, that's me") to the grand errors, the butt dials, the tweets that come out when the cat walks over the keyboard or the kid grabs the phone. If ZuccoTheParakeet were a real person anonymously typing "chirp chirp" in chat rooms in the nineties, ten years later that person might have created a fakester profile on Friendster or Myspace ("Favorite music: birdcall"), but an in-character personality like that on Twitter is likely to be automated as a bot (the creator of which might be anonymous, too). Some bots are abstract and evocative, like the unofficial Big Ben account that tweets "BONG BONG BONG . . ." on the hour. Others are comical, like Darius Kazemi's @HottestStartups, which automates text drawn from a corpus of Marxist texts and combines it with a pitch format ("Startup idea: The struggle for individual existence disappears") sometimes arriving a bit too on the nose ("Startup idea: Everybody thinks of his own welfare, and does not care whether by doing so he destroys the welfare of others"). Another artist, Everest Pipkin, created a bot called tiny_star_field, which tweets combinations of stars and asterisks that appear on a timeline like a sprinkle of confetti, a temporary break to the madness.

Despite all its clutter, its self-promotional detritus and eclectic assemblage, the pithiness of tweets—the billboard, bumper-sticker quality—made it ideal for organizing and activism. And, like a bumper sticker or a billboard, tweets could be viewed across various cultures. Whatever one's political affiliation, generation, or ethnicity, the blip-like limitation to the content, mixed with the variety of people on the platform, meant a lot of different users could see one another. Twitter users, unlike other online communities and platforms, were not so strictly situated in echo chambers. Communities based on identity are porous, and many users participate in a few at once ("Film Twitter," "Policy Twitter," "Black Twitter," "Media Twitter"). If I followed someone for their commentary on climate change, and they also tweet in "Horse Twitter," with various photos and tweets about riding, I could ignore those tweets or find the opportunity to see this side of a person as actually kind of delightful. But like message boards, Friendster, Usenet, and other internet communication before it, pulling tweets out of the mess that was the platform was like isolating thread from a tapestry. To look back on a post in the archive is to see it stripped of contextual meaning, such as what was in the news that day, who are the people I follow and who follows me, and what were my followers talking about that day. All of that context is gone later—all a lurker sees of an archived tweet is the tweet.

Despite the multiplicity of uses, and many kinds of users, early criticism of Twitter could be distilled to a single (ironically tweet-like) sentence: "No one cares what you had for breakfast." It was always breakfast. Never dinner, never snacks. Perhaps it stuck because it implied how Twitter was on a twenty-four-hour cycle, and heavy users tweeted shortly after waking up. It was a "no one cares about your dreams" admonishment for the twenty-first century. The reason for this antagonism has to do with the specifics of Twitter's hold on the media. Twitter, with its broadcasting purpose, became a natural platform for journalists; meanwhile, users from outside the media—without media training or background—took on a media-like role just by being on it. They, too, could share breaking news. This tension was alleviated, somewhat, with the introduction of user verification, creating a class of user known as the "blue checks," for the icon that appeared on the platform, the proof that this person submitted a government-issued ID to Twitter customer service and links to sources that explain their notability. It is a cardboard gold crown, but it helps in certain cases; for example, Twitter support will prioritize intervention requests when trolls attack a blue check. Twitter takes the media professionals on it for granted. They don't leave, even when it grows toxic, because promoting work through the platform is almost compulsory as a modern journalism job requirement. Meanwhile, journalists can get played by people with even more power, like Marc Andreessen, a venture capitalist and the cofounder of Mosaic and Netscape, who told *The New Yorker* that he loves the platform because "reporters are obsessed with it. It's like a tube and I have loudspeakers installed in every reporting cubicle around the world."

Now world events drive Twitter conversations, like writing prompts. Riffs on users' own lives and personal concerns seem inferior, too trivial to remark on, not worth adding to the ongoing stew of reactions to disasters, scandals, tragedies, and world chaos. Sometimes the concentration of attention leads to positive change, such as raising awareness for worthwhile causes. More often than not, Twitter now feels like endless punditry from low-information voters. Conspiracies and rumors spread easily, just like worthwhile stories, because one person's misinformation that sounds correct to an ignorant person is amplified and shared without a second glance. Had the commentator class allocated column inches early on to interrogate the company policies and leadership rather than the users around the world using 140 characters to describe burnt bagels, things might look different now. Public scrutiny might have resulted in stronger moderation and anti-harassment measures, implemented early enough to be effective. It is too late now, as the spread of rumors and misinformation is now part of Twitter's deal, let alone that Nazis, actual Nazis, have gone wild on this platform—examples that make it even harder to understand why anyone ever shamed people for tweeting what they had for breakfast ten years ago. At least those users kept in their lane. I am the expert of this bowl of oatmeal in front of me and not the emoluments clause or what's happening in Myanmar. Here's a selfie.

It is always easier to blame other people for discomfort than it is to blame systems, structures, and abstract processes like "design." I mean, I get it. I get annoyed with other people online, too. There is a trope in science fiction stories that telepathy burdens people with too much knowledge; if you could read people's minds, it would be unpleasant to have all that noise in your head. Maybe Twitter, as the receptacle of people's random barreling thoughts, opinions, drives, and desires aired out for the greater public, is this concept borne out. Nevertheless, idle cynicism should never be confused for a grand unified theory about the internet, because when users are scapegoated, Silicon Valley is left off the hook.

And still my iPhone sleeps beside me. Horrible habit, but I can't seem to break it. "The Internet seems so much more ridiculous, pocket-sized," was the first tweet I composed with my first iPhone. I didn't tweet much until the device was in my hands; once it was, it never left, and I retained that Twitter habit, too. Twitter was different in 2008, 2009. Would you believe that I once felt like I had nothing sincere enough to post to Twitter? That I was *too mean* to tweet? I wasn't above talking about my breakfast. I was below it; my voice felt misaligned with the sincerity of other users. Now I feel like I need to coat everything in a layer of sarcasm, despair, and anguish just to engage with Twitter. That's why I don't use it much now, and when I do, I look at it only on my phone. I find, in moments when the world feels especially unfathomable, the sensation of putting my phone back in my purse, or back in my pocket, is comforting, just as it was to slam a telephone receiver down in its cradle. What does it matter what the president has tweeted if this is a tiny phone, and everyone is a screw-eye-size icon? It's a coping mechanism, but what isn't.

■

The narcissism that social media users have been accused of since the beginning of social media is usually the projection of those imbued with a far more tedious and anti-intellectual trait: misanthropy. Reading over the copious "Who cares what you had for breakfast" anti-Twitter screeds that were published ten years ago, I couldn't help but imagine a simple "I know you are but what am I" retort: *Who cares what you think about tweets about other people's breakfast?* Plus, dismissing Twitter users as "narcissists" just for sharing their everyday experiences meant the word lost its teeth by the time Instagram coaxed its users into participating as perpetual spokespeople of their own lives.

Instagram began as an app behind a velvet rope. It was available only on the iPhone in 2010, when the iPhone was in its semi-exclusive, semi-luxury period. It made the frictionless act of photography on the iPhone friction-full, with a gimmick straight out of Spencer Gifts: a suite of filters—"1977," "Lo-fi," "Walden," among others—that distorted the temporality of an image. A picture with the right filter—fractured yellow, the illusion of a sepia bath—could look like it was taken decades ago, at a time when paper photographs showed their age. Music videos and fashion photographers often artificially aged images for a similar nostalgic effect, but here was the technique available for anyone to tinker with at leisure. It was eerie and exciting; the app wordlessly embodied all the confusion in a moment of rapid dematerialization: record stores were closing and e-books were selling, and both trends seemed inevitable. Instagram, as faux old parlor game, was antithetical to the atemporality of digital images, in which everything years ago, or years in the future, is the same file format, made of the same pixels, and absent the grain and markings of a physical image. In New York—where I was living at the time; a city endlessly embracing and denying its history, sometimes on the same block—it was curious, poignant even, to see my photographs look as though I'd captured moments in the seventies or eighties. Yes, that was my breakfast, but it looked like Patti Smith and Robert Mapplethorpe might walk by at any moment. It is the same gag offered by any novelty portrait studio from Deadwood to the Tower of London, but without costumes (the image itself was in costume) and for a different audience—city hipsters, the kind who might have a Holga camera on the shelf just for show. And the images could be shared, online, at once, with other design- and style-conscious Instagram users.

After it cinched up a tailored cool audience, in 2012, Instagram courted the masses and made the app available to Google Android phone users. Facebook acquired it that year, and by then, the novelty had faded, like every novelty. While users grew tired of the photo time warp, another trend emerged on Instagram: #nofilter. This hashtag indicated more than just an eschewal of vintage filters. It was a proclamation of authenticity and soon, an off-screen slang ("We need to talk. Hashtag no filter"). After the nostalgia games, Instagram evolved and eventually became the top photo-sharing social network. I find myself thinking about "#nofilter" now like an ad campaign slogan. It was Instagram's "Just do it," but users came up with it. Features on Twitter like the @ reply to respond to another user, or the hashtag to note a topic, or even the retweet (RT), were ideas that came from users. But in this case, the social network's brand image was written by the users. Because Instagram's base switched from vintage filters to #nofilter or more subtle use of filters—from the vintage photo effect to an ordinary digital image—if a user has been around a while, the images look older the farther you scroll down their page. The images, pseudo-atemporal then, now demonstrate age over time, after all.

Instagram was the only social media platform that got better on weekends. Outside work, left to one's own devices, a person's interests and habits came through in the images they shared. Flush with new Android and Facebook users, it began to take over the lifecasting that happened on other platforms. Twitter users were now more likely to link to articles they deemed important or comment on world events and politics (if they ever were tweeting breakfast). Instagram had no retweet-like function, which kept a feed specific to a user's own personality, rather than amplifying someone else's life. A visit to a user's Instagram feed felt like a direct portal to their experience: pets, hobbies, vacations, what their houses look like, the clothes they wear, parties, and yes, breakfast. People with unusual possessions and daily routines came to prominence. A Tumblr called "Rich Kids of Instagram" compiled examples of private jets, dressage competitions, and other markers of a stratosphere of luxury from users documenting their lives in Southampton, Saint-Tropez, Dubai, or St. Moritz. Celebrities took to Instagram to preempt paparazzi. A famous actress, taking pictures at her home (#nofilter), welcomed a user into her life in a way the media could never access, on her own terms, in an intimate domain. Instagram, with its focus on individuals as individuals, encouraged users to maintain parasocial relationships—lurking, digital people-watching—while also keeping up with the lives of friends. It used to be that camgirls on the internet were approximating fame; then all celebrities became camgirls.

The arrangement and presentation of any image, #nofilter or not, is rarely as spontaneous as it might appear, but this isn't necessarily an act of inauthenticity. It was once very unusual to see a person's apartment if you knew them only casually. After all, privacy was the point of building homes. Just as you might clean up your room before a guest arrives, a user might gently (or aggressively) edit their world before sharing it with their followers. A selfie is the swiftest way to express one's feeling without using emoji, which in certain cases is a bit too cute, too wry, or too comic book. Why not share it? Perhaps someone took a hundred selfies before they decided which one to share. What's the difference between that and revising a paragraph a hundred times? That's what humans do; they self-edit.

The problem with Instagram lies in how user identity entwines with commerce. Those prone to envy find Instagram challenging, as the keeping-up-with-the-Joneses mentality among users is more sinister than the anxieties examined in so many midcentury John Cheever stories. Status is calculated in counts of likes, comments, and followers. These numbers are not for nothing. The difference between five thousand and five hundred followers could determine whether a hiring manager at a fashion magazine even bothers to read the résumé of an applicant for an open editorial assistant position. Follower count status also plays out on Twitter, but there, a user performs the identity of distributed punditry. On Instagram, the product, the content, and the information to share comes from a user's own life—there's nothing more personal. That follower count is a grade of your life. Brands commonly pay people with large followings to wear their dresses or use various products in Instagram pictures, as personality payola. Some celebrities disclose paid affiliation—#sponcon ("sponsored content")—but without this hashtag it looks like the ultimate endorsement: a high-status person uses this. Among power users, it seems that everyone is selling something, whether that is clothes, fashion, dessert, design, or themselves. That blend of real and staged, where #nofilter meets #sponcon, sets the terms for casual users. From kinetic sand to overnight oat bowls, regular people feel pressure to make their lives eye-catching, adopting what was a professional skill to make things appealing.

YouTube and Twitch are some of the other platforms where user identity can balloon into riches or the dream of it. Vine, a video platform that lasted slightly longer than the six-second clips people posted on it, had its own cadre of elite "Vine stars." The most viral among them made millions of dollars in brand affiliations, or whatever ad people call it these days. A few of them rented apartments at a luxe complex in Los Angeles, 1600 Vine, at the corner of Sunset and Vine. It was a Hollywood dream that ended as Hollywood dreams almost always will.

Most influencers frighten me, those Ariana Grande clones with skin shellacked and Photoshopped to smooth marble, morphing under flower-crown and puppy-face Snapchat filters, who traipse through social content theme parks like the Museum of Ice Cream. (Although, who am I to judge? Myself, the idiot who once tried to channel Logan Tom in Friendster avatars.) And I worry about them. Micro-fame has a momentary shelf life in contrast with the structure, protection, and filthy lucre of traditional celebrity. There might be a windfall, but platform celebrity has no resilience; this stardom is unlikely to transition into the magazine covers, awards, and prestige we associate with cultural legends. Ann Powers, in a *Los Angeles Times* profile of Lady Gaga in 2009, described how the star had "tapped into one of the primary obsessions of our age—the changing nature of the self in relation to technology, the ever-expanding media sphere, and that sense of always being in character and publicly visible that Gaga calls 'the fame'—and made it her own obsession, the subject of her songs and the basis of her persona." In retrospect, Lady Gaga's response to the mirage of micro-celebrity horizontalism became a sensation because she was already ensconced in a dying model of a hierarchical stardom. Viral celebrity without the wealth to afford privacy and institutional support for protection is mere visibility, and fragile at that. Lady Gaga explored "self in relation to technology" from a position unattainable for most users.

While fame attained through social media comes with no institutional backbone, users on the platform see these Publishers Clearing House winners only while they are winning—the social media algorithms filter out the users left empty-handed and hungry. The spotlight blinds the winners, and their success is negligible. Now that being an internet user is no longer special, being popular on the internet is also not uncommon. Creating a blog used to be unique enough to merit attention, but the ratio of influencers to influenced is tilting toward a world in which every user is broadcasting for no one. Instagram, like YouTube and other broadcast platforms, is used by Academy Award–winning actors and the most popular boy at a small school in a rural town alike, to keep in touch with fans—both are striving to maintain relevance in this changing world. It is shallow personage. The internet democratized being a nobody.

A few years ago, when I was a contractor at a traffic-driven online magazine, I complained to a technologist friend about the pressure I was under to deliver page views above a certain threshold. Some of my co-workers had tens or hundreds of thousands of Twitter followers, and could take self-promotion for granted, but I was at the mercy of whoever happened to surf over to the website that day or whether the publication decided to promote my work. I made a joke about a service in Russia where people could buy traffic to their YouTube videos, saying that perhaps I could buy a hundred thousand clicks to my articles. "I could probably build a botnet to drive traffic to your stories," my friend said. But I didn't take her up on it. The publication let me go shortly after (it was not exactly a great work experience). All of this was instructive: I realized none of it mattered.

That I might have held on to my job if I paid off Russian hackers or asked my friend to build a botnet is reflective of the incoherence of the clickbait economy. My influence, or lack thereof, impacted my livelihood. Visiting a page says nothing about whether the user accessing it actually enjoyed what they read or not (as the old Myspace Spyspace website explained, "Some people just like clickin' around"), but this traffic is data that tells a story to decision makers. I could write objectively better stories and receive quantifiably fewer page views and build reader loyalty, but my employer prioritized numbers first. Advertisers prioritized these numbers, even if they could not identify a relationship between web ads and moving inventory. And, of course, the traffic could be faked. Followers can be bought. As social media makes everyone media, traffic, likes, followers, and engagement mean more to users than popularity. When metrics determine having a job or not having a job, those who seem thirsty, and desperate to influence, are owed some sympathy. The difference between thousands of followers or not could provide a month of insulin treatment through GoFundMe or not. It is grotesque, but an influencer's *influence* may have the stakes of life or death.

It is possible to be an Instagram user far away from all of this. A number of my friends say that Instagram is the only social network they actually like. They follow no celebrities or "influencers," only people they know—they are there to see the lives of people they care about. As for me, I dropped it years ago, and feel no withdrawal pangs. But I'm useless for advice on surviving an Instagram detox. The reason I bounced was that I was harassed by someone prominent in my field. All the while I was receiving obsessive, thoroughly inappropriate messages from him, his Instagram feed told another story, of beach vacations and romantic dinners with his partner. Every image on his feed looked to me like evidence that people would not believe my accusation. Disgusted by the disjuncture of this person's life, and with no interest in carefully pruning which of our mutual friends I should unfollow or block, I worked to build my life outside Instagram. I have thought about going back, but it would be too hard. This experience made my head spin and practically split open; and yes, it is difficult for me to disentangle my experience with one particularly toxic user of the platform from my feelings about the platform itself. I'm trying my best not to mistake my bad experience for the totality of all user interactions. Instagram use isn't Instagram abuse, but it is the property of Facebook, which means that no matter how you use it, your activity is tracked and sold.

Instagram is only one example of how photography figures into sharing as a conversational practice. Picture-taking is casual in the smartphone age, rather than planned, and the ease fuddles conventions of propriety. Pictures found online that convey a style or design or capture a user's interest can be stored and shared with the same digital tools to maintain an archive of one's personal photography. But a user sharing found images has created a new story, and a new context, independent of the original photographer's intent.

Photographs are an interpretation of reality presented as reality, and like the internet, fertile for misrepresentation. In her autobiography, responding to critics who thought her children looked severe and eerie in her photographs, Sally Mann revealed pictures taken just seconds before, in which they appeared relaxed and normal. She had selected the severe photos; a twitch of a facial expression and stiffness in the shoulders is all it takes to shift the mood of an image. "When only one photograph survives, its authority is unimpeachable, and we are in the position of jurors who have to decide a case based on one witness's unchallenged testimony," she wrote. I thought of Mann's comments when a picture of Sasha Obama standing with a young man at a buffet went viral, with social media users adding commentary like "mfw cutie makes a plate." This image was cropped from a picture of the entire Obama family serving Thanksgiving dinner to veterans. Those who shared the images with similar tweets and comments had failed to read the original news caption, that the former president's younger daughter, looking bright-eyed and having a good time, was standing next to her cousin Avery Robinson. How embarrassing for her that users rushed to interpret her facial expressions as conveying anything else.

Reaction images started as a trend on Tumblr, a platform

where scrapbooks became an interactive experience. In the beginning, Tumblr was general, like a blog but faster. The Tumblr browser extension could quickly highlight and post text and images from elsewhere on the web. It was a platform for political commentary and personal diary-like entries at first. Occupy Wall Street even had a Tumblr, "We are the 99%," that was its online focal point, where activists shared their faces and their stories of financial hardship. But writing original text and uploading original images felt slow, too slow for this particular platform, so capture and collage became a more common way of communicating on it. The perspective was also different from blogging in its thematic adherence. Tumblr users often had multiple Tumblrs, buckets for various ideas, interests, and presentations.

Tumblr may have longed for a wider reach, but by 2013, nearly half of its users were between the ages of sixteen and twenty-four. That's the age of those who collage their bedroom walls with pictures torn out of magazines, and that's what they were doing in pixels. Pinterest, in contrast, was slightly more grown-up, like Tumblr's basic older sister; a destination for brides-to-be, Mormon moms, and glamorous models who inexplicably all seemed to live on farms upstate. Tumblr had a more pointed youth-focused social justice bent, and its users seemed to be more progressive about gender identity than those on other corners of the internet. While nonbinary people, those who identify as agender, and men—cis and trans—were present on Tumblr, there was an unmistakable femininity that came through as well. Photographs of icons like Anna Karina and Grace Jones were commonly reblogged, collaged with whatever else, be it Kardashian paparazzi photos; mash notes; images from Astronomy Picture of the Day; decay and ruin displayed like beauty—like images of run-down Borscht Belt hotels turned Ballardian, with broken chairs piled in empty swimming pools; as well as the confessions one might only whisper if one were to speak them aloud at all. There was something active, rather than passive, something literary and aesthetic about Tumblr. Its users found connections between images and jumbles of juxtapositions. A certain kind of Tumblr user was "an Arcades Project of her fragments," wrote Kate Zambreno in her book *Heroines*. She identified how the platform, like LiveJournal before it, summoned a "new sort of subjectivity." For "these spaces operate as safe havens to be all sorts of identities at once, to be excessive, to feel and desire deeply," Zambreno continued. Tumblr's currency was images as vessels for arguments, stripped of context and applied with new meaning depending on what the user wanted. Unlike Instagram or Twitter, follower counts were hidden from all but the user themselves. People could guess which users were more influential than others, based on how often they appeared in their feeds, but there was no exact number to capture status and commodify it. It evaded much of Instagram's poseyness; plus, it was possible to be anonymous there—visible, ad hoc, but still part of a community.

Tumblr also lacked a big money data-mining operation. Yahoo bought the platform in 2013, and its attempts to introduce autoplay video ads alienated Tumblr users. In June 2016, it dropped from the top one hundred free iOS apps in the United States. Now it is the property of Verizon, which bought Yahoo in 2017. Harassment has become a problem on the platform, and with no suitable blocking tools, it is pernicious. Features that were Tumblr's signature—reblogging, like photocopying—have become a nightmare in its later stages because users can never completely delete their old posts.

In December 2018, Tumblr issued a ban on all "adult content." The decision came after Apple removed its app from the App Store, because of an incident of child pornography that was discovered on the service. The app was reapproved for the App Store following this ban. Another factor that may have contributed to Tumblr's decision was the Stop Enabling Sex Traffickers Act (SESTA) and Fight Online Sex Trafficking Act (FOSTA), passed in Congress that year, which amended U.S. law Section 230 of the 1996 Communications Decency Act to make an exception for "sex trafficking." To back up, Section 230 is how social sharing is even legally possible in the United States. It classifies platforms more as libraries than publishers. As the Electronic Frontier Foundation explains it, "This legal and policy framework has allowed for YouTube and Vimeo users to upload their own videos, Amazon and Yelp to offer countless user reviews, Craigslist to host classified ads, and Facebook and Twitter to offer social networking to hundreds of millions of Internet users." While there is no evidence that SESTA/FOSTA impacted "sex trafficking," the amendment disrupted the livelihoods of sex workers, who lost clients and the safe methods they had developed to screen them through the internet. But what was devastating to Tumblr's own communities was the term "adult content"; it seemed to cast too wide a net. Tumblr's queer and marginalized contingent, familiar with similar policy on other platforms, in which anything remotely queer-ish—say, two men holding hands—might be flagged, felt hurt and orphaned by a platform that once resembled something like a safe space.

■

Zambreno's *Heroines*, published in 2012, connected Tumblrs and LiveJournals with art and literature, an all too rare contextualization at the time—especially bound in a book. Self-declared intellectuals, and those who believed themselves to be concerned with the sanctity of books and culture, commonly dismissed the internet, in its entirety, as a sphere of the lowbrow and amateur—when they bothered to acknowledge it. To them, it was all junk, all grubby and artless. The internet, in their minds, defiled people and coated users in sewage that never washed off, or else it was the realm of the uncouth masses: endless unsolicited pitches and slush. Richard Ford, channeling Brad Paisley, told *The New York Times* that he never looked at literary blogs. Why would he read criticism written by "some guy sitting in his basement in Terre Haute"? In 2010, the publisher of *Harper's Magazine*, John R. MacArthur, challenged those who believe the internet is a "bottom-up phenomenon that wondrously bypasses the traditional gatekeepers in publishing and politics who allegedly snuff out true debate." Rather, as he put it, "most of what I see is unedited, incoherent babble indicative of a herd mentality." The title of a public event, organized by *The New Yorker* in 2013, drew a line in the sand: "Is Technology Good for Culture?" A few authors bought into these terms, and made a point to declare themselves pristine. A cliché marker of writerly genius in magazine profiles at the time was that the "author doesn't carry a phone" or "doesn't use the internet." This asceticism, conveying little more than an individual's communication preferences and boundaries with other people, was delivered as evidence of an individual's dedication and superior creativity. Can anyone imagine a profile of the sort extolling the virtue of any other deliberate ignorance? ("The author is so committed to his craft that he can't name a president after Nixon.") This non-debate about the internet's deleterious prospects for culture ran out the clock through vital hours, at a time when the media—including culture critics—should have focused on issues of user consent, monopoly power, harassment, and all of the internet's actual problems. Instead, the internet-haters of the highbrow persuasion flaunted their ignorance: bereft of language to describe it, they consequently could not differentiate the worst parts of the internet from the internet itself. Users and corporations were one and the same; no distinction was made between art and advertising or sharing and writing. The line in the sand was between internet—everything and everyone on it—and not-internet. This was no technology criticism; it was general-purpose classism.

This hostility toward the internet and the people on it might explain why there are still so few novels and films that deeply engage with the internet experience and all the emotions it entails. Granted, technology—especially internet technology—is a challenge to narrativize and depict in traditional media. Some of the best examples of art and literature that express what it means to live a digital life are works of words and images, often with formal qualities that do not neatly divide into either art or literature. Kate Zambreno understood this when she wrote about Tumblr. Mendi and Keith Obadike's eBay intervention, *Blackness for Sale*, and Ana Voog's Anacam are fine examples of internet art. I wonder if Natalie Wynn's "ContraPoints" commentary on YouTube will hold up as video art if in the future people stop using YouTube. Spalding Gray had Jonathan Demme and an empty theater, but the comments left on Wynn's page and the recommended videos that appear in the sidebar (many from the sort of incels she satirizes) feel integral to one's encounters with—and appreciation of—her performances. Another stunning work is *Why's (Poignant) Guide to Ruby*, a poetic, transgressive, and strange online document, with illustrations and recursive humor, that also happens to be one of the first guides to the Ruby programming language. The author, who was known as Why the Lucky Stiff, or "_why," had a restless Pynchonian humor (and disappeared from public life, like him). Other work just never materialized, like Ted Nelson's impossible dream of Project Xanadu, a goal since 1960 for universal electronic publishing with version control and unbreakable links—hypertext vaporware, which lives in the hearts of many internet old-timers, like Alejandro Jodorowsky's unrealized film of *Dune*.

Unfocused internet-hating in culture writing happened alongside uncritical, even fanboyish reporting on the tech industry that appeared in business sections. As result, there was an absence of worthwhile criticism. The sum total of internet users was climbing, major internet companies gained leverage and power, and calls for digital abstinence became less realistic day by day. Still, several years passed before the media responded appropriately. Sara Watson, author of the *Columbia Journalism Review* report "Toward a Constructive

Technology Criticism," identifies Edward Snowden's leaks in 2013 as a transformative event that fostered more pointed and nuanced coverage of the internet. Instead of vague stakes like "is it good or is it bad," moving forward, commentary about the internet involved specifics like diminishing privacy, the fallout of security breaches, and how platforms manipulate user behavior. As Watson explains, what "blossomed out of [the Snowden story] was an understanding of how much more the technology industry deserved investigative attention and journalistic resources. Since then, investigative efforts have exposed labor practices at Amazon, detailed Google's extensive lobbying efforts, uncovered Uber's means for dealing with harassment, and surfaced discriminatory decisions and predatory practices of algorithms."

In a 2011 appearance on *Late Night with Jimmy Fallon*, Winona Ryder admitted she was "afraid of the internet," as a new iPhone user. "Googling is very terrifying for me," she said. "I have this fear that I'm going to be trying to find out what movie is playing at what theater and then suddenly be a member of al-Qaeda." Ryder's comments weren't hateful or hostile to users who got online before her. Rather, she identifies an experience that rings true today, unlike so many high-minded anti-internet screeds at the time she said it: how hard it is to feel in control as a user.

There is one reliable method to control one's identity; it is imperfect, but it is not hard to do. That method is to use a locked account. Similar to the difference between a private book like a diary, or a book authored under a pseudonym, most social networks allow users to "go private" and control who follows them, and keep all their posts hidden from public viewing. It is building a house for your content, protecting your online identity on your own terms. Locked online accounts are for whispers and sympathy, and lurking means something different there.

On the internet, sharing is conversation, sharing is image-making, sharing is *sharing*; but when it comes to the tech giants that control centralized platforms, sharing is taking.

# 5

# Clash

Anyone active on Twitter in August 2013 might have seen the beginnings of a movement. It started with Mikki Kendall, a Chicago-based writer, who posted a series of tweets tagged #SolidarityIs-ForWhiteWomen, messages that depicted how white women instantiate anti-blackness and other forms of discrimination in feminist communities. Her tweets opened up a conversation of 75,465 messages in just the first four days. Contributors were other black women, indigenous and Native women, trans women, women who work as sex workers, Muslim women, queer women—in that moment, all kinds of women marginalized by the mainstream white feminist discourse raised their voices and found community with one another. The hashtag unfolded in pieces, as Twitter content does; each tweet became a node and junction, representative of the larger systemic issue. These were opinions and personal stories told in brief, interlinked with a wider appeal, as the platform allowed. The hashtag was a keyword and hyperlink to a community and context, which meant that no one experienced it the same way or followed the hashtag to completion. It was a shared experience, despite the fragmentary delivery, like passing a kaleidoscope around a campfire.

Harnessing Twitter algorithms and filters, the hashtag-driven conversation distributed information in the absence of traditional media. The contributors could direct attention to their commentary, without permission from media gatekeepers or customs of publicity. Twitter users who might not know or even follow Kendall, or any of the other primary contributors, could still find the conversation and add their relevant concerns. For anyone could access these tweets. White people and men might have noticed because women of color they followed were contributing to it, but also, because it was such a popular hashtag, it was listed in the sidebar under "trending topics."

As a white woman, it was not my place to contribute, but I lurked on the hashtag as it accelerated. It played out like a free lesson in how not to be a bigoted hypocrite, and that happens to be one of my goals in life. After #SolidarityIsForWhiteWomen followed its course, complementary campaigns, like #NotYourAsianSidekick, #BlackPowerIsForBlackMen, and #NotYourNarrative, in which Muslim women posted about their experiences with stereotypes and racism, took over with more specific ranges of concerns. So many users were contributing to these hashtag campaigns, it alleviated the stigma against speaking out. An individual, alienated and fearful of backlash if she raised these topics on her own, could post something knowing the hashtag offered context and strength in numbers.

Social justice hashtags were a crash course in intersectionality, a framework developed by Kimberlé Williams Crenshaw and further elucidated by writers and scholars like bell hooks and Audre Lorde. The word has stretched out in recent years, but "intersectionality" as a concept—at its core, as Crenshaw named it—refers to the overlapping injustices and biases to which black women are subordinated, and how, as she wrote, they are "excluded from feminist theory and antiracist policy discourse because both are predicated on a discrete set of experiences that often does not accurately reflect the interaction of race and gender." With regard to #SolidarityIsForWhiteWomen, the word "inclusive" might be more appropriate than "intersectional," as it applied to women of color more broadly. In any case, it highlighted how people who benefit from one privilege can be hindered by other forms of oppression in other contexts, or contribute to the oppression of another community. What might have been an uncomfortable conversation delivered by other means came through with stunning poignance and dignity. I learned from it. A lot of people did.

It was a summer of portents. Edward Snowden had just appeared on camera from a hotel room in Hong Kong, and a few months later, Chelsea Manning was convicted, after a court-martial predicated on a judge's failure to understand how the internet actually worked. #SolidarityIsForWhite-Women was groundbreaking and whistle-blowing, too, but due to the nature of its distribution—over Twitter, using hashtags—its significance is often undermined. These events are linked, in my mind, as instances in which blindfolds were ripped off; problems that were intuited rose to the surface; things that one might assume but never be able to prove were now out in the open and impossible to ignore. Swift, though incomplete, change has spun out of hashtag activism. But history has a tendency of erasing the incremental struggles that result in what is called progress after concerns reach critical mass. People who were brave and spoke out first faced retaliation and ostracism, before they were replaced with more accommodating voices, capitalizing on and neutralizing hard-won justice.

Another famous hashtag traces back to 2013: #BlackLives-Matter. Three black community organizers, Alicia Garza, Opal Tometi, and Patrisse Cullors, founded the movement as an online campaign in response to the injustice of George Zimmerman's acquittal for the murder of Trayvon Martin, and it germinated into demonstrations against other instances of police brutality, such as the killings of Eric Garner and Mike Brown in 2014. Black Lives Matter activists coordinated online and offline protests; networks of people connected through the hashtag could also unite in activism on the street. The murder of Mike Brown was particularly galvanizing, because the Black Lives Matter movement would not let anyone forget. Moreover, legacy media could no longer ignore police brutality in America, as social media, newly dominant in the lives of everyday Americans, provided constant reminders.

The press did not ignore these activists, but media coverage was often skeptical, identifying Twitter hashtag movements and online activism as a peanut gallery in a state of "outrage." The online magazine *Slate* embodied this sentiment with an interactive package called "The Year in Outrage" that was published before the holidays in 2014. It was designed to look like an advent calendar for the entire year, with each box representing an "outrage" that happened that day. A corresponding reader poll was used to determine whether each example was "outrageous" or "overblown." Votes were tallied on a meter graphic with two emoji-like faces representing the ends of the spectrum: an angry red "outrage" face and a yellow eye-rolling face to mean "overblown." The interactive was designed for a user to scroll through quickly, which imbued the content with a perverse leveling effect. Abhorrent injustices like the death of Eric Garner, who was killed by a New York City police officer, were nestled alongside celebrity scandals, and nothing but the vote tallies differentiated one from the other. Each appeared with an outrage meter and poll ("Was the incident a truly justified outrage or was it overblown? Click a face to vote"). This charade of insensitivity did little to contextualize outrage, but it unintentionally revealed the racism, transphobia, and other bigotries animating *Slate* readers. Issues related to people of color and trans people—including an example of a trans woman who committed suicide after an unethical reporter betrayed her—were rated "overblown." *Slate*'s interactive was a near-perfect focus group for Park Slope politics in 2014. The ire its readers felt about, say, anti-vaxxers (yes, very bad!) didn't extend to examples of suffering that marginalized communities faced.

"Outrage" is often a stealth accusation of insubordination. People don't talk about the "outrage" of their bosses or the "outrage" of billionaires. It is the great unwashed who outrage away, typically on their Twitters and the Facebooks. Some thoughtful and eloquent people are accused of "outrage" because they choose to face struggles head-on rather than compliment the powerful and maintain the status quo. As the feminist scholar Sara Ahmed has put it, "you are perceived as being pushy when what you are pushing against is not perceived." If the powerless and disenfranchised are indignant, well, why wouldn't they be? The opposite of outrage is calmness and complicity. There is no way to disrupt hierarchy—patriarchy, white supremacy, aristocracy—without outrage.

The outrage over "outrage" was a symptom of media growing pains. Those with comfortable legacy media perches as staff writers and editors might have used the internet, but they did not identify as *users*—at least not in the way that someone posting a grievance online would be. The pain that was exhibited in hashtag campaigns like #SolidarityIsForWhiteWomen was "not perceived"—at least not yet. Collective grievance was conflated with mob behavior and moral panics online. The many grades and variations of power were brushed aside to condemn internet outrage as an oversize threat. As a classic example of this conflation, Jon Ronson, while promoting his 2015 book *So You've Been Publicly Shamed*, routinely stated that internet users are collectively "worse than the NSA."

Another tipping domino, in 2013, was Sheryl Sandberg's

book, *Lean In: Women, Work, and the Will to Lead.* However, it was the criticism it garnered, rather than the actual text, that made a lasting impact. Facebook's chief operating officer had big plans for her first book. It was going to be a movement with "Lean In circles," and networking and mentorship events for women in business. To hype the book and a newly launched nonprofit with the same name, Sandberg invited twenty writers associated with women's publications to an off-the-record dinner in Tribeca. Needless to say, the feminist billionaire was a plum contact for the members of the media. Perhaps *Lean In* would proffer nicely paid contract work; maybe Sandberg could fund new publications or sponsor documentaries and conferences, or otherwise materially support these writers in their careers. I can't confirm whether any of them made it to the Lean In Foundation payroll, but a few published impassioned defenses of the book against early criticism, so Sandberg got what she wanted out of that dinner.

At first glance, *Lean In*'s advice seemed sensible, if a little staid. Among its recommendations, there were calls for women to be more assertive rather than cower in impostor syndrome. "Don't leave before you leave" was a frequently quoted suggestion, meaning, don't give up on your career too far in advance of having a family, but cross the bridge when you come to it. Okay, sure. But at second glance—for anyone except the Tribeca dinner-party-goers—it was obvious that what Sandberg offered was relevant only to women leaning in to a princely tax bracket.

Melissa Gira Grant was the first critic to address *Lean In*'s myopic notions of class and race, and the homogeneity of its assumed readership. As a former reporter at Valleywag,

Grant was very familiar with Sandberg's career and leadership style. Facebook's COO, Grant wrote, failed to consider that women are also "child-free, unmarried, lesbian or bisexual, transgender, or working in the many thousands of jobs outside the halls of global capital's leadership." Furthermore, she concluded in her piece for *The Washington Post*, "women and our social movements do not need a better boss but a more powerful base, from which we can lead on our own terms." Grant's criticism sounds a lot like contemporary #TimesUp and #MeToo demands, but when this piece was published, she was met with scorn. Women who attended Sandberg's dinner sarcastically subtweeted Grant and began treating her coldly at social functions. They had been hand-selected by Sandberg's PR team as influencers, after all. Other popular feminist writers roundly attacked Grant's reasonable op-ed for daring to criticize their new queen bee. "Skirting feminist self-parody," Michelle Goldberg wrote in *The Daily Beast*, "Grant proceeds to complain that Sandberg fails to grapple with the struggles of domestic workers, the unemployed, people whose caretaking duties extend beyond children to aging parents as well as 'close friends and extended families,' women who can't have children, and those who are lesbian, bisexual, or transgender."

Yes, and? What good is feminism without them? Several other high-profile feminist commentators circled the wagons and defended Sandberg in *The Nation*, *The New Yorker*, and other publications. But as the year went on, Susan Faludi, bell hooks, Sarah Leonard, and other writers followed up with criticism aligned with Grant's key points. They highlighted the labor, race, and class dimensions that the book and "movement" ignored. Critics even pointed out the faulty advice in its own title—suggesting that an individual "lean in" to change denies the structural problems that fortify gender bias in the workplace. None other than the *Harvard Business Review*, the publication affiliated with Sandberg's alma mater, weighed in, calling out the book for perpetuating the myth that women merely lack the confidence to negotiate their salaries. The piece, reviewing a survey of forty-six hundred randomly selected employees across eight hundred workplaces, concluded that "women do 'ask' just as often as men. They just don't 'get.'" Now "lean in" is slang for futile optics that are ultimately useless at preventing structural gender discrimination. Some of the writers who sprang to Sandberg's defense early on have casually disavowed her book; others quietly distanced themselves from it. Goldberg even echoed Grant's original points in a review of Ivanka Trump's 2017 book *Women Who Work*.

*Lean In* was a publicity machine, but real results were coming out of existing feminist activism in technology. Communities of women tech workers, several steps ahead of Sandberg, were inclusive, adapting to the needs of queer and trans people, disabled people, and people of color, and aware of how aspects of identity exacerbate sexism. Among these groups were the feminist hackerspace Double Union, an unconference called AdaCamp, and a blog and wiki called *Geek Feminism*, which included an exhaustive number of articles with information like how to write a code of conduct to use at a conference, or the best practices of explaining nonbinary inclusion in "women's spaces." Theirs was no "Got a lot done, Hitlerina" boosterism, as a character in a Caryl Churchill play once put it. These groups, many based in the Bay Area, were having conversations more advanced than those of women's media based in New York (typical 2013 headline: IS BEYONCÉ *REALLY* A FEMINIST?). If I were a Malcolm Gladwell type of thinkfluencer, I might try to weave a grand unified theory around why women in the tech community seemed more likely than professional feminist commentators in New York to address intersectional concerns. Perhaps it has something to do with networks (TCP/IP and bell hooks, yeah, there's a scholarly dissertation in there somewhere). Whatever it was, their organizing, rather than Sandberg's failed feminist movement, is more broadly reflected in women's media today.

Many of the feminists in tech wrote op-eds and posted them for free on Medium, the hybrid platform-publisher-platisher-platypus free-for-all. Evan Williams, the founder of Medium, had previously founded Twitter and Blogger, but his new platform, which launched in 2012, was inscrutable. Medium, in its early years, seemed like a comprehensive list of every rejected *Wired* pitch, either stories that were too outlandishly techno-sociopathic ("What If Trayvon Martin Was Wearing Google Glasses?" was the title of an actual piece a Medium user published in 2013 that argued the device might have saved the teenager's life) or commentary that ever so modestly addressed sexism in the tech industry ("Hi, pardon me, sorry, but could guys at software conferences please stop sexually harassing me?"). Later, a few of the popular feminist Medium writers went on to create a publication of their own called *Model View Culture*. It was both a quarterly printed edition and an online site. Here is how the editors summarized the first issue:

> [We] discuss the connection between Facebook and NSA surveillance, explore network dynamics in London's Tech City, and investigate identity as labor in startup culture. We analyze the search for the next Zuckerberg, challenge monolithic approaches to social justice in tech, and examine the link between online harassment and platform features. Plus, an open letter to marginalized people beginning their careers, Q&A with Ada Developers Academy, a political cartoon about VC funding, and a look at the role of critique in our community.

The publication ran vital pieces month after month. Unfortunately, a year later, a cofounder of *Model View Culture* left because of what she claimed was an emotionally and verbally abusive environment. While this backstory is disappointing, the writing published was typically excellent, and it remains an essential archive for critical perspectives on technology at a time when such commentary was rare.

*Model View Culture* was crucial context for emerging scandals, including a sexual harassment and gender discrimination case at GitHub that broke shortly after its first issue in early 2014. Julie Ann Horvath, an engineer at the code collaboration platform, spoke out about a jumble of toxic office behavior: she was targeted by a range of people, her work was routinely undermined in gendered ways, the wife of a GitHub cofounder—who was not an employee—bullied her, that cofounder was confrontational and escalated the situation, and when she turned down a co-worker's request for a date, he ripped out some of her code, erasing her contributions to a project they collaborated on. (After an investigation, the cofounder, Tom Preston-Werner, was found to have acted inappropriately toward Horvath and he offered his resignation.) What happened at GitHub wasn't easy for outsiders to follow, but the heap of examples—of varying graduations of misconduct—and muddled nature of it were relatable. Many women, including myself, could see experiences of their own—experiences that perhaps they were unwilling to label as harassment at the time—in Horvath's allegations. TechCrunch, ordinarily a Silicon Valley cheerleading rag, and seldom one to rock the boat, published a remarkably sympathetic piece documenting the abuse she experienced at the company, concluding that the "situation has greater import than a single person's struggle: Horvath's story is a tale of what many underrepresented groups feel and experience in the tech sector."

The story of Horvath's exit had a long media cycle, including coverage in publications rarely concerned with Silicon Valley or its products at the time. Readers outside the tech industry learned about GitHub's bizarre policy of "holacracy," the so-called decentralized management structure that is a clusterfuck in practice, where no one is responsible for anything and everyone is responsible for everything. Few reporters could resist a jab at GitHub HQ's replica of the White House Oval Office, complete with a circular carpet emblazoned with the words "The United Meritocracy of GitHub" (the company's gift to itself after a one-hundred-million-dollar investment from Andreessen Horowitz). A year later, Ellen Pao's gender discrimination case against her former employer Kleiner Perkins Caufield & Byers went to trial, and the topic of "Women in Tech" became unavoidable. Reporters and pundits began to connect the dots to show that the industry (like every other industry, including the media) was run by white men (CEOs and brogrammers) and yet they were creating the apps and websites that shaped and structured our society and culture.

To deter scrutiny, many tech founders and insiders assumed the mantle of responsibility and attempted to diversify their teams (rather than turning to existing feminist organizers in Silicon Valley, like Double Union). They prioritized capitalism-compliant optics over real solutions, the polite over the combative, and the conciliatory over the activist, just like *Lean In*. Championing "diversity" was also a diversion tactic. Throwing money at diversity programs was less fraught than examining the causes for the lack of it (patriarchy, white supremacy, and capitalism). Heartwarming images of ten-year-old girls learning Python could temporarily overshadow other issues that Silicon Valley was increasingly held accountable for, like the vast and growing economic inequality in the Bay Area, the omnisurveillance that Edward Snowden's disclosures brought to public attention, surveillance capitalism, and how the tech industry exacerbated lack of public trust in institutions. Capitalizing on intersectionality isn't an altogether bad thing. It's just complicated. It is wonderful, for example, that Google provides pads and tampons in men's rooms of some of its offices. Google also lets people announce their pronouns with stickers at tech conference check-ins, but meanwhile Google donates money to anti-LGBTQ politicians. These companies don't have a user's best interest at heart, or else they wouldn't be these companies.

The press didn't break the story of Horvath's exit. She

went to Twitter first, a platform where she would later receive heaps of online abuse for daring to speak out as she had. Twitter fully exhibited the double-edge sword of visibility: there, attention came at the expense of safety. Yes, a user could broadcast a message across contexts—as hashtag activism demonstrated—and get people who would not normally consider an issue to listen. However, because Twitter is designed to accommodate all kinds of people, this cross-context eddy drew the attention of hostile people as well—the kind who might flood a user's account with rape threats, death threats, and other violent statements. As use of Twitter grew, user demands for support and moderation—labor that requires hiring people and suspending users, practices believed to choke off engagement—went unheard.

Earlier social networks and social digital environments benefited from smaller, segmented communities: no obligation to participate, IRL intervals between logged-in sessions, and more flexible online identities. It is not so much that the early internet had no Nazis as that they tended to huddle in their own poisonous spaces. Usenet and other early chat rooms and forums were not natively suited to mediate harassment issues or ban trolls from platforms. If mediation occurred, it was initiated by a community as a restorative justice approach, which was possible only because of the intimate sizes of these communities. With the exception of extreme cases of harassment, including a vile instance in 2006 that culminated in the suicide of Megan Meier, a thirteen-year-old girl, Friendster and Myspace were never quite as intertwined with individuals' lives as Twitter and Facebook have come to be. Someone experiencing harassment back then could, reasonably, take a break from the platform if things got to that point. It was still possible to log off.

Corralling people into massive international multimillion- and multibillion-user platforms heightens interpersonal conflict (that jerk you can't avoid), as it leaves a user vulnerable to attacks from strangers. Hostile users can wield @ replies like bumper cars at a carnival. There's nothing designed to throttle a person motivated by malice from driving full speed into another person's digital life. This clash between users is revenue: generating "impressions," the term of art for the number of views of a particular piece of content. If wide use is a company's goal, harassment is not necessarily in opposition to that goal. Abuse, hate reads, coordinated harassment, and yes, *outrage* all lead to online rubbernecking—monetized clash. Advertising is sold by quantity of eyeballs, and interfering with the flow of content—moderating, mediating what is shared—comes at the expense of click-throughs.

Impersonation is one of the cruelest strains of online harassment. A friend of mine noticed an obscene example when she participated in the #NotYourAsianSidekick campaign, which was a follow-up to #SolidarityIsForWhiteWomen. The majority of people using the hashtag were Asian and Pacific Islander feminists, but among their tweets were comments from new accounts that had to be fake. On Twitter, an avatar is a user's image. Not everyone uses a face, sometimes it is a random design—flowers, a cat, clouds in the sky—but there's nothing to differentiate the photograph of an Asian woman who uploaded her own photo to the website from a photo of an Asian woman uploaded by some jerk who googled around for it and added a fake Twitter bio. The real and the fake are both two-dimensional profiles appearing on a screen. As Lisa Nakamura observed in her book *Cybertypes*, it was racist when white men assumed the identities of Asian women in cyberspace chat rooms and message boards, playing out geisha stereotypes and reinforcing these stereotypes in dialogue with other ignorant users. Impersonations on Twitter were even more sinister; it was a practice to deliberately exploit racist hierarchies, at a time when identity—online and off—was assumed to be consistent and stable.

Some fake accounts used the hashtag #NotYourAsianSidekick to insult the real people contributing to the conversation. Other fake accounts used the hashtag to post racist remarks about black women. There were multiple kinds of fake accounts, too. Trolls impersonated specific users contributing to the discussion: they would copy that user's profile image and create a near identical Twitter handle (for example, the username @lovecats2013 would be duplicated as @Iovecats2013, with an uppercase *I* replacing the lowercase *l*). My friend said that she was most disturbed by the fake accounts impersonating Jewish or black users, exaggerating stereotypes of them, while accusing the women on #NotYourAsianSidekick of anti-Semitism or anti-blackness with grotesque straw man arguments.

These tactics of impersonation-as-harassment were the groundwork for a coordinated attack on all women of color using Twitter, in June 2014. It was called #EndFathersDay, a fake hashtag campaign that the 4chan community invented and attributed to the #SolidarityIsForWhiteWomen community. It trended on Twitter, just like #SolidarityIsForWhiteWomen, but the accounts were either fake or bolstered by users asking questions like "what the hell is #EndFathers-Day?" Fox News and other conservative news outlets were first out of the gate with condemnation of "PC culture out of control." It didn't occur to them to look skeptically at these accounts, because the hashtag confirmed their low opinions of internet users concerned with social justice. Again, the attack was designed to divide women on Twitter. A fake account tweeting things like "#EndFathersDay bc it's a slap in the face to single mothers everywhere," with an avatar image of a woman of color, would be used to pick fights with white women. One of the people responsible for the fake hashtag explained his methods in a men's rights activist message board:

> We bait [people of color] into agreeing with us as we subtly move them more and more to the extreme. The purpose is to make moderate feminists turned off with the movement, as well as cause infighting within the group. [We] pose as women of color and argue with white feminists. We "check their privilege" to the point that they are fed up. For example, if they say "it's not our time to talk, white ladies, it's our time to listen," we say "the last time white women just listened, George Zimmerman walked free."

They failed on the first count. Women of color saw through this coordinated attack immediately. The fake users had coined terms like "transracial" and "Poos (People of Oppression)" that might sound authentic to readers of the Daily Caller but looked ridiculous to anyone who thinks critically about issues of race and gender. Shafiqah Hudson, I'Nasah

Crockett, and several other black women on Twitter launched a counterattack, identifying the impostors using the hashtag #YourSlipIsShowing. They posted screenshots from 4chan, in which the instigators openly discussed their tactics and intentions. Unfortunately, the second goal of 4chan's attack was successful—in the short term, at least. Sydette Harry, a community researcher who has worked with Mozilla and the Coral Project, noted on Twitter how 4chan seemed to have a "grasp of the tectonics of feminist interaction" better than some would-be allies, as they recognized how black women and other women of color can be ignored or scapegoated in feminist spaces. Remember, in 2014, it was still considered acceptable—worthwhile, even!—for feminists to debate things like whether trans women are women. It was rare to see women of color speaking at feminist conferences or listed on the masthead of feminist publications. The coordinated attack exaggerated divisions between white cis women and everyone else, but a disturbing outcome of this trolling campaign was that a few white feminist pundits wrote about #EndFathersDay as a broad attack on all women on Twitter, completely ignoring the existing fissure that it was designed to amplify.

In this book, I use the word "lurking" only in a positive context. Lurking is listening and witnessing on the internet, rather than opining and capturing the attention of others. Actions by 4chan users against feminists on Twitter were developed through reconnaissance and stalking of them, the negative aspects of observing the behavior of others. It is revealing that the 4chan users assumed these women would never see their own public discussion. This ignorance is what ultimately derailed the coordinated harassment—#YourSlipIsShowing had outmaneuvered them. I remember feeling exasperated at the time that few people noticed the complexity of this style of harassment, and I wasn't even one of the people receiving this abuse. Two years later, similar tactics by Russian trolls were counted among factors that threw an election to Donald Trump. But I can't compare women of color on the internet to a canary in the coal mine, because in that idiom, the canary isn't ignored.

Gamergate began that August. In short, it was a conspiracy about women in video games. Eron Gjoni, bitter over his recent breakup, posted a screed of about nine thousand words to a blog. The subject of his rancor was Zoë Quinn, an indie game developer. He falsely accused her of cheating on him with gaming journalists for favorable coverage of her work. The outcry resonated with some of the worst internet users, and it acted like a Katamari Damacy ball, collecting other women in gaming as targets. Put on negative pedestals, they would go on to receive unending rape and death threats, among other forms of harassment. Any old misogynists, transphobes, or racists—many with no prior interest in gaming—could latch on to its rationalizations, for the loose online movement that would come to be known as Gamergate insisted it was something, while never forming coherent goals, or even coherent concern ("actually, it's about ethics in journalism," was the near continual refrain when Gamergate supporters spoke with the media).

Visibility brought about this harassment, but anonymity does not explain the attackers. As Sarah Jeong pointed out in her book *The Internet of Garbage*, "harassers are almost always depicted as anonymous strangers. Never mind that Kathy Sierra's most prominent harasser, Andrew Auernheimer, has always had his legal name connected to his online pseudonym, 'weev.' Never mind that the campaign against Zoë began with and was egged on by an ex-partner." The attack on Sierra, like #YourSlipIsShowing, is instructive to consider now that online harassment is more commonplace. In 2007, she was about to turn fifty: not just a rare woman in the tech industry, but ever rarer—she was a woman in tech with seniority. Sierra was a prominent Java programmer and instructor, who wrote bestselling books on software design and published a blog focused on her professional talents. It was on her blog, *Creating Passionate Users*, that death threats and rape threats began to appear, some including images of her, altered with vulgarity. Auernheimer became a public figure after his involvement with Sierra, leading to profiles in *The New York Times Magazine* and *GQ*. Sierra, however, quit blogging and even left the tech industry for good.

Anonymous attackers could be just as brutal as those with a platform. "I watched them, live, pore through reams of private information in an attempt to discover who I was. Being trans made me particularly vulnerable to having my private information used in a campaign to terrorize me. They found my deadname, eventually, but only by combing through the obituary of my mother," Sarah Nyberg wrote in a 2015 essay about the horrors she endured as a Gamergate target. Nyberg's friends and family received threats, sometimes to their home addresses; the attackers dug up photos of her before her transition and distributed those as well as pictures of her loved ones, including people who had passed away. Her previous life online was available for Gamergate to exploit. Jokes and ironic "edgelord" trying-to-get-a-rise-out-of-people comments she had posted to forums and in chat rooms long ago (for example, that her computer was "seized by police") were taken out of context by the Gamergate mob and used as evidence in this travesty of a crusade. "It's never about the truth, but instead what they can twist, distort and lie about in an attempt to destroy and silence us," she concluded, noting that "these campaigns are structured so the damage is permanent—all of that information is compiled on sites, wikis, defamatory tabloid style blogs, and Youtube videos."

Gamergate revealed how reductive the discussion of online "outrage" had been up until that point. Meanwhile, other coordinated online harassment campaigns received media attention, like the hacking of A-list celebrities' nude photos and their dissemination on Reddit. Media commentary began to address various degrees of harassment experienced by different communities, including how women of color and trans women were subject to exponentially more harm in these situations. Nevertheless, this has become a regular format to stoke hatred online. Just look at President Trump's 2019 tweets attacking Congresswoman Ilhan Omar; it is the same conspiratorial thinking and target-creation as Gamergate exhibited just a few years before.

Trump trolled Rep. Omar. Now, "troll" is a common accusation and often an inaccurate one. A resolute internet hater might assume that every user is a troll. An author might be upset to find a one-star review of their book on Goodreads, but that doesn't make the person leaving that comment a troll. Perhaps this person went to work, came home, fed the dog, picked up a book, didn't like it, and posted a review to alert their friends. It happens. That's not online abuse or trolling—it is having an opinion someone doesn't like. Or maybe a reviewer leaving a single star did so in a subversive manner, like a fake "Abe L" on Yelp reviewing Ford's Theatre. In this case, calling the individual a "troll" is something of a compliment—like a "buffoon" or court jester, creating anarchy and destabilizing the pious.

Bundling terms helps no one, so to define it clearly: a troll—the bad, inhumane kind—is a user deliberately acting in bad faith, deliberately attempting to provoke another. "Flaming" and "griefing" were earlier terms for that, the latter associated with role-playing games and virtual worlds like multi-user dungeon games and Second Life. "Abuse" happens when there is a power differential. Online abuse can be the labor of one person or many. The abuser could be someone you know or a stranger. A coordinated attack is a flood of online abuse from multiple users. The users that make up a coordinated attack might not be real—one can suffer from online abuse that is the work of sock puppets and bots—which means something that looked like a coordinated attack could be the work of one person. Some coordinated attacks are like road rage in gridlock. Picking out an individual from comments is like picking out a jerk in traffic, who might act completely differently in other contexts. The severity of coordinated attacks depends on conditions of the power differential. For example, while the status of a victim of online abuse relative to the status of the perpetrators of abuse matters, volume and visibility of abuse is another condition of severity. Celebrities have been run offline after waves of abuse from multiple accounts. Celebrities can also direct mobs of their fans to attack individuals (for example, if a famous singer with many "stans" were to call out a music critic's bad review). The content of discussion matters, too. If someone calls you a racist after you say something racist, that is not online abuse. If fifty people on Twitter are telling you plainly that a comment you made was racist, consider that a free schooling rather than an example of "bullying." "Doxing" leverages the inexact relationship between our online and offline identities, as the practice of retrieving a person's private information (such as an address or a social security number) and distributing it online with the intention of fomenting a mob to harass a victim in physical space, with phone calls and items sent in the mail. "Swatting"—spoofing a 911 call so a SWAT team will arrive at someone's house—has led to the death of harassment victims. Trolls can be president of the United States or they may have little to no power or wealth, in which case they might still assume power in numbers.

■

There was a time when 4chan's users seemed to pick worthwhile enemies, including institutions like the Church of Scientology. Its activist arm, known as Anonymous, or "Anon," grew away from the shitposting platform while also being the cohort of users who were, for several years, most closely associated with it. Anon, highly stylized with Guy Fawkes masks and the catchphrase "Expect us," engaged in hacktivist attacks on the Recording Industry Association of America and the American Israel Public Affairs Committee, actions in support of Occupy Wall Street, and allied with the

Steubenville rape victim. Anon's avant-garde structure and affect—anonymous, multiauthored, existing everywhere and nowhere, with the potential to absorb anyone—was irresistible to a few new-media theorists. Anon was "trickster-like," as they put it, a twenty-first-century game of exquisite corpse, upending Westphalian sovereignty and authorship and so forth. Over time, Anon's power diffused into endless splinter sects ("Operation Monsanto," "Operation Killing Bay," "Operation DarkNet"). The election of Donald Trump, and his fomenting of online hate groups—many active on 4chan—tarnished Anon's Robin Hood reputation by proximity.

The troll behemoth 4chan is amorphous; it is no institution. It has nothing like Facebook's money or massive Menlo Park campus, but to borrow a line from *Videodrome*, the anonymous image board "has a philosophy and that is what makes it dangerous." In its early years, the website footers linked to a manifesto by a user known only as "Shii," who created an earlier anonymous board, which 4chan was based on. "Anonymity counters vanity," Shii wrote in the text. "If there is a user ID attached to a user, a discussion tends to become a criticizing game. On the other hand, under the anonymous system, even though your opinion/information is criticized, you don't know with whom to be upset. Also with a user ID, those who participate in the site for a long time tend to have authority, and it becomes difficult for a user to disagree with them. Under a perfectly anonymous system, you can say, 'it's boring,' if it is actually boring. All information is treated equally; only an accurate argument will work."

It was anonymous, but for a time it wasn't quite leaderless—or public-figureless, rather. Christopher Poole ("moot") came out as its founder in 2008, and provided the media with a perfect foil to Mark Zuckerberg—they looked alike-ish, while Poole held beliefs in direct contrast with the Facebook founder's anti-privacy, one-identity inflexibility. In 2010, he even gave a TED talk entitled "The Case for Anonymity Online." Zuckerberg and Poole also differed in wealth. Conference stipends only go so far, and meanwhile he was responsible for a website that made advertisers wary—4chan was just about impossible to monetize. Given his spotlight, compounded with decisions as a leader to comply with DMCA requests and turn over IP addresses to authorities, Poole lost the confidence of the 4chan community. Users were further incensed when he banned Gamergate content. Finally, in 2015, Poole gave up on the project and sold 4chan to the founder of 2channel, the Japanese site that it was based on. By 2016, he was working for Google.

Anonymity was a smoke screen. Hostility to sincerity was 4chan's through line. This proved to be a natural stance for bigots, which is how it became an alt-right breeding ground. Many 4chan users had already cut their teeth on the goon humor of Something Awful forums or shock sites like the Stile Project. There, a user, part of a collective but sitting elsewhere, could laugh at a screen or focus on a spectacle, alone in one's room but with company online—one had the privacy to say things that might not fly in polite society.

In 2010, the danger that underscored 4chan's insincerity poked out as it instigated the harassment of an art student in Chicago named Natacha Stolz. A video of her performance *Interior Semiotics* was available on YouTube. Over the course of the eight-minute video, the artist smeared SpaghettiOs on her top, cut a hole in her tights at the crotch, fingered herself, and removed her top, using it to clean up the mess. Fellow students at the School of the Art Institute of Chicago might recognize this piece as an homage to Carolee Schneemann's *Interior Scroll.* There looked to be about forty people in the audience, at rapt attention, each of them dressed the way people who go to galleries tend to dress. Perhaps performance art like this piece is not to your taste. That's fine. Offline, you can decline to attend such an event, but what's more likely is you wouldn't know about it or get an invite in the first place. Someone on 4chan found Stolz's video and shared it, just to get the community to "rage" at its perceived pretentiousness. The video received more than two hundred thousand views in forty-eight hours. That's volume beyond what an independent gallery ever expects through its doors—an audience size more comparable to a modest cable TV program. It is an understatement to say the video was not to the taste of most of these visitors. The video eventually received more than two million views, with heaps of derogatory comments about Stolz as well as the "hipsters" in the audience.

The 4chan response to *Interior Semiotics* revealed the collective 4chan mind-set: they believed in one identity online, like the flip side to Mark Zuckerberg's famous musing that "having two identities for yourself is an example of a lack of integrity." The video posted to the internet was not theirs; it wasn't created for their consumption, but to 4chan users, as content on the internet, it was on their turf. The 4chan community reacted to *Interior Semiotics* as a gentrification of the internet they perceived as theirs and theirs alone.

While the world has changed in ten years, the 4chan ideology is resilient in its regressiveness. Whether "alt-right" or 4chan shitposter, these bigoted persons and collectives are—ironically—triggered by the rest of us internet users, as they were by the art student in Chicago. They are sad that the internet is not their own private island; it is not their "safe space," if you will. "The internet is not reality," tweeted the neo-Nazi online playpen Gab, in its official statement after the 2018 Pittsburgh synagogue attack, because fascism is, among its dangers and evils, also profoundly corny. These new fash want to believe the internet is an escape hatch to the unreal; but it's not the internet that is.

Much of how members of the 4chan and the alt-right behave suggests they are not serious when they say they are not serious. In early examples of networked trolling, like the coordinated abuse directed at the families of Mitchell Henderson, a seventh grader who committed suicide, and Nikki Catsouras, a teenager who died in a car accident, the confused and diffused nature of attacks heightened the outright cruelty of these actions. Henderson and Catsouras both died in 2006, and the harassment their families experienced operated outside expected social norms and behaviors. This was evil so extreme and so freakish, it was hard to accept, hard to explain, hard to tell as a story so another person might understand and offer sympathy. Henderson's father talked to *The New York Times* about phone calls that continued for a year and a half after his son's death. Anonymous callers would say things on the phone like, "Hi, I'm Mitchell's ghost, the front door is locked. Can you come down and let me in?" *Newsweek* reported that Catsouras's family had to stop using the internet because of the harassment. The coroner felt the accident was too gruesome to allow the family to identify her, but nine photos of the accident scene had been hacked or leaked, and trolls, pretending to be clients of her father, would email him copies. There was no name for this kind of harassment yet. There were no cyber-anthropologists who had ethnographic studies these victims could refer to back then; they suffered this perverse cruelty alone.

In the same *New York Times* story, the reporter Mattathias Schwartz talked with self-identifying trolls who said they were operating in the tradition of trickster gods. It was all a "social experiment," they said. I've referred back to Schwartz's piece many times since it was published in 2008. It is comprehensive and well written, but the framing always bothers me. It is one of the first pieces of its kind—a sit-down with the networked enemy—and Schwartz makes a mistake that is representative of this kind of literature, for he doesn't interrogate the conditions under which the trolls opened up to him. Would his subjects have spoken to a black woman journalist all the same? Plus, one of the key people in the story was Andrew Auernheimer, who revealed himself therein as an instigator of online harassment against Kathy Sierra, and without on-the-record comments from her, it felt incomplete and insensitive. Since then, "weev"—described in the piece as influenced by "Coyote, Loki, and Kali"—has gone full, unironic neo-Nazi; he's even the sysadmin of the Daily Stormer website. He isn't Loki or Kali, but a garden variety fascist-racist. It is hard to imagine now that Auernheimer could ever have been profiled so cavalierly, but that was a different time. In 2009, there was even a photo-sharing and wardrobe-ranking start-up called Fashism that counted

Ashton Kutcher among its investors. The name of that app says everything about how the tech industry took its market-compliant liberal values for granted.

Certain subcultures that came to the internet early had issues with white supremacy just as bad, if not worse, than contemporary gaming (hence, the Dead Kennedys song "Nazi Punks Fuck Off!"). A friend of mine who was part of the New Jersey punk scene in the 1980s remembers how white nationalist and Marxist skinheads dressed identically except for the shoelaces of their Doc Martens: white or red. The white supremacists were there in the fringes, bobbing in where they had purchase, attending shows for white power bands like Skrewdriver or creating a headache for Madness, who despite their anti-racism, were embraced by white nationalists as the only ska group composed of white guys. "After a while . . . casual, even ironic embrace of the totems of bigotry crosses over into the real poison," wrote Lester Bangs, in an essay, "The White Noise Supremacists," that ran in *The Village Voice* in 1979, and could just as well be about the hate groups congregating on Reddit and YouTube today. The racists were out in the open. Maybe not in the center, but around, nearby. They were there. Not your friends, at least, as far as you knew. But looming near, at the same gigs, the same comics shops, riding the same subway trains, drinking at the same dive bars. Later, they were on the same internet. Bringing people to the internet meant bringing the wide swath of humanity's capacity for good and evil into this eccentric communication space. In the early years of the internet, there were no grand funnels like YouTube and Twitter, in which people with widely diverging values shared the same stream.

Perhaps young fascists in the nineties would spread their hatred on forums like alt.music.hardcore, but usually they were segmented apart from the general internet population. That's still too close. In the nineties, AOL even hosted a page for the Texas branch of the Ku Klux Klan. The online provider prohibited racial slurs in search and user profiles, and yet this was a First Amendment issue, AOL insisted. It happened at a time when AOL install discs arrived as junk mail and fell out of Sunday newspapers. AOL was too busy laying down the welcome mat for new users to pull it away for problematic ones, and the company didn't see how that was counterproductive. Racist rage at "identity politics" and progressive campus activism isn't a new thing, either. Books like *Cyber Racism* by Jessie Daniels offer countless examples of early racist memes and racist communities—examples that should put to rest any theory that contemporary online racists are reacting to "Tumblr feminism" or that they are newly radicalized because of "performative wokeness." Racists have been online from the beginning, just as racists existed before there was an internet.

The alt-right's self-narratives are inconsistent with their behaviors and methods, which adds another layer of confusion. The alt-right would like for us to blame their rise on Tumblr and feminism in general, but these are their irritants, rather than causes. Ultimately, it is useless to ponder what motivates the alt-right, because there is no candor to their hatred. We can judge them only by their behavior rather than their own rationalizations for the way they behave. If one had to look at causes for the alt-right, obvious factors might include systematic forces like rising unemployment, the Great Recession, the climate crisis, and the nihilism and doom-mindedness that has resulted from a culture rapidly spiraling into an apocalypse. Young people are rendered futureless, fighting for scarce resources, and among them—like many cowards before—some choose to punch down rather than up. Then again, plenty of white supremacists come from money. Richard Spencer was a rich kid, and Mike Cernovich collected "seven figures" in alimony from his ex-wife. An anonymous writer who goes by the handle Immolations posted an essay to Medium in 2017 on the class mechanics that were in play in media coverage of Milo Yiannopoulos. "He has been afforded the privilege of being rendered as a 'unique voice', 'charming' and 'provocative' simply because he shares a similar background to many of those in the media," Immolations explained. Their coverage demonstrated a "refusal to acknowledge that those from similar backgrounds can indeed be the figureheads of such disgusting politics and a need to paint bigotry and hatred solely as working class phenomena"—analysis that extends to media's initial angle on Spencer as a "dapper" fash. Upholding race- and class-based allegiance, certain members of the media might see themselves as the antagonistic peers of Yiannopoulos and Spencer—splitting hairs with scolding banter—while they were no company to the people put in danger by what these men say.

Whatever their class background, any hateful person looking for a sense of purpose can enlist themselves in troll militias. Those users are put in motion as little cogs in a machine of chaos, in events ranging from distributing naked photos of Jennifer Lawrence obtained without her consent or making an ordinary person's life miserable on Twitter. Much of the mid-aughts tech enthusiasm took the self-organizing free labor of users for granted, but here is how it landed: one of the best known examples of "peer production" is Gamergate, and QAnon is, perhaps, the world's only successful work of "transmedia storytelling."

One characteristic has distinguished the racism online today from yesterday's innocent-ish little cyberspace: online patronage—fund-raising on Patreon or their own crowdfunding platforms when Patreon kicks them off. Social media and crowdsourcing platforms, and today's internet of micro-fame and grift, appeals to the vanity of racists as much as any other deluded Instagram influencer. Someone who is dreaming of a Cernovich-style media empire might hold on to a poisonous ideology long after they have ceased to believe in it. An amoral person, feeble-minded and of limited means, might be tempted to hitch a ride on the violence of others. Of course, the line between amoral and immoral is a fine one, a question philosophers have pondered through the ages. And to be sure, recognizing scarce resources as a condition exacerbating hate and racism is not the same as absolving someone of them.

It is important to point this out because—believe it or not—bad things on the internet are often somewhat less bad when there's no profit motive for badness. Decentralizing the internet, alone, is not enough to rid the internet of its worst users (take, for example, Gab, the social network just for Pepe Nazis); it only decenters the problem. As it stands, platforms like Twitter, YouTube, and others tend to capitalize on viral content, which means something super-vicious can go super-viral, while posts are promoted to trending topics and ranked lists of what is popular. YouTube algorithms and autoplay even act as a feedback loop—when they're not an on-ramp—for hateful content. As platforms incentivize conflict, they foment hate, providing entry points, from the alt-light (Jordan Peterson) to the unambiguously dangerous (Alex Jones and Richard Spencer). Platforms have to ban these bad actors outright, and some have, but only those who are poisonous beyond the point of no return, not the intro-level bigots.

The politics of resentment, as the adage goes, might also be described as the politics of taking poison and waiting for the other person to die. Online, that looks like devoting all one's energy to making others suffer. Trolls on 4chan, far-right conspirators, men's rights activists, white supremacists, abusers, and hateful users are not a monolith, but the internet and the world would be better without their menace. What a beautiful day it would be if they all woke up to the error of their ways. And then . . . and then . . . well, then what? I don't know what to do about contrition, forgiveness, and redemption, any more than I know how to convince them to change. This net is cast so widely already, I'm not even sure who should be included—Trump voters? Yes, them, too. And some might change as a result of unsavory motivations. I find myself dreading who will be the first "cured all right" ex-alt-right guy to cash in on a hateful past—with book deals, TED talks, and CNN commentator gigs—parading through publicity infrastructures, their conversion enshrined as a media event. Anyone honest about stepping into the light would have to eschew all of this. To make a break from this past, one has to be humble and accountable, rather than shift to a new grift.

Since I don't have the answers myself, I will do the thing everyone does, facing tough questions: I call for this conversation to happen. Because there is a conversation to be had about redemption and forgiveness. Any restorative justice needs to start with the victims—what are their needs and what does safety look like to them? Reform does not begin with forgetting. I don't mean reminding people of their past offenses at every minute, but refusing to forget, accepting it as part of the totality of their identity—some parts good, some parts bad, all human. There's a fine line between encouraging redemption versus acting as an enabler, but I don't know where the line is drawn, and it is not the same line for every single person. Always, it is the case that holding someone accountable is caring about them. And by the way, no one should ever make the mistake of using someone's own victimhood to minimize the impact of their abuse of others. "Hurt people hurt people" is an old chestnut that reminds us to open up to forgiveness, but it is not a write-off or an excuse.

In less freighted examples, we can always make room for others to do better. That would involve listening carefully rather than defensively. Change is normal. I know I have changed. Perhaps that's why this section is so difficult for me to write. I have slowed down my speed of typing. I feel awkward and insecure about what is to be put down on this page, because I know that I have been complicit, myself. When I look back at pieces I wrote or edited ten years ago, I am horrified by some of the language I thought was suitable. For example,

I once published a piece on an artwork inspired by Brandon Teena that includes the term "biologically female." I didn't know back then, but my ignorance was itself an expression of my privilege. Even worse, there was a time in my early twenties when I said hurtful things, which I felt no responsibility for because I thought it was clear that I was kidding. But I was lucky, because on one occasion, a friend stopped to tell me a joke I told wasn't funny. I was startled at first (*Who, me? But I don't really mean it*). Then I was embarrassed. Then I changed. I'm glad he's still my friend. That's the difference between calling someone out and calling someone in. A number of white people and cis people, like me, who have grown up on the internet have come to reassess the irony and humor common in online forums and chat rooms that were never even as extreme as 4chan. Lee Carter, the Virginia state lawmaker, once addressed this in a long thread on Twitter in 2018. "I'm an elder millennial and an internet early adopter," he wrote, "so my formative years happened on the internet. I said horrible things without realizing the harm of them. Homophobic, transphobic, sometimes sexist or racially insensitive. Wish I could undo that harm, but I can't." This comment was in reference to unfair or baseless "personal smears" on political candidates like Julia Salazar and Alexandria Ocasio-Cortez. He mentioned it in a list of events in his personal history that he expected could be used against him in his own reelection campaign. I doubt he will be the last politician to make an admission like this.

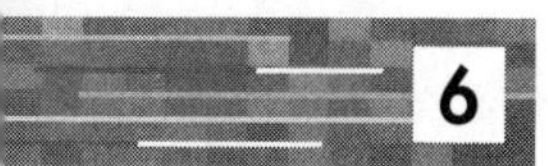

# Community

HAS FACEBOOK FINALLY INTRODUCED "WHO'S LOOKING AT YOUR PROFILE"? asked a coy headline on the London-based blog *Shiny Shiny*. The post, from December 2010, questioned a feature that was part of the latest Facebook redesign. A sidebar, containing the avatars of ten friends, appeared on user profile pages. Anna Leach, who wrote the post, speculated that these avatars were not-so-randomly selected. "You only need to refresh your profile three or four times to see that the same group of people comes up again and again," she wrote. "Out of my 421 friends, the same 15 come up." Five of them were users she contacted regularly on Facebook, but the other ten she barely interacted with at all. She assumed the sidebar revealed which mutual contacts most frequently clicked on her profile. Leach quoted a friend of hers who had similar suspicions: "These two girls keep turning up on my friends list—but they're not people I interact with on Facebook—so I think they must fancy me."

Comments poured in from readers who had noticed similar patterns:

> WOW! I was already thinking this because a guy who's profile I have been avoiding looking at and haven't interacted with publicly since early last fall kept showing up on my list . . . So I decided to try snooping on my ex's profile, refreshing about 10 times, but I didn't see myself show up, and now a half hour later, I checked again, and I am showing up on his list. Wierd.

> I think (and at least hope) it's based on who has viewed your profile. I've recently split with my ex, and have gone a little mad. Been off work the last week and have looked at her page constantly throughout the day. She does not appear in my friends during the day (when she would be at work and facebook is blocked) but DOES appear at night, presumably as shes looking at my profile.

> I LOVE THIS FEATURE, I dont really care who can see me on their friendslist or know Im creeping, this is the

life of facebook and we are supposed to creep. If you dont like people creeping you, then dont have a profile. Or put them on super limited

I would love to figure out what's happening!! I have this one guy who 9/10 times shows up FIRST on my friends list. . . . we don't have any sort of fb interaction (just lots of common friends)! It drives me crazy. . . . no matter how many times I refresh the page he is always there, which makes no sense!

It is undoubtedly based on who is looking at your profile. My list is almost all guys who I haven't interacted with since we became friends years ago. I never look at their profiles, like their posts, comment on their page, send them emails, or communicate with them through private email. All are men I would assume might have a crush on me. There is no other explanation than they are looking at my profile. Interestingly, people I do interact with regularly do not show up at all, so clearly it only has to do with profile viewing.

sooo this guy in my class i think liked me and when i got home he was on my friend list i think he clicked on my profile and then it showed up in friends listtt i had no intaction with him and never talk to him

Hahaha this has turned from FACEBOOK FRIENDSLIST CHAT into DATING ADVICE 101 :)

Facebook's press office contacted Leach to dispute her speculations. The company insisted that the avatars of contacts were organized in the sidebar "according to who you have had the most public interaction with in the past month and a half." It was unusual that the press office would reach out to her at all. Normally it was Leach calling them for a comment—and unsuccessfully. She included the Facebook representative's note in an update to her post, but the company's response felt incomplete, even deceptive. The people commenting on the *Shiny Shiny* post also doubted Facebook's official statement. If the sidebar calculated "public interaction," then why were crushes showing up? The people you "fancy"—and who fancies you—are as secret, implied, and decidedly not public as social media gets.

An extended conversation unfolded in the comments of the *Shiny Shiny* post, and it would continue over the next four years. The people leaving comments mobilized unorthodox research methods like counting page views and creating charts, while scrutinizing every inch of the Facebook interface for patterns or anything odd. Their collaboration was an attempt to reverse engineer the Facebook algorithms, if not expressly named as such. One of the commenters guessed that the people showing up in your profile sidebar were selected by a combination of two factors: how much they look at your profile, and how often you look at theirs. To test it, some of the *Shiny Shiny*-ers stopped clicking on other people's profiles—some stopped interacting on Facebook entirely except to look at their own pages. This drained Facebook of their reciprocal data, and in their estimation, forced the social network to calculate sidebar inclusion based only on the people who visited their profiles. Another tactic floated was to create an alt-account, which they used to visit their main account. If this fake account were to appear in their sidebar, there would be proof that Facebook's statement was a lie.

Many of the commenters sounded young—teenage young, college student young—with talk of seeing a crush after class or in class or on the way to class, right before their beloved's avatar made an appearance in that Facebook sidebar. I wonder if they had any idea that they were among the first to puncture Facebook's public image and address its use of algorithms. Why weren't they taken seriously? Even if they were all teenage girls—so what? That would mean they were about the same age as Mark Zuckerberg when he started Facebook.

A comment thread of this length and longevity is rare, and it is especially usual for a blog like *Shiny Shiny*. It was the flagship vertical of Shiny Media—a blog network that set out to be the Gawker Media of the UK—catering to a specific market: young women and gadgets (think a mixture of *Tatler*, CNet, and SkyMall, with a dash of the old *Saturday Night Live* skit "Chess for Girls"). Daily posts hyped anything Sony, Nokia, or Asus offered in metallic pink (Shiny! Shiny!). Featured products were bedazzled, bright, and celebrity-endorsed ("Samsung + Lily Allen = a netbook that looks like Victorian Wallpaper"). Acknowledging that women used gadgets and hiring them to write about them was better than nothing, but as Leach, the now former editor of *Shiny Shiny*, wondered back then—did the content have to be so bubbly, so baubly? Concerned that *Shiny Shiny* features pandered to its audience, she looked for alternatives to mix up the content, while adhering to its "women and tech" focus. Facebook, with its social implications, relative newness, and wide user base, was "grippy," Leach told me. Facebook was "always updating its interface" back then, and it rarely bothered to communicate these changes to its users, which meant that users looked to blogs and other media to understand what was happening. It was interesting to write about Facebook; plus, these posts were reliable page-view grabbers, so between updates on Swarovski-crystal-studded headphones and Hello Kitty flash drives, she would offer tips and observations about the social network.

So was this matter of the sidebar a tea-leaf read, or was there more to it? Even if the situation Leach described was a case of apophenia, the *Shiny Shiny* community soon uncovered more examples of Facebook algo-work bleeding through its seams. The top names listed in Facebook's chat bar seemed too familiar to be totally random. ("Anybody else tried testing the chatbar . . . I don't know if only the last three are the people most frequently visiting your page or are the last 4th & 5th person also counted? If anybody has any idea or proof, please do let me know," asked a commenter.) It, like the sidebar, showed crushes and past hook-ups, at least to the users leaving comments. Deep in the *Shiny Shiny* thread, someone noticed an interface element that the community nicknamed the "Mouseover 5," or "MO5." This was not a British Algo-Intelligence Agency, but the array of five avatars that appeared on the screen when a user rolled their cursor over their own profile image. The sidebar was finicky—after refreshing the browser several times, both crush objects and random people would circle in and out—but according to the comments there were no randos in the MO5. From this, the

*Shiny Shiny*-ers deduced that the MO5 was calculated by profile views alone, making it the ultimate who-is-lurking-on-you list.

Anyone who has ever been a teenager with a massive crush might understand how and why someone that age would take it upon themselves to learn the decision trees of social network algorithms before asking a desired person out on a date. The *Shiny Shiny* commenters just wanted to know if that cute person in biology class liked them back or not, and so they began card-counting profile views, to abate the potential agony of rejection. But, in many cases, it appeared their research only ramped up their anxiety. Abstaining from clicking on profiles on Facebook is like fasting inside a doughnut shop. One commenter said of the experiment, "it's making me crazy. i want to look! but i want to know if he's thinking of me!" Teenage drama it might be, but they did what so many other Facebook users did not back then: they tried to make sense of how data—their data—was administered through the platform. Although they lacked the language to ask pointed questions (the word "algorithm" was, for the most part, absent from their discussion), they understood, as users, that the platform had a pattern. It was not random. Facebook was calculating assumptions about their lives, their relationships, and their preferences, enacting decisions that could override their own choices and values.

The comments continued to flurry in, and by the summer of 2011, several months after Leach's post was published, there were more than seven hundred responses. The conversation crisscrossed with a community on Reddit that was meanwhile sorting out why Facebook prioritized certain users over others. That summer, a team of independent developers created a JavaScript bookmarklet "Stalker List," which scraped Facebook's JSON file that calculated the "affinity scores" of every user's contacts. After downloading the bookmarklet, a user logged into Facebook could click on it and see a full list of friends as Facebook ranked them. For example, your best friend, someone you message with frequently on the platform, might have a score like "78." Someone marked as a friend, but with whom you barely communicated on the platform, might have a score like "–5." It wasn't clear what factors added up to that number, but to look at the scores was to stare at Facebook in its bare essence: cynical and inhuman. Here was a list of the people in your life, aspects priceless and unmeasurable, tallied up like a grocery store receipt.

The *Shiny Shiny* community took to the "Stalker List" bookmarklet immediately. Finally they had control data to balance all the variables in their prior experiments. The comments—still piling up—began to sound like math homework:

> if you see a name you don't recognize on search bar for instance, said person will show up on stalker list as 9.08. If you have veiwed them in the past/mutual views you will see a jump from say 14.33–23.22 as Kava pointed out earlier. 9.08 is a reflection of your viewing the other site. That number will decrease at a rate of approximately 1.74 per day until. . . . I don't know. . . . I haven't tracked that yet. That seems to be the case when there is no mutual looks . . .

> I have two guys at the tops-both former/ongoing lovers whose numbers never change-for this week anyways. one I look at and send messages to-he is 147 and he appearss all over sidebar . . . first on all searches, his status updates, photos, etc. the second one, I haven't looked at in a month, nor have we spoken, nor can I see his friends lists or wall or photos-he remains at 60, and he shows up everywhere first and his friends show up on my search bar too.

I wasn't just lurking on this comment thread. In 2011, when I came across it, I tested it out and the results seemed legit—or at least plausible. Among my "MO5," I had dated three of them, and the other two were close friends. I barely used the social network, and I only had an account to maintain and edit the Facebook page for the nonprofit where I worked. I didn't leave comments or click on profiles very much, so what was MO5 calculating? How else could Facebook estimate the significance of these five people to me? I mentioned the MO5 to a co-worker that summer. She opened Facebook on her laptop and checked. "All of my exes!" she gasped. Something more than "public interaction" had to be part of its accounting.

After I discovered the *Shiny Shiny* thread, I became sensitive to Facebook's other robotic methods of organizing people. If I clicked on the full list of my Facebook friends, and opted to sort them as a grid of profile images rather than an alphabetical list of names, then all the Harvard alumni among them would appear at the top of the page. I suspect this happened because Facebook assigned a number related to how early a user signed up. If Facebook's "random" grid view sorted users based on that number, then naturally, the top would always feature Harvard students who joined the platform when it was exclusive to them. The sorting method was pseudorandom, but I could only guess its mechanics. Facebook wasn't going to tell me how it estimated—and therefore influenced—my relationships.

Then I tried out the JSON "Stalker List." The inaccuracy of the scores was as eerie as seeing the scores in the first place. The people in my "MO5" scored highly, but ranking just as high were random acquaintances and people from my past. Their assigned numbers were higher than my closest friends. People I actually prioritized, who knew that I avoided Facebook as much as possible, were aware that the best way to contact me was over email or text message. Facebook had a corporate ego: it assumed that Facebook activity was perfectly representative of the strength of a relationship.

A feature to de-anonymize lurkers is the ultimate be-careful-what-you-wish-for on social media. Fascinating and ego-boosting as it might be for the lurked on, it is just as potentially embarrassing for the lurker. When people learn who looks at them or not, profile views tend to grind to a halt. That's what Friendster learned after the company removed a layer of anonymity by force when it introduced a feature called "Who's Viewed Me" (it offered users the choice to opt out after criticism). Spyspace, the visitor-tracker for Myspace, was surreptitiously adopted, and never an in-house product. Currently, on Instagram, users can see what other users check their "Stories," but that is a particular feature to incentivize a temporary post, rather than a feature for the social network as a whole. What Leach suggested on *Shiny Shiny* in 2010 was different; it could have been an accident, after all, in which case Facebook exposed lurkers like a boom mic hovering in a frame.

In her original post, Leach wrote how frustrated she was that "Facebook isn't clear about the process." That was the underlying threat. Why was Facebook so dogmatic and opaque? Couldn't the company explain what kooky math went into deciding which avatars appeared? And would it hurt if a user could change it somehow, override it—whether feature or bug—for the sake of privacy? The Facebook sidebar was an everyday reminder that the user had little control over who the platform determined they liked best. Whether the interface elements appeared the way the Facebook press office suggested or the way the *Shiny Shiny* commenters suspected, it was readily apparent that Facebook was not guided by happenstance. Anyone perplexed by Facebook's algorithms might have stumbled on the *Shiny Shiny* comment thread, as it was a top Google search result for inquiries about the sidebar or whether there was a way to tell if people looked at your profile. The comments continued to accumulate on that post dated 2010. As recently as 2015, someone dropped in with a new comment. Why was her grandfather appearing in the sidebar? He had passed away two years before. Couldn't Facebook let her move on from his death?

The young women in the comments of the *Shiny Shiny* post had come together and formed a community. Ad hoc and anonymous, and united by a screwball common interest (concern whether Facebook algorithms controlled their fate), it was an unlikely community, yet true to what the word means. For a community can be a fly-by-night cohort, the specific uniting interest can be anything, and the participants need not share identifying information to partake (online especially, but also with anonymous support groups like AA). A community is not all persons ever in all the land. Whenever Mark Zuckerberg calls Facebook—the sum total of its users—a "community," we should understand this as flaunting the very thing his company will never be.

Zuckerberg clings to the word "community" because it "creates a flattened space where everyone is the same," Kate Losse, Zuckerberg's former ghostwriter at Facebook and the company's fifty-first hire, told me. The word "community" is used to describe Facebook employees, Facebook customers, and Facebook users, and therefore "assigns responsibility to everybody." Facebook values do not scale. It colonizes, but it does not homogenize. What it calls a "global community" is global user gridlock.

Following Trump's election, when Facebook's influence came into question, a consonant but mistaken narrative began to take shape in the media. This was a "techlash," journalists explained. According to this narrative, users were once very happy to share their lives on Facebook. The company was believed to be a net positive and a social good before election night of 2016, and only in recent years have users felt betrayed by the platform—believing it to be harmful to themselves as individuals, and harmful to society. It is a story that resonated with other members of the media who scarcely thought much about Silicon Valley until it was too late. This is the history of Facebook as its founder and CEO tells it, too.

In a 2018 interview with Kara Swisher, Zuckerberg said, "For the last ten or fifteen years, we have gotten mostly glowing and adoring attention from people, and if people wanna focus on some real issues for a couple of years, I'm fine with it."

Kate Losse remembers things very differently. When she reads about her former workplace in *The New York Times*, or in printouts of articles from BuzzFeed and other publications, she will underline sentences that perpetuate this error—sentences like, "Everyone used to love Facebook, but now people are afraid of it." Journalists make this point regularly, because it adds dramatic flair to a story, but "that's not at all how the reaction to Facebook has ever been," Losse told me. "Look at any particular year, and you could find a news article about a change to the product, then a negative reaction to the change." People's anxiety about Facebook "always came out first," she said, remembering the reactions people had to it, even back in 2005, when she began working at the company. New acquaintances would share their concerns about their data and their privacy, their apprehension about using the platform, or how unscrupulous they believed Mark Zuckerberg to be. At a dinner party, as soon as people learned where she worked, for two hours they would want to talk about "how terrible the privacy situation was at Facebook." If you had told someone in Silicon Valley you worked at Apple in those years, back when Steve Jobs was giving his blustery keynotes, they might have said, "Cool, I love my iPhone!" But not Facebook. No way.

For as bad as it was, and for as bad as it was perceived to be, it was never bad enough not to use. Losse recognized this "double condition" in place when she talked with disgruntled

Facebook users in its early years. They knew Facebook was a platform to interact with friends and socialize, and used it as such, but they also understood the company was not transparent and had some grandiose ambition that was only vaguely communicated, but probably scary. The platform was ideal for users because of its surface-level technical achievement and reliability (it had none of the lag problems that Friendster had with its servers, and none of Myspace's general cruddiness), but its proficiency didn't inspire equanimity. Rather, its frictionless interface was part of people's sense of unease about it. The better it worked, the more users wondered what was happening to their data to make it work so well.

Facebook pushed ahead no matter what, with its company watchword "move fast and break things" epitomizing its personal-boundary-breaking ethos. This is why Leach believes her *Shiny Shiny* posts about Facebook resonated with readers back in 2010. Whenever Facebook redesigned its interface, and provided no explanation to its users, the changes felt akin to noticing that someone had rummaged through their personal belongings. Users understood these surreptitious redesigns, as Leach put it, as cases of "Hey what have you done with my stuff?" In all its redesigns, Facebook maintained an ungainly appearance, and the ugliness was intended—well, sort of. Its interface aesthetics—the clunky minimalism, dull boxes, incessant alerts—were calming to people with authority. It looked as if a government body were running it. That made it attractive to institutions, municipalities, and private companies, and the individuals central to the running of these bodies. A single user could distrust

Facebook, but it appealed to the sensibilities of individuals as a committee, sitting together at a conference table on ergonomic mesh swivel chairs. A community might take to Facebook—for all its benefits to users as a group—but an individual might not like it. Like Google, Facebook prioritized one thing: scaling. The platform mobilized its platform as a platform of platforms; it assembled as a community of communities; it gobbled up businesses, schools, and other institutions, and put itself at the center. But Facebook is the very opposite of community; it decides a community for you. With no access to a user's innermost thoughts, it has to draw maps as workarounds, with algorithms that poke and prod users along. Those numbers in the JavaScript tracker the *Shiny Shiny* community played with revealed what the social network ordained. Facebook wasn't just ranking people in a user's life, but deciding for them how much of another person's content—another person's life—they would get to see.

In 2012, Kate Losse published the memoir *The Boy Kings*, covering the years after she dropped out of grad school and joined Facebook, feeling like the "humanist troll to the company's obsession with technologizing everything." Something she gleaned, in those decisive years, is that Facebook, unlike other platforms, told users what they care about. Facebook algorithms interpret a relationship in terms like "this person looks at another person's page a lot," Losse told me, "but maybe you don't even care. Maybe it's a mutual friend in a photo. There's no human knowledge. It isn't asking, 'Who do you care about?' It's trying to assume all of this." In her book, she describes sharing similar concerns with co-workers about the Facebook News Feed before its 2006 launch:

> It wasn't just telling me things quickly but telling me things I typically wouldn't know about . . . I wondered, then, if News Feed and the future of Facebook would be built on the model of how social cohesion works—what is comfortable and relevant to you and what isn't—or if it would be indifferent to etiquette and sensitivity. It turned out to be the latter, and I'm not sure Mark knew the difference. To him and many of the engineers, it seemed, more data is always good, regardless of how you get it. Social graces—and privacy and psychological well-being, for that matter—are just obstacles in the way of having more information.

News Feed dominated a user's full attention, which meant that Facebook dominated a user's full attention. As the company explained it, News Feed was a time saver; but to a user, it was a time vacuum. It was a simple idea and yet groundbreaking in its rollout: a daily briefing of all possible life events and gossip of your "social graph," like a micro-targeted digital experience of *This Is Your Life*—gossip compiled into a memo. And News Feed decided which of your friends were newsworthy.

Facebook developers also wrote algorithms to find logic in communities and the people who are part of them. "Google edgerank," said one of the *Shiny Shiny* comments in 2012. If you were to google it now, you would learn that Edgerank was the name of the algorithmic filtering system that *Shiny Shiny* users had an inkling of when they conducted their research. It was rudimentary then, with a method that could be sketched on a napkin: a summation sigma followed by three factors. These factors—"turning knobs"—together decided whether content would be seen or hidden: user affinity, type of action taken on it, and recency. So a post with no comments or engagement that was a week old probably wouldn't show up in a News Feed. "User affinity" was less obvious; it was assembled using factors that the *Shiny Shiny* community had been sensitive to, a calculation Facebook refused to reveal.

Friendster and Myspace were simple, and use of either was straightforward: add people, message people, click around. There were no algorithmic filters ranking and prioritizing what content a user would most wish to see. Granted, in earlier social media iterations, users had fewer online acquaintances. The first Facebook users arrived with an accumulation of preexisting online contacts—a list that was growing. It is hard to read every friend's every update when you have five hundred of them, but users came to Facebook with the expectation that a platform would do what they told it to, not the other way around. Facebook, meanwhile, was navigating and managing a user's experience. User control tends to be discussed in the context of echo chambers, but this concern should be broader: Why can't I decide what I see? Myspace let me choose my top eight friends; why does Facebook think it knows which people I value better than I do? Today, instead of Edgerank, convoluted machine learning determines the value of user content to other users. No everyday users, like the *Shiny Shiny*-ers, could detect its patterns on its own. But this filtering already changed users' expectations of one another. Through these algorithms, relationships maintained on Facebook become Facebook-branded relationships—shaped toward its methods of sorting, prioritizing, and categorizing people.

What's really troubling is the "People You May Know" recommendation box. It suggests users to one another, at times leaking things like a sex worker's identity to her clients, or a psychiatrist's list of patients. The reporter Kashmir Hill maintains a list of these examples, which go beyond context collapse: a robber to his victim, the mistress who broke up a marriage forty years ago; a man who once donated sperm to a couple saw their child as a recommended friend. Facebook's data gluttony and shamelessness created this tangled web. It makes these recommendations with what it has gathered from WhatsApp and Instagram data, of course, and scans cell phone contacts. Facebook even filed a patent to detect when two phones are in the same location, using accelerometer and gyroscope data to determine whether two people are facing each other or not. Facebook vacuums up call and SMS history on Android phones with Lite or Messenger apps, which a New Zealand–based software developer discovered after he downloaded and looked over his Facebook data (an option the platform made available to any user in 2018 to comply with the EU General Data Protection Regulation [GDPR]). "Somehow," he tweeted, "it has my entire call history with my partner's mum."

My friend Heather McDonald once found her father in the "People You May Know" box. It had been twenty-seven years since she had seen or heard from him. The avatar, with her father's name, showed a metal mask—no face; she wouldn't have recognized him anyway. His back is to the camera in the one photo she has of him, and all she can remember now, vaguely, as she wrote in an essay about the experience, is "glasses, a beard, nondescript sandy brown hair." She was settled with their estrangement. He is not part of her life, and that's how things go, and yet here was Facebook, forcing him back in, opening up the possibility of a conversation she did not want to have, but would nevertheless think about and daydream about after the social network reminded her that he is out there, just another internet user. She could ask him right now about, say, his medical history. Now she knows he lives 450 miles away. She didn't need or want to know that.

As she explained in her essay for *The Rumpus*:

> Facebook's neat labels and algorithms cannot begin to account for all the forms of kin, community, and history among people. The complexity of relationships flattens with the ability to find out what an old flame is up to, or what the bully does now, to rekindle old friendships, settle disputes, or start new ones. Facebook was built on the core assumption that everyone wants to be connected, that every single human interaction and connection matters and has value.
>
> Maybe they don't. Maybe they don't have to. Maybe that's okay.

Stephen Hawking joined Facebook in the fall of 2014 and answered questions on the platform in a company-sponsored event. As he spoke with the users, Hawking volleyed his own question to the Facebook founder. "Which of the big questions in science would you like to know the answer to and why?" Zuckerberg answered:

> I'm most interested in questions about people. What will enable us to live forever? How do we cure all diseases? How does the brain work? How does learning work and how we can empower humans to learn a million times more? I'm also curious about whether there is a fundamental mathematical law underlying human social relationships that governs the balance of who and what we all care about. I bet there is.

All the numbers the young *Shiny Shiny* commenters had struggled to unpack amounted to something after all: this linear approach to the unknowable and ambiguous, his rough drafts at a "fundamental mathematical law underlying human social relationships." These attempts to draw blueprints of human relationships became thirst traps for users. The product wasn't just sticky, it was quicksand. Facebook shoehorns values into patterns, removes nuance, and presents it as ruled by a "fundamental mathematical law." It offers a coherent story on the internet, where confusion and uncertainty rule. Connections are "friends," a user is in a relationship or not. Content is liked or it isn't liked. Yes or no. Friend or Unfriend. When it comes to ambiguity, Facebook conjures up what it believes are answers; because even if the answer is wrong, the company can try again, iterate, and get closer to it—or further away. A wrong answer is not nothing; a wrong answer is content. A wrong answer is something the company can sell ads against.

In his ascent to power, Zuckerberg spoke of Facebook as a social good, a change agent. It connected everyone and democratized the world, people met their spouses and had kids because of it, they kept up with friends halfway across the world with it, they found community there. There were "meaningful communities" for Facebook users, like private support groups for people with rare diseases (never mind that one of its many privacy dustups involved a loophole for marketers to harvest names of users in private patient communities). "Don't be evil" was always bunk, but at least Google's old watchword boasted about its tolerance for dissent. Facebook's company culture was an ouroboros, posing that its virtue rested simply in being. Evil, to Facebook, festered in the absence of Facebook. All this time Zuckerberg was practicing rhetorical usury of his users, for with every rare-disease support group coming together in empathetic harmony, there were white supremacists and actual genocide enablers, uniting and forging their own "communities." Facebook profited from their clicks, too.

Mark Zuckerberg's creation, which is compared to the suburbs and "tract housing" just as often as Myspace was once called "trashy," was indifferent to the internet as subculture, let alone the internet as culture. Zuckerberg even clashed with those who saw the internet as culture. One of his first public appearances was at South by Southwest in 2008. He was just twenty-three years old, stilted and awkward onstage, speaking in bottomless corporate jargon. The Web 2.0 hipsters, many of them a generation older, weren't buying it. "Talk about something interesting," someone heckled, halfway in. The audience laughed and disparaged him while using Twitter as a backchannel, before a battery of questions about privacy during the audience Q&A. Fast-forward ten years later to May 2018, amid the Cambridge Analytica scandal, fury over "fake news," and the platform's role in the Rohingya genocide, when Mark Zuckerberg appeared unbothered in his keynote at the Facebook developer conference F8. "What I can assure you is we're hard at work making sure people don't abuse this platform, so you can all keep building things that people love," he said with a smirk. A few weeks earlier, Congress had grilled him about all of Facebook's scandals and blunders. It might have been the first time since SXSW that he interacted professionally with others who displayed anything other than subservience. But at F8, he turned that experience into a joke, and laughed at a photo of himself in the hot seat before moving along to new products and developments.

In this span of ten years—far too long a window between humiliations for any mere mortal—Zuckerberg had time to shape his errant philosophy that the social network was a medicine for the world, which he alone could administer. Never mind that Zuckerberg was a temperamental fellow, that early employees reported he walked around with a samurai sword and threatened to attack them for unsatisfactory work (joking, but nevertheless). Instant messages he sent when he was nineteen and just founding Facebook were leaked to Business Insider:

**ZUCK:** yea so if you ever need info about anyone at harvard

**ZUCK:** just ask

**ZUCK:** i have over 4000 emails, pictures, addresses, sns

**FRIEND:** what!? how'd you manage that one?

**ZUCK:** people just submitted it

**ZUCK:** i don't know why

**ZUCK:** they "trust me"

**ZUCK:** dumb fucks

Mark Zuckerberg is tied with Bill Gates as Harvard's most famous dropout, and as with Gates—as well as Jeff Bezos, Elon Musk, and plenty of other tech industry titans—family wealth spurred on his success. The dorm room eureka moment might be what the company touts as its own origin story, but the "initial working capital" Dr. Edward Zuckerberg offered his son in 2004 and 2005 meant the company could make a play for the virtual souls of students at other Ivies, all while the younger Zuckerberg was leaving analog Harvard.

Zuckerberg confirmed the "dumb fucks" comment in a 2010 *New Yorker* profile. In lieu of an apology, he offered a curious justification, submitting the success of his company as evidence of his path to a moral high ground: "If you're going to go on to build a service that is influential and that a lot of people rely on, then you need to be mature, right? I think I've grown and learned a lot." While he might use different language now, Zuckerberg never stopped treating his users like "dumb fucks." In 2011, the year after his non-apology, Zuckerberg began a practice of rewarding his favorite company partners with bundled user data that revealed things like relationship status and photos. This data was a "bargaining chip," as an NBC News report explained.

Facebook's incomprehension of the meaning of "community" is compounded by its endless ethical quagmires. There was a very public and messy scramble in June 2014, when Facebook-affiliated academic researchers announced they used the platform to conduct a test on 689,003 users, tweaking their feeds to include content deemed cheerier or gloomier, depending on which group these users were randomly sorted in. The experiment tested whether an "emotion contagion" would take effect, that is, if the sad-sorted people would come to post sad things, or happy-sorted people might share happier content. The researchers announced the findings with no ceremony, as if it were a totally normal white paper, and they were met with proper internet outrage. This study, as countless op-eds railed, wasn't just creepy but overwhelmingly manipulative and exploitative. What if one of the users was prone to suicidal ideations? Someone could have died! Maybe someone did die! What right did Facebook have to rearrange a digital world for someone without their consent?

Later that year, Facebook's reputation continued to sink, culminating in a long-drawn-out standoff with drag queens, who were kicked off the service due to its stringent and restrictive "real names" policy. The policy also alienated trans users, Native Americans, and other users with names that were not expressly white and cis normative. These users had to go through intense check-ins with Facebook customer service, sending in passport photos and other official documents, an absurd overreach from something that was not a government body, but a private internet company run by a dude in a hoodie. Notice which communities were singled out when the platform cracked down on "inauthenticity." Facebook had no similar hard line against the widespread practice of law enforcement creating actual fake profiles as a tactic to infiltrate activist communities like Black Lives Matter.

The real names policy was a tool for harassment, but this harassment was structural, too. White supremacist groups flagged Native Americans and others for deletion as a form of abuse, but the platform's indifference bore out the consequences of this harassment. "Facebook workers—particularly those who live outside of the United States and Canada—may not be familiar with Native naming conventions. To an employee in Germany, for example, the Shoshone surname 'Has No Horse' might lack context and appear to be fake," explained Aura Bogado in a piece for Colorlines. When Oglala Lakota Facebook user Lance Browneyes was kicked off the service, he sent in proof of identification, and Facebook reactivated his account. However, a Facebook admin inexplicably whitewashed his username as "Lance Brown" when his account was reactivated. Only after he threatened the service with a class-action lawsuit and launched an online petition did Facebook allow him to use his actual "real" name. "They had no issue with me changing my name to a white man's name but harassed me and others, forcing us to prove our identity while other people kept whatever they had," Browneyes commented, identifying the platform itself as the source of injury. Regardless of who flagged the account, the hoops he had to jump through with the service were institutionally racist. Online harassment had, up until this point, been primarily discussed as a user-to-user conflict; but Facebook stoked its own problems—with its real names policy, the platform harassed its own users.

Facebook eventually offered an apology to the drag queen users who had protested outside its Menlo Park headquarters and received media attention. Facebook's chief product officer, Chris Cox, wrote a post defending the policy while extending an olive branch to those it alienated: "The spirit of our policy is that everyone on Facebook uses the authentic name they use in real life. For Sister Roma, that's Sister Roma. For Lil Miss Hot Mess, that's Lil Miss Hot Mess." It was too little and too late. By then, some of the queer, trans, and drag queen users had skipped off Facebook and reorganized on Ello. Facebook was bleeding communities.

■

Ello launched in limited beta in 2014, the finest climate there ever was to unveil a potential Facebook competitor. It was timing as fortuitous as that of Facebook itself. The press responded in kind. It was a "Facebook killer," *Wired* proclaimed; it was "positioning itself as a network with a social conscience," said *The Guardian*. Its "idealism might be the real deal," chimed PandoDaily. Amid the real names scandals, the LGBTQ community led the switch, but plenty of other users, annoyed with Facebook for a plethora of valid reasons, also signed up. Ello processed thirty thousand sign-up requests an hour. These are numbers that start-up founders dream about.

The catch was that Ello had a tricky ideology expressed in its design and approach to community. The website looked like it could have been hawking limited-edition footwear or obscure coffee-making equipment. It was founded by several white dudes based in Vermont and Colorado. One of the seven cofounders, a serial entrepreneur, had only just emerged from an internet scandal of his own after he was accused of copying designs from a rival indie bike company. But Ello had ideals; it was elastic about usernames, ad-free, and pro-user—at least, according to the social network's "manifesto," which read as follows:

> Every post you share, every friend you make and every link you follow is tracked, recorded and converted into data. Advertisers buy your data so they can show you more ads. You are the product that's bought and sold. We believe there is a better way. We believe in audacity. We believe in beauty, simplicity and transparency. We believe that the people who make things and the people who use them should be in partnership. We believe a social network can be a tool for empowerment. Not a tool to deceive, coerce and manipulate—but a place to connect, create and celebrate life.

What Ello proposed was similar to the "If You're Not Paying, You're the Product" catchphrase often bandied about in online privacy and data discourse at the time. For a while, a number of prominent tech-critic types would say things to the effect of, "I'd like to pay twenty dollars a month for an ad-free Facebook experience," as if that wouldn't only result in an equally evil Facebook and each user twenty bucks short. Like many a great phrase, it was always too clever by half. It was clever enough that Ello could appropriate the "you're the product" slogan as their own start-up pitch. Yes, the lack of surveillance was appealing. But the start-up's manifesto failed to mention that its proposal to build a social network where users are not the "product that's bought and sold" was venture capital–backed. It had to return on the VC investment eventually; either it would exploit you somehow, or it was vaporware. It was a public-benefit *corporation*, which is not a nonprofit, let alone some worker/user–owned co-op utopian project.

Right after I signed up, I started gaining followers—hundreds and hundreds overnight. All but a dozen were strangers. Ello featured my image and avatar on the login page, along with a handful of its other "favorite users." I was flattered that I had become an influencer on it already without even doing anything. Here was my chance to be to Ello what Tila Tequila was to Myspace (except for the whole going-Nazi thing). I felt obligated to make use of this small-batch soapbox. So I started blogging on it. Most of my blog posts were silly tech-culture observations, too long for Twitter and too short to write as an essay. People often left comments on my posts, which didn't necessarily speak of how compelling my Ello blog posts were, but rather, that people on Ello were bored and wanted something to do on it.

In my first few weeks as an Ello influencer, I realized I could use my visibility on the platform to address its shortcomings. It struck me that the platform wasn't doing right by the community that brought about its media adoration. It was safer than Facebook, simply by being not-Facebook, but Ello wasn't actively building a safe space for its marginalized communities. One tactical solution they failed to engage seemed so obvious to me—why didn't they hire one of the drag queens chased off Facebook to work as a community manager, to keep that community engaged, involved, and heard? (As just a start to its issues with diversity.) Worse, it had a laissez-faire approach to moderation that seemed dangerous, like it was set up for an inevitable Gamergate-style clash. As a VIP Ello-er, someone cool enough in their mind to be featured on the login screen, I figured I could start a dialogue about this. So, in a short post, I stated my concerns and summarized, "This is another social network built by a team of cisgender white dudes. These crowds aren't homogenous because people are nice. It is because they have, in the subtlest ways, filtered others out."

The response to my post was overwhelmingly positive . . . at first. Dozens of women and people of color on Ello responded in comments that they also noticed a very white male point of view that was coming across in Ello's design and approach to community. It hindered their desire to participate on it. "This was my thought exactly after I spent some time scrolling through the 'discover' page. It is like . . . beards . . . beards everywhere," wrote one woman. "YES! [My friend] and I have been talking a lot about this with regards to Ello's lack of privacy features: how would they be expected to understand what minorities need if they aren't really familiar with our culture and our struggles?" responded another woman.

While the first dozen comments were enthusiastic and in support of my observations, things got dicey from there. A man in the comments told me I was "white-hetero-male shaming." Another tried to convince me that "cisgender" is a slur. An Ello cofounder who went by Cacheflowe came across my post and engaged in the comments, but rather than doing the work of community management—deescalating the abuse that was ratcheting up—he added fuel to the flames. He goaded on the people leaving harassing comments, and responded to me as though I had instigated everything. Startled by the Ello cofounder's hostile messages, I immediately stopped using Ello. I wonder how much longer afterward I was listed among the "favorite users" on the login screen.

Four months after the last time I logged into Ello, I received a notification that the Ello cofounder mentioned me in a new comment. He was responding to an Ello blog post, written by an acquaintance of mine, the social media theorist Nathan Jurgenson. Their discussion was regarding an essay Jurgenson had written elsewhere, in which he explained that "with nearly every Ello headline being equally about Facebook, Ello's entire existence is understood through the lens of its orientation to the bigger social network." Because Jurgenson's piece was an obituary for the service Cacheflowe cofounded, distributed on that very service, I can see why Cacheflowe was annoyed. What I didn't get was why I had to be tagged, and thereby looped into this conversation. The response he posted was typical haters-gonna-hate logic, including an inexplicable jab at the worst Ello-critical meanie he could think of, and that would be me.

I emailed Jurgenson and explained my previous unpleasant encounter with Cacheflowe. So Jurgenson blocked him. He blocked the Ello cofounder on Ello.

Cacheflowe responded with a series of creepy emails to Jurgenson, pointing out that it was his website and he could always unblock himself. He went on to brag about all the young women he mentored, and insisted, "Most people I know would say that I'm one of the nicest, most empathetic people they know. My romantic partner would tell you that I'm a model feminist." I've seen the emails and felt alarmed that Cacheflowe continued to mention me and my "demeaning post about [Ello] being 'cisgender white dudes.'" I was grateful for Jurgenson's attempts to deescalate the situation, but the Ello cofounder only grew more incensed. Sensing he had driven Jurgenson off Ello for good, Cacheflowe started harassing him on Twitter, even inserting himself in conversations he had with others, with comments like "Nathan likes to provide critique, but not receive" and "How's your self-righteousness doing?"

The Ello cofounder's behavior is an oversize example of a start-up leader acting improperly. However, the platform is sometimes cast these days as a David that failed to topple Goliath. "Ello's rapid downfall occurred," Nick Srnicek, author of *Platform Capitalism*, wrote in 2017, "because it never reached the critical mass of users required to prompt an exodus from Facebook—whose dominance means that even if you're frustrated by its advertising and tracking of your data, it's still likely to be your first choice because that's where everyone is, and that's the point of a social network."

But let's not forget Ello had a favorable climate and opportunity, and a tremendous number of sign-ups, all of which it fumbled through sheer incompetence. Which, yes, I say as the person cyberbullied off Ello by an Ello cofounder. I might laugh about it now, but if Ello had taken off and properly killed Facebook, and with its leadership the same, it could have become a real problem for me.

Ello is still around, in some kind of "creator-focused" capacity. In recent interviews, the founders insist that its micro-size community was the point. Maybe it was, and maybe it is all for the best, but when I looked at the website the other day I found it interesting to see a post from the company that said, "Ello Celebrates Diversity." It is still ad-free, but in 2015 the company was caught using Facebook-targeted ads to encourage new users to sign up. It stood for nothing.

A "Facebook killer" isn't the right way to image Facebook's demise; it would just mean moving on to a new set of problems on another platform. The only solution to Facebook is for Facebook not to exist and for nothing Facebook-like to pick up in its absence. Unfortunately, media commentary tends to zero in on tactical questions like whether it is right for Facebook to ban Infowars, or how to solve the problem of fake news with fact-checkers, or what kind of affiliations of fact-checkers are acceptable. Tech reporters act like Facebook's "Loyal Opposition," as the writer and academic M. R. Sauter has put it: bantering over its problems, expecting it will always be there, attempting to lock horns—while they are ants in proportion to its size.

After all, who benefits when the story is that the crisis of Facebook is a new one? This problem is not a "techlash," as new-tech journalists and tech pundits positioned it. The "tech beat" scarcely existed four years ago, although Facebook and other poisonous platforms had cursed beginnings in the aughts. The legacy media analogue to virality—a news peg, an angle, decisions over what is newsworthy—is a factor in how commercial platforms gobbled up so many industries, including the very same news business that largely ignored Silicon Valley's ascent. What would Facebook (or Google or Twitter) look like now if there had been more thorough media attention and investigation of these platforms and their practices years ago?

It won't be easy to destroy Facebook, and part of the reason is that it is by design next to impossible for users to quit. Facebook has taken over for community services such as community papers and community corkboards at community cafés. All sorts of people depend on it for updates about office hours, snow days, town halls, and street cleanings (not to mention all the gossip). Then there is its insidious "free basics" program, which offered internet service to developing countries for free through their platform—hooking in vulnerable people as users and locking them in, as well as their relatives in the diaspora who sign in to keep up with family back home. All of these individuals are subject to Facebook's crass sorting methods. It is a privilege to delete Facebook, because the social network is built to be coercive. The network effect is that everyone is stuck, some more than others.

We can, as individuals, always do our part to make the social sacrifice of leaving Facebook less painful. For example, someone creating an event page on Facebook might also set up another page on the web, just so non-users can see it (services like Eventbrite let you do this). Such tactics are better thought of as harm reduction than a boycott. Instead of quitting outright, you might choose to reduce what news you consume there and what friends you communicate with there, just to minimize the Facebook lens on your world, which is intent on cannibalizing and repurposing your life. Or just use Instagram or WhatsApp. They'll have your data, but you can keep your mind. Think of it like Facebook pescatarianism; some people just can't go all the way. I say this as one of the privileged ones. I don't use Facebook. Yes, life as a non-user is sometimes an inconvenience. I am often late to hear personal news from less-than-close friends, and I seem to hear about parties only after they happen. But the sanity I maintain is worth it. I just can't stand the feeling of being conscripted inside its bleak mines of friend-affinity scores and fascist math about people. And I'm lucky. I routed my life around Facebook, and I was able to do that only because of choices I made a long time ago and a lot of understanding from the people in my life.

Facebook provided a map of human relationships that no one asked for but that many now believe they could never live without. It offers an illusion of control when what a user really gets is a more compressed living space. Through it, the intensity of real life is condensed into a legible, seemingly rule-bound interface. While Google is omnivorous, eating any dimension of the world it can make fit and discarding data when it is no longer needed, Facebook's organizing principles are more concrete. Google claimed it was building a mirror of the world when it wasn't, but Facebook is nearly there, mirroring all the people in the world and locking their identities in the platform. Even non-users are represented; their gaps have profiles, too—"dark profiles," which Facebook began documenting in 2006. "We were using every technical means at our disposal to create a database of all the people in the world," Losse explained in her book. The people who are not tagged in photos, the phone numbers that Facebook does not identify, the gaps, the missing pieces: all of these compose the shadow qualities, like the people represented as gray outlines in snapshots in the opening titles of *The Leftovers*. For

Facebook sees all the people in the world as users, even what it calls "nonregistered users." The only way to not be what Facebook deems a user is to never have been born, or to have died before it was invented.

Because life is never as thematically tidy and straightforward as a chapter in a book, it should be noted that there are plenty of examples of individuals enriching their lives using Facebook as a tool. I remember reading about a little boy in Arkansas with vitiligo, whose mother reached out to the owner of a dog with vitiligo in Oregon, who she found on Facebook. Later, the boy traveled to meet the dog and the resulting photos were so sweet that I cried reading the story. It is a nice story! But why should Facebook, the company, and Zuckerberg, the head of it, get any credit for this? These people made the connection through the internet, on the World Wide Web, which Facebook is floating within. Crediting Facebook for what the internet already provides is like praising a pinworm for something its carrier did.

In this book I have tried to maintain a consistent tone of criticism that is not openly combative, less "this is wrong" than "isn't it interesting how wrong this is," but I have found it next to impossible to maintain this distance when it comes to the topic of Facebook. I hate it. The company is one of the biggest mistakes in modern history, a digital cesspool that, while calamitous when it fails, is at its most dangerous when it works as intended. Facebook is an ant farm of humanity. It's so unsubtle in its horribleness that I think of it in terms of unsubtle Banksy-like metaphors: ANT FARM OF HUMANITY! Of course, I hate it. Who doesn't? Now that it has received proper scrutiny and attention, its reputation has taken a tumble. Facebook was listed ninety-fourth on the 2019 Axios Harris Poll 100, which ranks the reputation of companies according to a sample of 18,228 Americans. To put it in perspective, the Trump Organization is ranked ninety-eighth on the same list, Philip Morris is ranked ninety-ninth, and the U.S. government was ranked one hundredth. I feel cheap leaning on populism; nevertheless, this is a company—which has a mission about *friends and community*—that the American public likes less than Goldman Sachs (ninety-third on the list). There are many angles one can take on why it is bad, such as media manipulation, data harvesting, and good old-fashioned colonialism—or even its holdings like WhatsApp, which demonstrates how the velocity of sharing is another problem, when users forward rumors and misinformation. But at its worst Facebook is fully parasitic of everything human, while also, with its preset filters and artificial groupings, bulldozing the agency of users as individuals.

No, Facebook isn't a community; it is impossible at that scale. It is an infinite ant farm. Even if we took it broadly that every Facebook user is united with an interest in Facebook (or is frustrated with it)—well, it fails again. Because, discounting factors of ascribed status, all worthwhile communities have this in common: participants are always free to leave.

7

# Accountability

In 1855, a man escaped his bondage through the Underground Railroad. As a free man, he wanted a name of his own, and from that day forward, he was known as Sheridan Ford. A century and a half later, his great-great-granddaughter signed up for a Wikipedia account and claimed that name for herself.

Kyra Gaunt, Wikipedia's SheridanFord, made her first edit in 2007, with a minor update to the page for NBC's *The Apprentice*. She added a citation to an academic paper about racism in the workplace and the corresponding dynamics on the reality show. Now the host of *The Apprentice* sits in the

Oval Office and Gaunt continues to address Donald Trump's racism through Wikipedia, in addition to a wide assortment of other topics. The pages she edits range from table football to Los Cabos. On the "Twerking" page, she once argued with other editors that it had to be put in the context of African dance and African diaspora choreography, rather than characterized as a discrete trend that emerged after the Ying Yang Twins. Gaunt, a professor at the State University of New York at Albany, and a musician and ethnomusicologist, enjoys the opportunity to make a difference through the platform. She was one of the first academics to teach hip-hop, and she was early to see potential in Wikipedia, too. The platform isn't perfect, but two aspects appealed to her from the start: anybody can read it and anyone can make it better.

Gaunt calls her work on Wikipedia "knowledge activism," and it relates to her broader concerns about how people access information or who gets to speak and who is taken seriously when they do. Take for example one of her former students: he's an international student with a Ph.D., who came to the United States to earn another Ph.D. His English is imperfect and Wikipedians constantly reverted his edits whenever he tried to contribute. This student is bright, his contributions to the online encyclopedia were important, yet the community noticed the surface flaws in his language before the concrete value of the information he contributed. On Wikipedia, the "text stands in for you," she told me. While she knew the value of her student's work, those who encountered him as a user in the edit history dismissed him as inexpert for these cosmetic reasons. The earlier Sheridan Ford might have encountered similar hostility. Gaunt told me about a beautifully written letter her ancestor composed after his escape. It is not perfect English, she explained, but what it communicated was "profound, high English." After all, he was sounding out words he hadn't seen, and with tremendous skill considering all the barriers he surmounted in pursuit of literacy. As we talked, she connected her feeling about how her student was judged to John Dewey's theory of the "assumptive world," which explains how experiences and point of view shape our values. I was unfamiliar with the concept, and when I looked it up later, I came across the Wikipedia page for "Transactionalism." There was SheridanFord again in edits.

Her username embraces and deflects aspects of Gaunt's identity at once. The "assumptive world" offline might presume things about her as a black woman, but "SheridanFord," at first glance, as a username on Wikipedia, reveals nothing about the person behind it. Someone could visit the SheridanFord profile page and learn who she is, as she has posted biographical details there, but she's shielded from the snap judgments of other Wikipedians in the day-to-day activity of revision. The opportunity to avoid typical aspects of harassment—the sort that happens in online spaces where a user's identity is linked to their image—is another part of Wikipedia's appeal. In a heated "edit war," trolls might attack her with racism and sexism, or they might simply take issue with her approach to information and how she chooses to edit. Trolls and antagonistic users she has encountered in the past "were not coming for me simply because of my identity," she told me. "They were also being gatekeepers of the standards that Wikipedia stands for."

The best way to define what Wikipedia is might be to

list what it is not. One of its many pages listing content policies (actually called "What Wikipedia Is Not") does just that. When the page was created in 2001, it was a solid list of ten items: Wikipedia is not propaganda or personal essays; it is not a usage guide—it is "not in the business of saying how idioms, etc., are used." It is not discussion forums or a chat room. It is not a collection of links. It is not a dictionary and it is not just for hackers. Since then, the anti-about page has expanded the list of things it does *not* do and does *not* contain. Wikipedia is not paper, so "there is no practical limit to the number of topics Wikipedia can cover or the total amount of content," but with respect to the slow download speeds of readers visiting through dial-up or mobile service, it is best to keep pages at a reasonable word count. It is not a "publisher of original thought" or a soapbox. It is not a blog or a social network or a directory or a guidebook or a textbook. It's not indiscriminate, but it is not censored. It is neither anarchy nor an experiment in democracy, nor a laboratory. It's not even total bureaucracy, because Wikipedians can follow the rule "ignore all rules." It is not compulsory; you don't have to create an account to read its pages, but—and here's where the Wikipedia page stops and my own editorializing takes over—there is something compelling about it that brought this entirely implausible project into existence.

■

Long one of the top ten most-visited websites, Wikipedia differs widely from all other major internet players because its content is collectively vetted and not monetized. Founded in 2001, its business model and editorial strategy seem like nineties cyberspace holdovers, inheriting that generation's optimism along with its blind spots. It carries the torch of John Perry Barlow's principles in "A Declaration of the Independence of Cyberspace," and in addition to what it is not, Wikipedia isn't anticapitalist. The founder, Jimmy Wales, like many cyber-utopians, was a libertarian (albeit his Twitter feed now suggests that, like a lot of libertarians in the Clinton years, he's since moved to the left). In the nineties, he organized a forum on Ayn Rand's philosophy of objectivism, and he was interested in Austrian economics. His online encyclopedia experiment is libertarian without corruption, libertarianism as libertarians imagine liberty—an endeavor that is impossible to sustain as anything other than a thought experiment, except for this rare exception in internetland, and a massively imperfect one at that. Wikipedia works by harnessing the great "small l" libertarian tradition of endlessly arguing on the internet for nothing. It is global and open, transactional and pluralistic, chaotic and rule-based, and anonymous apart from usernames and IP addresses. While beset with problems including harassment, the platform is robust and self-sustaining. Unfortunately, the Wikipedia model is next to impossible to replicate, as it is held together with luck and Popsicle sticks.

Wikipedia's strengths emerged from its decentralized command. In 2003, Wales curtailed his leadership and transferred all Wikipedia assets to the Wikimedia Foundation, a nonprofit responsible for Wikipedia and its related projects. Wales seemed to have had no real desire to be an oversize founder-god (his net worth was last reported as one million dollars, not un-rich by any honest measure, but not a stratospheric bubble of comfort, either). As a nonprofit, the organization is largely funded by its readers. It has no advertising. Without an ad model, there is no accelerant, nothing to incentivize clicking or compulsive activity on pages. Notice that Wikipedia is a community of "editors," rather than writers: the work is custodial and selective rather than prolix and free-for-all. On Wikipedia, the labor is deciding (and arguing over) what is worth publishing. Information is culled so that each page is definitive for its subject and each subject is deemed necessary for inclusion. Each page must meet a recognizable need.

On Wikipedia, users work to cull and create, unlike on Facebook, YouTube, Twitter, and other digital public spaces owned by private companies. Those noxious plate tectonics manifest in the proliferation of content prioritized over the value of it; a post might be harassing another user, it might be espousing conspiracies or peddling disinformation, and yet commercial platforms can sell ads against it. But Wikipedia has none of these incentives. A Wikipedia page is not considered more valuable because more people visit it. More people edit the page for Justin Bieber than the page for Pascoag, Rhode Island, and Bieber's page has more visitors, but that does not correspond with more revenue. Both pages meet Wikipedia's notability guideline, which does not reflect where the internet traffic is raining down at any given moment. This also explains why Wikipedia wasn't a vector for QAnon or Pizzagate conspiracies. Its standards for notability and reliable sources help prevent the spread of conspiracies and hoaxes—unreliable information is deleted.

There is only one Wikipedia page for each subject. There's no redundancy. The single page might seem simple and obvious (it is an encyclopedia, after all), but in today's media environment, this constraint means attention is siphoned to a page that can be maintained and guarded. There are few shared experiences these days like watching Walter Cronkite on the evening news each night; but if there's a major news story, a substantial number of internet users are reading the Wikipedia pages of related subjects, whether it's a person or a location or other entity. In such cases, Wikipedia proactively locks pages that are undergoing a mass revision or in the middle of a breaking news story. Contrast that with Yelp and TripAdvisor listings, which also have only one page for each subject, but host consumer reviews, and can get overwhelmed with positive or negative fake reviews, such as the comments that piled up on user-review sites for the Red Hen in Lexington, Virginia, after the restaurant refused service to White House press secretary Sarah Huckabee Sanders in 2018.

In addition to its eschewal of surveillance capitalism and tracking, another aspect that distinguishes Wikipedia from other internet platforms with traffic at its scale is its accountability mechanisms. Again, all of this is imperfect—bad at times, terrible even, and an object lesson in transparency as tumult—but the mechanisms exist. There are rules, and these rules are easy to find. Some users might adhere to the rules more strictly than others, but these rules are transparent and worked out by the site's own community of users. There are rules nested in rules nested in even more rules. A first-time Wikipedia editor might begin with the rules called the "five pillars"—"Wikipedia is an encyclopedia" (it is "not a soapbox, an advertising platform, a vanity press, an experiment in anarchy or democracy, an indiscriminate collection of information, or a web directory"), it is written with a "neutral point of view," the content is free for anyone to use and it is freely licensed to the public, civility is important, and lastly, "Wikipedia has no firm rules." The rule about neutral point of view (NPOV) falls under another heading, that of the "Core content policies," under which "No original research" and "Verifiability" are key, although "notability" could also fall in here. Wikipedia's rules for civility boil down to "no personal attacks" and "assume good faith." This is just the beginning. There are endless sets of "principles" posted to Wikipedia, some doubling up or condensing rules that have already been published (like the "five pillars" precursor, "remain neutral, don't be a jerk, and ignore all rules"). It is a platform with self-loathing as part of its culture. Wikipedia's own rules decree that it is, itself, "not considered to be a reliable source."

Wikipedia is free for everyone, available to anyone, and can be read and edited by anyone; and—as happens with many internet spaces designed for pluralism—it does not benefit everyone. A particular kind of user takes the lead. Wikipedia's "neutral point of view," an institutional voice assembled out of hundreds of millions of edits and revisions, doesn't speak as a blend of the thirty-four million registered users. Rather, the voice is flattened by the type of individuals most active on the website: users who are white and male and, presumably, straight and cis. Bias is an ongoing problem, and one that can develop myriad neighboring complications as Wikipedia becomes common element in machine-learning data sets. But, in some cases, Wikipedia has changed for the better. In 2013, when Chelsea Manning came out as transgender, editors battled over how to address this on her page before decisively editing it under the heading of her new name and proper pronouns. A new rule or procedure becomes a new drainpipe for a deluge. The following year, an anonymous user, identified in the edit history with an IP address that traced back to Congress, was banned from Wikipedia for more than a week, after deadnaming Manning and making other transphobic updates. Anyone else working in the Capitol Building that day, with that IP address, was blocked from editing Wikipedia.

I asked Kyra Gaunt if she'd seen similar progress on Wikipedia over the years. Could it be that Wikipedia editors are growing more diverse? She thinks that progressive changes, such as how the Chelsea Manning page emerged, could also be the work of a number of white-guy Wikipedia regulars. Maybe some of them have developed a more enlightened "neutral point of view," but there is a sport to it. Issues of racial justice and trans rights are in the news, and "if it's in the news, they want to be the first person to get it on Wikipedia," Gaunt said.

Even still, the platform is not devoid of racism, transphobia, or other kinds of bigotry or harassment. That happens in the edits, and largely stemming out of its hierarchical structure. It is hostile to newbies, so people of color and women joining today, almost twenty years after it launched, might be intimidated by the possessive and insidery habits of the community of longtime users. There's a learning curve, after all, and it is accelerated by the voracious pedantry of the fervid. A black editor, new to the service, making a simple mistake, could be singled out as a "vandal"—and even worse, get upbraided by a Wikipedian who prides himself on "hunting vandals." After a bad first encounter with Wikipedia like that, it would be fair to decide that one's volunteer labor just isn't worth it.

Another factor compounding bias, besides the homogeneity of its editors, is Wikipedia's insistent policy that users assume good faith in one another. That is a core principle—not a rule that can be dodged with the "ignore all the rules" rule. The alt-right and other modern bigots ran the floor with it. In 2015, five editors attempted to clean up pages related to Gamergate and its targets, but soon they were banned from editing. One of them, a man in Alaska who "had no idea who Zoë Quinn was or what a social justice warrior was six months ago," as he told Lauren C. Williams at ThinkProgress, was later doxed and harassed like any other Gamergate target. He was a longtime Wikipedian, editing the site for ten years, and simply volunteered his time to remove links to obviously disreputable websites like Breitbart and delete inappropriate, harassing language ("I don't want [anyone] calling people a slut on the world's most-read website," he said at the time).

Wikipedia "assumes everyone is acting in good faith," wrote Michael Mandiberg in an article for *Social Text Journal*, which left the community "unprepared for the Men's Rights Activism spawned from Reddit, 4chan, and 8chan." This extends to harassment *on* Wikipedia, and how Wikipedia is organized to respond to it. Users who experience harassment, stalking, or intimidation on Wikipedia have no formal process of filing a harassment case. Instead, they are encouraged to solve all problems themselves, before turning to ANI ("Administrators' Noticeboard/Incidents") dispute resolution, which is run by a team of volunteers. Then the onus is on users to demonstrate attempts to deescalate the abuse that was directed at them, with links to edit histories and talk pages and other documentation. Much worse, users have to tell the other party that they are filing a case, or the ANI won't even look at it. As a consequence, the actual process of filing a case can be an act of harassment. Agitators can use this public method of reporting a dispute to stigmatize and intimidate others, especially those less familiar with how Wikipedia works.

Solutions to Wikipedia issues with hierarchies, demographics, and representation tend to come from outside organizations like Art+Feminism. This group's project began in 2014, with a gathering in New York and more than thirty satellite locations, to work together to add more biographies of women and nonbinary artists to Wikipedia. It has blossomed into hundreds of edit-a-thons around the world, year after year, including annual events at museums and universities. (I met Kyra Gaunt at one such edit-a-thon at the Museum of Modern Art in New York.) The Black Lunch Table is a similar initiative that organized edit-a-thons for black history, and events have been organized for World AIDS Day, among other efforts to make Wikipedia content more inclusive. Art+Feminism and the Black Lunch Table create community at an actual community level, rather than a sum-total-of-users level. People come together with shared purpose and goals. Those with authority use it for mentoring and advice, rather than hectoring new editors. Meeting in physical space, in an environment designed to be welcoming and inclusive, helps offset the anxiety Wikipedia newbies might feel. Volunteers are there to talk them through the various mazes of Wikipedia and all its inevitable hiccups, whether that means a procedural dispute, or an editor accusing them of messing up the tagging structure or entering a URL incorrectly—or less vague forms of harassment happening digitally.

Here's an example of the power of the Art+Feminism project. In 2017, the city of Los Angeles removed Sheila Klein's public sculpture *Vermonica* from the East Hollywood parking lot where it had stood since 1993. The piece was an assemblage of decommissioned streetlamps, a cross section of poles from different eras and neighborhoods, with different heights and shapes. It was enchanting to come across it by accident, especially when it was all lit up at night. If this installation sounds familiar, you might be thinking of Chris Burden's *Urban Light*, the much-Instagrammed piece outside LACMA that was erected fifteen years after *Vermonica*. Whether or not Burden lifted the idea from Klein, he undermined her previous work, because he failed to reference or acknowledge it in any way. I much prefer Klein's piece; *Urban Light* is too Disney—selfie-ready before there were selfies—but *Vermonica* spoke to its unlikely location and context. The name is a riff on its location, the intersection of Vermont Avenue and Santa Monica Boulevard. Klein first imagined a pastoral setting for it, but she changed her mind after the 1992 riots. "I thought it has to be right in this place where things had burned down. I remember driving by that strip mall and seeing the sign that said, 'We are rebuilding!'" she told the *Los Angeles Times*. *Vermonica* is part of Los Angeles's story of solidarity and repair, which makes its ending all the more infuriating. The artist wasn't even notified before it was taken down. Later, the city reinstalled it in front of the Bureau of

Street Lighting office, but it was site sensitive—in another location, it wasn't the same piece.

After I heard about the destruction of *Vermonica*, I clicked over to Wikipedia, intending to create a page for it. I didn't have to—someone had already published it. Not only that, a Wikipedia editor prominently noted that *Vermonica* preceded *Urban Light*—on the page for *Urban Light*. (Chris Burden might have been ignorant of Sheila Klein, but from now on, no art student working on a term paper about him has any excuse.) Both edits happened at an Art+Feminism-adjacent event called Unforgetting Los Angeles. The city of Los Angeles could destroy *Vermonica*, Chris Burden and LACMA could ignore or deny it, but Wikipedia is designed for facts.

While anyone can read Wikipedia, not many people participate; but this distinction isn't a bad thing. The logged-in users "run the place," Kyra Gaunt told me, and the difference between them—an actual community with norms and habits, and the people who edit pages anonymously (marked only by IP address)—is the difference between "night and day." When someone edits under a username, all their contributions are added to their profile, which makes a user's page almost like a portfolio; they can be part of the wider community of editors. But someone editing with only an IP address to identify themselves flutters in and flutters out. Another group of users, outside the community, includes all people who neither log in nor edit—the readers, the lurkers. Wikipedia regulars generally don't take issue with those who look but do not edit. They are the public this work is created for; rather than sponging off their work, lurkers might even make it easier for the editors—it is hard to imagine the already fragile Wikipedia ecosystem sustaining itself if every single internet user on the internet took an active role. In the early years of enthusiasm for peer production, techno-utopians talked about this dynamic as the 1–9–90 or "1 percent rule"—that is, in collaborative online spaces, roughly 90 percent of people only read content, 9 percent edit the content, and another 1 percent actually create new content. As I reviewed the Wikipedia page for the 1 percent rule, an anecdote jumped out at me. It read (at least, it did the last time I checked):

> The terms lurk and lurking, in reference to online activity, are used to refer to online observation without engaging others in the community, and were first used by veteran print journalist, P. Tomi Austin, circa 1990.

According to the anecdote on the Wikipedia page, Austin was at the time in her thirties and engaging in a chat room with users in their teens and twenties. Going by the username "Bilbo," she identified herself to the participants as a chat room novice "lurking" to better familiarize herself with their culture, etiquette, and habits.

Now, I had spent several years researching this book when I happened to find this origin story in the summer of 2018. This was the first I had ever heard of P. Tomi Austin. Unfortunately, the chunk of text, posted in 2013, concluded with two striking "citation needed" tags. I searched the internet for relevant clues—an essay, blog post, some kind of archival community news story, anything at all. All I could find was aggregated content quoting that same Wikipedia entry.

So I turned to my last resort: Facebook. I logged in with an alt-account I use only for reporting, and sent a message to the one person in Facebook's entire database with that name. I noticed she was based in Utah, and remembered that the text about the coinage of "lurking" came from an anonymous user with an IP address tracing back to Utah. I already knew this edit broke Wikipedia's "no original research" rule; perhaps it flouted the ban on "conflict-of-interest editing," too?

Her profile photo, with a vintage glow that was no filter, revealed a young Asian American woman with a bright smile, dressed in a stylish wine-colored blouse and flowers in her hair, singing into a mic. The image was captioned, "Salt Lake City Arts Festival main stage, 1985, I think? Maybe '87? One of the best gigs ever." Her profile description read, "Writer, photographer, editor, university tutor, former law-enforcement (former certified police officer), grandparent, caregiver for a number of seniors, bird rescuer & rehab-er (parrots/hookbills), parrotrent to 8 parrots from 'tiels to Cockatoos, dog rescuer, I love most animals, except not so big on cats, am allergic to cats, am very pragmatic, have unusually good common sense, a deep sense of compassion, kindness, and a very strong sense of ethics and morality." Her public Facebook updates were very, very Utah: a mix of anti-abortion news stories ("high court in Ireland rules an unborn baby has a right to life," announced one post) and her own strong words about the president ("Trump needs to be, MUST be prosecuted for human rights violations"), especially with regard to his policy on immigration.

Austin responded to my message the following day, and agreed to take my call. On the phone, she told me about her experiences decades ago as a staff writer and photographer for local press and Catholic publications. As a journalist, she often wrote about domestic violence, drawing on her previous work in law enforcement. Later, she became interested in gaming. She built a computer on her own, and went back to school to study computer science. She was warm and funny, but demurred when it came to the story that made it to Wikipedia. I had hoped she could direct me to a personal essay she wrote or a local news story where she might have been quoted. However, it appears that only she and the chat room participants would know about it. "My memory just isn't what it used to be," she explained. The story was true—she went by "Bilbo" in a chat room thirty years ago and she did tell everyone online that she was "lurking"—but how it ended up on Wikipedia, she could not say.

Wrapping up the call, Austin asked me what brought me to that particular Wikipedia page. I told her about this book.

"Do you have a working title?" she asked. She laughed when I told her.

I ended the call, still wondering about Austin's chat room anecdote. There was not much I could do other than take her word for it that the world will never know which Wikipedia editor, with an IP address in Utah, added this anecdote about her to the page for the 1 percent rule. Google shut down its newspaper archive in 2011. I could fly to Salt Lake City and review the microfiche for various local Catholic publications, if any relevant papers are even archived. That's hours and hours of time for a question unlikely to be answerable. Wikipedia did what it was supposed to: it flagged information in need of citation. It just happens that in this instance, the original research—which wasn't supposed to be there—was more valuable to me than the vetted content on the page.

Austin's peripatetic career, wide range of interests—nerdy interests, like the reference to *The Hobbit* years before the Peter Jackson movies—and sweet sense of humor reminded me of the kind of eccentric curiosity and friendliness of people in chat rooms from the nineties. As we talked, I found myself nostalgic for the pre-social-media internet of chat rooms and Usenet, where people could talk with others, despite their differences, before a time of political polarization. Naturally, this conversation also benefited from formality and specific purpose, with no need to discuss politics or approach issues like abortion or policing—topics that couldn't possibly go down as warmly.

After the call, I snapped out of it and realized that the internet I felt momentarily nostalgic for is an internet that never actually existed. There was never a chat room where I could have talked freely with people the age of my parents, who also held vastly different views on politics and religion. That's how the internet was first sold to me, but it was never how I used it. As far as I have come in this research, even I catch myself trying to believe in the lie of cyberspace as a respite from identity, where people from all walks of life could find sanctuary despite their differences. Perhaps these mythical anti-echo chambers existed, but the reality of the internet has always been that anything untrammeled online gets trammeled eventually. Even spaces like the much-lamented LiveJournal had trolling and hatred, and platform-specific toxicity, like the "Nonuglies" communities, where users, in cutting and anatomized detail, rated the attractiveness of other users. Pleasant internet communities are brief junctures, when they are not airbrushed by history. Some old Usenet group or forum that was once tight-knit and happy could get blighted with spam, or some creep denying the Armenian genocide; then everyone would drop out eventually. Chat rooms, forums, listservs, and other communities have expiry dates, whether measured by time or personal fallouts.

I have come to realize that when I think I feel nostalgic for the internet before social media consolidation, what I am actually experiencing is a longing for an internet that is better, for internet communities that haven't come into being yet—certainly not on a mass scale, and even then, nothing lasting. The traits that make a community idyllic at first are the same traits that make it momentary. To build a better internet means work, not simply dreams and wishes. That is the labor of mediation, vital to all online communities, but undervalued; the work of professional community managers or volunteer moderators, people who can hold users accountable to one another.

Kat Lo, a Ph.D. student at UC Irvine, studies the functions of moderators and the labor of maintaining online communities. She has worked with companies like Instagram and Microsoft, and organizations like the Southern Poverty Law Center and Girls Code, where she often draws on her background as a volunteer moderator of various online groups. As a teenager, she spent time on some of the internet's most unruly quarters, like 4chan—a different place when she was in high school—and later she went on to moderate the GirlGamers subreddit, which she founded. Reddit, home to the Gamergate indoctrination project /r/KotakuInAction and the alt-right Trump meme factory /r/The_Donald, is not exactly a warm and fuzzy venue for intersectional feminists who enjoy video games. Nevertheless, Lo and her cohort have been able to carve out a space for themselves through it. Newcomers can find their subreddit easily, and she doesn't have to code her own forum or pay for hosting to keep the community together. There are layers to inclusion as a way to ward off trolls. Someone who joins and participates in /r/GirlGamers is hanging out at the equivalent of the front porch of a party. To get to the kitchen, where the better conversations are taking place, a user must apply to join their Discord server, a private text-chat channel using freeware popular in the gaming community. An applicant submits a posting history of at least three months to moderators, who review their posts and decide whether the user seems legitimate. The Reddit-to-Discord conduit is porous where it needs to be. It is laborious to hostile people, while welcoming to like-minded new people. Much of the social internet is moving to spaces like Discord and Slack, which a user needs an invite to access, but it is good to keep some windows open along the way, so people in remote places and circumstances, without other girl-gamers as IRL friends, can still find their people. This process mitigates the openness of the Reddit channel, and while it does not perfectly prevent trolling on Discord, it is manageable.

Diverse as its communities are today, Lo thinks of Reddit as inheriting "forum dwelling behavior." The culture on this platform was set by "young white men who were already on forums." These first users had plenty of alternatives when Reddit launched; there was already Digg, Slashdot, and Something Awful—all built for a certain sort of online guy.

But these "forum dwellers" preferred Reddit, and their loyalty is what brought other communities along to create their own subreddits. In Lo's words, Reddit has "idiot libertarian" founding principles; it did nothing to improve the diversity of its users; it did nothing special for them at all—it was just easy for everyone to use. Someone like Lo, who had better things to do than whip up a platform in PHP from scratch, could use Reddit to get an online community up and running very quickly.

One of its most common ongoing features is called "Ask Me Anything," where celebrities and politicians, and people with odd jobs or unusual experiences, take questions from Reddit users; but original posts in forum threads are often structured as question-prompts as well. Some of these discussions are genuinely beautiful, humane, and engaging, like the long thread that came out of a question, "What is the smallest amount of power you've ever seen someone abuse?" Name a culture, community, or experience and it is represented in Reddit as a subreddit. It might not be as active as Reddit's famous poisonous corners, but these users are on Reddit, too, however quietly. There are subreddits for people dealing with addiction and illness, as well as resources and tactical advice for those at risk of unemployment or homelessness.

It is harder to make grand pronouncements about Reddit, as one might about Facebook. The variance that comes through in communities—communities, as in plural—has everything to do with how the platforms are tended to and organized. Lo thinks of the difference as a dichotomy: Facebook is a "network community," in contrast with Reddit, a "forum community." On a forum, "people have to do some collective types of negotiation [or] the inertia of a community can take place." These aren't strict categories. Facebook groups might resemble Reddit forums, but they lack the ad hoc anonymity; users are Facebook users before they are users of a specific Facebook group. Anonymity makes the Reddit experience wildly different from activity on Facebook. Perhaps usernames foster "forum communities." A user known only as tardigradefan96 is not so unknown if you have been chatting with that person for months in a subreddit. Reddit offers extreme examples of positive and negative use of online anonymity (subreddits that range from r/homeless to r/beatingwomen). The difference between a Reddit forum and a Facebook group is the difference between a masked assembly in a forest glen while the apocalypse rages a mile down the road and a group meeting inside a panopticon—or maybe it is not so stark. Reddit ad-tech was minimal until recent years, but now its users are subject to "personalized" targeted ads by default. Reddit feels more hands-off than Facebook with its ever-present filters and monitoring, and its data collection practices are nowhere near as gargantuan, but the "forum community" tracks its users, too.

On Reddit—or any forum—the habits of one space aren't the same as another, nor are the habits transferable, just as friend groups form bonds according to many different criteria and develop different in-jokes. The way to be a good mod is to develop localized tactics for individual online communities. What works for the GirlGamers subreddit might not work for other forums, which receive other kinds of abuses and have other problems to filter around. These nuances can be spotted and understood only by members of a community.

Moderating GirlGamers isn't a full-time endeavor for one person, let alone teams of thousands. Kat Lo's workload is in proportion to the size of her community. The community might choose to dissolve if it ever required more maintenance. Besides forums for specific communities, moderation increasingly falls on internet users, who find themselves called to intervene when a conflict breaks out in all sorts of online communities, such as mediating a spat over PTA meeting notes posted to Facebook or attempts to deescalate racism posted to Nextdoor. It is care work that is part of an ordinary social life online, and imperfect as it is, even in intimate community settings, it is a form of labor that does not scale.

Reddit was, for a long time, an extreme example of a platform committed to "free speech." Yishan Wong, the CEO of Reddit from 2012 until 2014, once refused to ban any content that was legal. That's the "easiest way to host a forum because you invest no resources," Kat Lo told me. In the past five years, it has banned a number of extreme subreddits, including r/beatingwomen and a forum for QAnon, and it has "quarantined" others like r/The_Donald. Other tech companies and platforms are strongly censorious when they choose to be, given examples like Facebook's quick deletion of users with Native American names in 2014 but its resistance to banning Alex Jones until 2019. It took Apple quite some time to remove Alex Jones's *Infowars* podcast from its iTunes listings, but in 2012, Josh Begley's Drone+ app—a simple project that provided users with updates on drone strikes and their location on a map—was swiftly purged from Apple's App Store. The company told Begley, "We found that your app contains content that many audiences would find objectionable, which is not in compliance with the App Store Review Guidelines." Begley appealed to Apple, only to see his app, renamed Metadata+, rejected or removed from the platform several more times until it was finally accepted in 2017 . . . until it was rejected once again. As recently as 2017, Twitter locked out users for joking about Elon Musk in their usernames, as well as activists and sex workers for benign offenses, but Donald Trump can harass Ilhan Omar on the platform with no repercussions. This double standard reveals who the platforms pander and cower to, and which users are taken for granted.

Moderating platforms today involves a combination of human labor, algorithmic filtering, and methods such as whitelisting or blacklisting users or content. Pro-ana content—like the aslant GeoCities pages I stumbled on as a teenager—has long confounded internet censors. Tumblr and Instagram, like Yahoo and other services before it, have issued policies to ban content that glorifies self-harm, only to see these users misspell common hashtags or otherwise evade bans through in-community secret language or signaling. More execrable content calls for specialized content moderators, labor that platforms usually contract out. It is grinding and traumatizing work. The contractors' task is to clean the platforms of snuff images, child pornography, and other things I'd rather not think about. No one should have to do this job, even if it is paid (which it is, but not particularly well). The content moderators and the PTSD they suffer is evidence enough that it is impossible for these platforms to ever clean themselves up.

Accountability on the internet, for the internet, and for users collectively depends on the tension between privacy for a few and openness to newcomers. We can create spaces for ourselves and our friends and call them "safe spaces" or "sanctuaries," but what use is that if like-minded people are still left in the cold? A sanctuary isn't going to look the same for everybody. Maybe it's Echo, still thriving, thirty years on, with users typing in the same key commands as they have for thirty years. Or it is learning the Wikipedia ropes and clearing room for students to participate without fear, as Kyra Gaunt does for her classroom. The ideal internet experience looks different user to user. It isn't all that much different from the search for safe spaces offline; but an additional thorn is the need to circumvent a platform's profit-seeking agenda.

I fear that the media's delayed—and often misplaced—concerns about technology has fostered an endless ping-pong of surface changes and tactics, rather than focus on structural changes like decommodification and decentralization to enact a better internet. Worse still, Silicon Valley—handed this truncated timeline of its ills—is already working to coopt and neutralize the "techlash," similar to how it weakly responded to the matter of diversity just a few years before. Calls for "ethics" are coming from inside the big tech houses, and with an agenda that favors optics over solutions. When tech executives appoint themselves as the stewards of the industry cleanup, they carry on with the same spirit of contempt for outsiders—and users—that unleashed the problems in the first place.

Yet failure to anticipate the consequences of the internet is not the same as accepting, loving, or yielding to the internet in its current state. None other than Tim Berners-Lee—he of the modest 1991 Usenet announcement about a project that "comes without any warranty whatsoever"—has expressed disappointment about what has become of it. The World Wide Web was built following the ethic of a decentralized internet; concentration of power, which Amazon, Google, and Facebook have shored up, once seemed impossible to him. "Happily, the Web is so huge that there's no way any one company can dominate it," Berners-Lee wrote in 1999. Twenty years later, the World Wide Web Foundation, with his approval, would fund research about social hazards online—largely because of companies he predicted would never gain a foothold on it. Half the world's population has become internet users, which means the internet is still growing. Berners-Lee worries how these new users will be further marginalized. In a *Vanity Fair* profile, he drew a graph to display inequality in vectors of privacy. At the top right was a mark to represent "Elon Musk when he is using his most powerful computer." Lower on the page he drew a mark to represent "people in Ethiopia who have reasonable connectivity but they are totally being spied on." Ever the optimist, he pointed to the center of the graph and told the interviewer, the "goal is to fill in that square. To fill it up so all of humanity has total power on the Web."

Google and Facebook alone account for more than 70 percent of the internet traffic, a share that has steeply climbed since 2014. These companies have taken over functions of a state without administering the benefits or protections of a state. Nation-states might appear today to be as fragile and theoretical as anything digital, but the difference is not small. Google might secure contracts with the defense department, but the company does not authorize drone strikes. Facebook can't put you in prison. Apple doesn't run black sites. Amazon's foul treatment of its factory workers is iniquitous, but it is not extraordinary rendition. Infrastructure is power, but it is not the law, which means there is still an opportunity for users—as individuals and collectives, and working with government bodies—to hold platforms accountable.

Some well-intentioned leftists have suggested nationalizing big tech. While admitting it is an unrealistic demand, Sarah Jaffe has argued in favor of nationalizing Amazon for its infrastructure and logistics. Its efficiency is valuable. In a piece she wrote for The Outline, she explains that a call to "nationalize Amazon is to challenge the idea that Amazon should have more power than the democratically-elected governments of states or countries." A similar argument can't quite be made for the major companies focused on communication and online communities. Nationalizing Google would be devastating: further entrenching the biases of its search algorithms and binding its unethical pursuits to the future. Nationalizing Facebook would be to conscript all future generations inside an IRS for friendships. No thanks.

Regulation is another incomplete solution. At best, policy for the internet could be like what seat belts or HOV lanes were for the highway and driving, or even the digital equivalent of pedestrian-only zones. But Facebook is not an automobile, it does not move individuals from one place to the next; instead, it entraps them inside its feedback loops and mazes. Facebook has entrapped two billion individuals—a user base so vast, it is virtually impossible for this platform to ever be effectively governed. The most urgently needed regulation—an outright ban on targeted advertising—could bring it to its knees, maybe. Mastodon (a Twitter and Facebook alternative) as well as PixelFed and PeerTube (decentralized attempts at Instagram or YouTube) are viable alternatives, which are free, open-source, and self-hosted. The challenge is convincing people to use them.

Another possibility is antitrust action, which might, for example, divide Google and YouTube or split up Instagram, WhatsApp, and Facebook. A short-term result of this might be a decentralized commercial internet, as it was in the nineties—better but still no paradise. In 1994, Carmen Hermosillo, an internet user who went by "humdog," posted a manifesto to the internet, "pandora's vox: on community in cyberspace." It has been widely shared and reblogged ever since. Adam Curtis even quoted the manifesto in his miniseries *All Watched Over by Machines of Loving Grace*, and talked about the prescience of this text on a 2011 radio show hosted by Jarvis Cocker.

"[When] i went into cyberspace i went into it thinking that it was a place like any other place and that it would be a human interaction like any other human interaction," Hermosillo began, tearing down The WELL's self-mythologizing as a utopia, and instead painting a picture of cyberspace as large as a vampiric spectacle:

> i have seen many people spill their guts on-line, and i did so myself until, at last, i began to see that i had

> commodified myself. commodification means that you turn something into a product which has a money-value. in the nineteenth century, commodities were made in factories, which karl marx called "the means of production." capitalists were people who owned the means of production, and the commodities were made by workers who were mostly exploited. i created my interior thoughts as a means of production for the corporation that owned the board i was posting to, and that commodity was being sold to other commodity/consumer entities as entertainment. that means that i sold my soul like a tennis shoe and i derived no profit from the sale of my soul. people who post frequently on boards appear to know that they are factory equipment and tennis shoes, and sometimes trade sends and email about how their contributions are not appreciated by management.
>
> as if this were not enough, all of my words were made immortal by means of tape backups. furthermore, i was paying two bucks an hour for the privilege of commodifying and exposing myself. worse still, i was subjecting myself to the possibility of scrutiny by such friendly folks as the FBI: they can, and have, downloaded pretty much whatever they damn well please. the rhetoric in cyberspace is liberation-speak. the reality is that cyberspace is an increasingly efficient tool of surveillance with which people have a voluntary relationship.

What have users traded in a search for belonging, in communities owned by corporations—with million-dollar or billion-dollar operations? Words posted online "were made immortal," as humdog forewarned—not as a legacy but as a haunting. "i suspect that my words have been extracted and that when this essay shows up, they will be extracted some more," she concludes. She passed away in 2008, and since then, the prophecy of her words in 1994 has been realized. The text has been posted to VC-backed blog platforms and GitHub. The clip of Jarvis Cocker and Adam Curtis is available on YouTube. Links to this content are shared on Facebook and Twitter regularly. Decentralization isn't much without a noncommercial mission, but now we're back to the demand, beneath the gloss of social internet, from cyberspace to social media: How does society dismantle hierarchies, bring about progressive social change, and negate corruption, bias, exploitation, and injustice—problems born online or there all along?

Regarding these age-old questions, I often think about Kim Stanley Robinson's definition of utopia—it emerges from abolishing all but the "necessary" human tragedies. That plus online is utopia online. Utopia is an impossible condition, on the internet or offline, but the internet can provide moments of solace. It might be found in messages users send one another in real time or in words in digital archives or old websites that offer comfort to a person in the here and now. The solace almost makes it all worth it.

# Closing: End User

Among the many YouTube subcultures is a group that produces self-recordings known as transition journeys. In these videos, members of the trans community share their experiences with hormone therapy over time, sometimes documenting the changes in their appearance in time-lapsed final montages. These videos tend to be filmed for other trans people, as a service to those deliberating this momentous life step. "These types of transition montages were helpful to me, so I wanted to pay it forward," a woman told The Verge, explaining why she shared this private experience with a kindred but unknown public.

A computer science professor in North Carolina discovered these videos through one of his students. Then he gathered thirty-eight clips from YouTube, and created a database with more than a million images for the purpose of improving accuracy in face recognition research. He failed to see the unique vulnerability of this information—it was no ordinary data or broadcast, but images and messages cherished by a specific few, and not for him. Later, following criticism, he realized the intimate nature of the videos he had collected, and cut off access to the data set. He apologized for what he had done. But it was too late. People who appeared in the videos now might find their faces illustrating related scientific papers, despite never giving their consent to be identified this way. Depicted was a personal change, rare and weighty, of a significance and liberation that few of us will know or understand, that someone chose to share through a platform, to a stranger who would get it. A community of users expressing care for one another became useful bits to an outsider. That's not lurking; it's exploiting.

Here is where users get used: as scrap metal, as data in a data set, as something less than human, as actual tools. Priceless experience, lived online, can be boiled down to a price, which tends to be fractions of pennies. I, personally, might have a sense not to disturb someone whose boarding pass I found, but these boundaries are my own, not ingrained as custom online. Such boundaries do not always exist in academia or the media, and are definitely not the custom at Google or Facebook, inevitably spinning up data at this minute, similar or just as exploitative as the—

noncommercial!—project known as the "HRT Transgender Dataset."

My life, before I was aware of the bargain, is up for grabs, because I lived online before I realized what the internet takes from me. Myspace sold user data to the ad-tech octopus Viant—later part of Time Inc.—in 2011. What might come of it? I can't even rule out the possibility that something stupid I did on AOL won't resurface in the future and embarrass me. Like the North Carolina project, IBM scraped Flickr archives without the consent of users—many of whom may not have checked the site in years—to create another facial recognition training set. These are memories. Photos from birthdays, graduations, weddings—and from a while ago, because internet platforms now have history. This exploitation of our past is becoming more commonplace. Sometimes a user can request to opt out, but you would have to have heard about the data capture first, which is not always possible when unknown traces of yourself are floating around in a fickle ether.

It is a haunting. A user animates their internet representation through comments and images; so when a user is split from their content, what is left is what binds them to the conditions of the internet. Like ghosts in a house, the ghosts of the internet are stuck within its walls. Whatever the data, wherever it is chained, enough of this data is going to outlive me.

These systems were broken at the beginning; now the systems are broken and rusty. What actions can be taken toward developing greater privacy protection and user consent? Even our vocabulary frustrates attempts to express this desire; there isn't even a word in English for enjoying time alone—for enjoying privacy. Just to speak of it must count for something.

A better internet could accommodate us all like a public park: a space for all, a benefit to everyone; a space one can enter or leave, and leave without a trace. Then again, public parks are valorized for benefits that are unevenly fulfilled. We know which populations—playing a game of chess, enjoying a picnic lunch—are more likely to have cops called on them for no good reason. Studies have shown that Jim Crow laws and more recent instances of racism have led to a black population wary of public parks and less likely to visit them.

Public parks are a flawed ideal, but what about libraries? I often think about Amazon as the ultimate Wario to the public library. Like a library, it began with books, and later expanded operations to include Hollywood studio productions, cloud infrastructure, groceries, and space missions. A library is also more than books. Many librarians are now trained to administer naloxone, which is available at the front desk. At the New York Public Library, a person can check out a suit jacket, tie, or nice purse, should they need these items for job interviews or other events requiring formal dress. Other libraries loan bicycles and offer on-site medical services. Amazon, with its books-to-Mars trajectory, demonstrates the limitlessness of American avarice and exploitation, while for libraries to offer not only books but also suit jackets and bicycles upholds in perfect opposition the limitless spirit of compassion and generosity to those in need—a spirit that is curtailed only by the reality of municipal budgets.

Apple has even set up shop in an old library. You can

upgrade your phone at the Apple Carnegie Library in Washington, D.C., which opened in 2019. As Tim Cook announced, the company will "continue the legacy of this beautiful building as a place where people seek knowledge and a sense of community." Once it was home to ninety-five thousand volumes; now a customer can purchase a laptop there for three thousand dollars. Then again, there's a reason why it wasn't called the Central Public Library when Apple took over. Its very name—Apple *Carnegie* Library—demonstrates a problem older than the personal computer.

The differences between libraries and Google or Facebook are more subtle than the differences between libraries and Apple Stores. Libraries do not have customers; they have patrons. It could also be said that libraries have users. As Jessamyn West pointed out, there is no such thing as a library without librarians; but neither Facebook nor Google—despite having more money than all the libraries in the world—has anything like a librarian on staff. Neither company is structured for that type of role: a person who might meet users where they are and help provide what they need. Librarians are what the internet is aching for—people on task to care about the past, with respect to the past and also to what it shall bequeath to the future. There needs to be rituals in place online to treat people—users—with dignity, both the living and the dead. For to speak of the humanity of internet users is to recognize the impermanence, the mortality of that humanity.

Everyone is welcome in a library just for being. A person in a library is a person: homeless or not, hurting or not. My dream for the internet, as a final form, is a civic and independent body, where all people are welcome and respected, guided by principles of justice, rights, and human dignity. For this, users would express care in return, with a sense of purpose and responsibility to the digital spaces organized with these values. With the internet routing through a planet that is the origin of more than a hundred billion lives, such a project means information in abundance. Segmenting and clustering users and history into communities, rather than mass-purpose platforms, would be an integral component to this ideal internet in its cycles of maintenance and renewal.

Calls for regulation or even brand-new ventures might be too little, too late, but it doesn't hurt to dream. A public internet alone won't save us, a decentralized internet itself won't protect us; more than that, what users need are noncommercial localized systems of feedback, mutual aid, and accountability—commons guided with respect to user consent and privacy. Users need users, people need people. To borrow a slogan often expressed by health and disability activists, there should be "nothing about us without us." Communities online have to be shaped and minded by their very same communities. And the internet needs its librarians. Until then, the internet remains imperfect, a hell that is fun, ruled by idiots and thieves, providing users with slingshots for self-expression but no shield from the bile that rebounds. It is our potential, our conscription, and our reality: platforms that trap us, platforms that cannot accommodate us, platforms that don't deserve us.

# NOTES

## INTRODUCTION

Olia Lialina's 2012 essay "Turing Complete User" is available on her website: contemporary-home-computing.org/turing-complete-user/. The email from a Mechanical Turk worker to Jeff Bezos was part of a letter-writing campaign organized through the MTurk collective Dynamo. Will Oremus has written about Amazon as a surveillance company, with products like Ring and Echo, in the Medium publication *OneZero* ("Amazon Is Watching," June 27, 2019). Goodreads and Twitch, the livestreaming video platform, are Amazon subsidiaries, but their social media operations are small in comparison to services like cloud computing, logistics, and retail. A good explanation of the difference between users and customers can be found in "The Discovery of Behavioral Surplus," in Shoshana Zuboff's *The Age of Surveillance Capitalism*

(Public Affairs, 2019): "There is no economic exchange, no price, and no profit. Nor do users function in the role of workers . . . Users are not paid for their labor, nor do they operate the means of production."

## 1. SEARCH

In 2015, Google restructured itself and renamed its holding company "Alphabet," but no one seems to actually call it that other than its shareholders. There was an NPR segment in 2014 about the questions the New York Public Library fielded from the 1940s to the '80s ("Before the Internet, Librarians Would 'Answer Everything'—And Still Do," December 28, 2014). Note cards documenting the questions were also featured on the NYPL Instagram account at the time. I got the number "2,738 websites in 1994" and other figures from the website Internet Live Stats. Also, it should be noted that Archie was the first internet search engine—created by Alan Emtage in 1989. There were several web search engines in the 1990s, including Excite, Lycos, AltaVista, WebCrawler, Yahoo, HotBot, Infoseek, Inktomi, Snap, Direct Hit, Magellan, and Ask Jeeves. For years, I could have sworn HotBot had the most relevant results, and I was surprised to learn many, many years later that it was only the skin for search that the Inktomi database provided. In addition to the Lycos and Yahoo model of directories, there was a user-sorted directory called DMOZ, which shut down in 2017. Slashdot noted that the "site was so old that its hierarchical categories were originally based on the hierarchy of Usenet newsgroups" ("After 19 Years, DMOZ Will Close, Announces AOL," Slashdot, March 4, 2017). Mark Hansen and Ben Rubin's installation *Listening Post* was first presented at Brooklyn Academy of Music in December 2001. Rubin has a video clip on his Vimeo page. On YouTube, one might find a 2006 user-created video depicting a screen broadcasting live search results. Frank Pasquale, in a piece for Aeon ("Digital Star Chamber," August 18, 2015), provides more context about Google results: "For example, thanks to Federal Trade Commission action in 2002, United States consumer-protection laws require the separation of advertisements from unpaid, 'organic' content. In a world where media firms are constantly trying to blur the distinction between content and 'native advertising,' that law matters." Katie Benner and Daisuke Wakabayashi reported on Google's issues with sexual harassment, in their eye-opening piece "How Google Protected Andy Rubin, the 'Father of Android'" (*The New York Times*, October 25, 2018). For more information on the Google walkout, read Marie Hicks's "The Long History Behind the Google Walkout" (The Verge, November 9, 2018). The artist Andrew Norman Wilson wrote an essay about his experience, "The Artist Leaving the Googleplex," in the September 2016 issue of *e-Flux Journal*. For more information on the hierarchy of badge colors, there is a report by Mark Bergen and Josh Eidelson, "Inside Google's Shadow Workforce" (Bloomberg, July 25, 2018). The transcript of my interview with a Street View driver appeared on Medium as "An Interview with a Google Street View Driver," posted May 28, 2015. Robots, in addition to people, did photograph the inside of museums with the Google Art Project. The artist Mario Santamaria collected examples of their uncanny selfies on a Tumblr called "The Camera in the Mirror." In 2019, Google was ordered to pay $13 million after a class-action case that found Street View cars gathered passwords, emails, and other data from unencrypted household Wi-Fi networks that they passed. It is interesting to contrast Google's old "mirror the world" rhetoric with its recent eagerness to comply with censorship in China, including its Dragonfly project, which was reportedly shut down due to internal dissent (*The Intercept* has covered this ongoing story). The Marissa Mayer statement happened at the 2010 gathering of LeWeb, and she is quoted in TechCrunch ("Marissa Mayer's Next Big Thing: 'Contextual Discovery,'" December 8, 2010). My source for Gmail's lack of a delete option was a *Wired* story, confirmed by additional reporting at the time (Michael Calore, "April 1, 2004: Gmail Hits Webmail G-Spot," *Wired*, April 1, 2009). The Marissa Mayer interview about GOOG-411 was conducted by Juan Carlos Perez for InfoWorld ("Google Wants Your Phonemes," October 23, 2007). In 2010, the CEO Eric Schmidt said at the Newseum, "There is what I call the creepy line. The Google policy on a lot of things is to get right up to the creepy line and not cross it," according to a report in *The Hill* (Sara Jerome, "Schmidt: Google gets 'right up to the creepy line,'" October 1, 2010). The website Killed By Google (killedbygoogle.com) is a thorough database of the apps, services, and hardware that have been junked. It has been reported that Google shut down Google+ largely because it was easier to do than fix a security breach (Douglas MacMillan and Robert McMillan, "Google Exposed User Data, Feared Repercussions of Disclosing to Public," *The Wall Street Journal*, October 8, 2018). I interviewed Jessamyn West on August 10, 2017. Earlier she wrote about this experience for Medium (Jessamyn West, "Google's Slow Fade with Librarians," February 2, 2015). Information about the event I was part of at the Institute of Contemporary Arts is on its website ("The Influence of Technology," February 25, 2014), along with the dead YouTube link. The transcript of my talk is available here: https://archive.fo/OcY4H. In addition to the quotes from Sergey Brin about books in "That horrid Google on the prowl!!!," in Steven Levy's *In the Plex* (Simon & Schuster, 2011), and Ken Auletta's *Googled: The End of the World as We Know It* (Penguin Press, 2009, 124), I found Zuckerberg's statement "I don't read" in Katherine Losse's memoir *The Boy Kings* (Free Press, 2012, 6). In addition to Auletta and Levy's encounters with Brin, John Battelle says in the footnotes of his book *The Search* (Portfolio, 2005) that "in exchange for sitting down with me, Page wanted the right to review every mention of Google, Page, or Brin in my book, then respond in footnotes. Such a deal would have been nearly impossible to realize, and would have required untold hours of work on Page's part. Page and I negotiated for weeks over his proposal . . . In the end, Page relented." I entered the beginning of this passage into Google itself—just the words "In exchange for sitting down with me." The search engine did not recommend Battelle's or even Auletta's book (which quotes him). Instead, the first result, and the second, fourth, fifth, and eighth—there were only eight results—directed me to suicide hotlines, including the website of a major nonprofit and a YouTube video, "Dance Moms/Group Dance Suicide Hotline." Google algorithms must have parsed "In exchange for sitting down with me" as a cry for help (?). Nothing in my search history might have tipped this off, and it's such an unsettling instance that I thought I would mention it here. Google's "Year in Search 2017" is available on YouTube, in addition to its other annual roundups. Eric

Schmidt called multiple results a "bug" in an interview with Charlie Rose in 2005, which is further considered in a *Washington Post* piece by Gregory Ferenstein ("Google, Competition and the Perfect Result," January 4, 2013). Nitasha Tiku has reported on activism at Google ("Why Tech Worker Dissent Is Going Viral," *Wired*, June 29, 2018). An interview with Guillaume Chaslot, one of the engineers who worked on the recommendation system, in *The Guardian* ("'Fiction is outperforming reality': how YouTube's algorithm distorts truth," February 2, 2018) provides more information on how hateful content and misinformation spreads on the platform. Safiya Umoja Noble's book *Algorithms of Oppression* (NYU Press, 2018) is a definitive look at Google's bias. Jack Nicas reported on Fiskhorn's Google-instigated transition into "Fishkorn" ("As Google Maps Renames Neighborhoods, Residents Fume," *The New York Times*, August 2, 2018). Ellen Ullman has commented on how Google has shifted the meaning of the word "search." In her book *Life in Code* (MCD, 2017, 206), she writes, "Search is a part of us, one of the desires evolution has woven into us over the eons, to keep us alive." And in a 2013 interview with Maud Newton she commented, "Has Google appropriated the word 'search'? If so, I find it sad. Search is a deep human yearning, an ancient trope in the recorded history of human life" ("Meet the Flannery O'Connor of the Internet Age," *Salon*, January 23, 2013).

## 2. ANONYMITY

This chapter only briefly touches on the internet before the web. Anyone interested in the prologue should check out Janet Abbate's 1999 book, *Inventing the Internet* (MIT Press, 83), especially for its depiction of ARPANET as an example of the "variety of active roles users can play in shaping a new technology." The William Gibson quote comes from an interview in *The Paris Review* (David Wallace-Wells, "William Gibson, The Art of Fiction No. 211," 2011). "First" as a date and concept is often a fuzzy distinction. The World Wide Web is thirty years old, a date that is basically correct the year I write this (2019), the year this book will hit shelves (2020), and the year after that (2021); Tim Berners-Lee invented it in 1989, wrote the first browser in 1990, and released it to the public, per his newsgroup posts, in 1991. Among the first commercial online services, The Source launched in July 1979, according to the 1995 Washington Technology obit for its founder, William F. von Meister, which also reports that Isaac Asimov was in attendance at its launch at the Plaza Hotel event, where he said, "This is the beginning of the information age." CompuServe, according to its still-operational website, was founded in 1969 as a computer time-sharing service. The company website also explains that in 1979, CompuServe became the first service to offer email and "technical support to personal computer users." The Source brochure slogan is quoted in Walter Isaacson's *The Innovators* (Simon & Schuster, 2015, 392). The advertisement is available to view in Fredric Saunier's 1988 book *Marketing Strategies for the Online Industry* (Macmillan, 1988, 85). In 2003, the *Chicago Tribune* profiled the locals Ward Christensen and Randy Suess, who invented the BBS in 1978, mentioning that "in typical Chicago fashion, a snowstorm got an assist in the invention" (Patrick Kampert, "Low-Key Pioneer," February 16, 2003). The Katie Hafner quote about the BBS's "public broadcasting sensibility" comes from an article she wrote for *The New York Times* ("Old Newsgroups in New Packages," June 24, 1999). Information about AOL, including its description of channels, comes from "The Official America Online Tour Guide, Third Edition, 1997," a text that is available to read on the Internet Archive. Echo was a "conferencing service," but that is a "fine distinction" from the BBS, as Stacy Horn told me. This section draws on my interviews with Horn in March and August 2017. I also consulted Horn's memoir about her experience founding the company ("And Now," in *Cyberville: Clicks, Culture, and the Creation of an Online Town*, Warner Books, 1998). The community's 9/11 posts were republished on *New York* magazine's website on September 6, 2006 ("Item 245: Breaking News"). There was a profile of Echo in *The New York Times* (Trish Hall, "Coming to the East Coast: An Electronic Salon," January 28, 1990). Marisa Bowe wrote about the service in *Wired* ("Net Living: The East Coast Hang Out," March 1, 1993). More recently, Sandra Newman profiled the service in *The Atlantic* ("Growing Old in New

York's Snarkiest Early-Internet Community," May 2, 2017), and Claire L. Evans provided further context in her book *Broad Band* (Portfolio, 2018, 134–80). As the website for Echo explains, "Founded in 1990, we have over 3,000 members and 40% of them are female." According to Fred Turner's *From Counterculture to Cyberculture* (University of Chicago Press, 2006, 279), 40 percent of the users of The WELL were women, too. Julian Dibbell's "A Rape in Cyberspace," first published in *The Village Voice*, also appears in his book *My Tiny Life: Crime and Passion in a Virtual World* (Fourth Estate, 1999). My comment that "no legends or legendary work emerged from" New York's tech-media-art scene is a bit of a provocation, given that such things take time. Even in later years, hardly anyone has set their film or fiction in this time period and scene (notable exception: Thomas Pynchon's *Bleeding Edge*, 2013). Until then, we might look to nineties San Francisco for West Coast context, including Lynn Hershman Leeson, who made the film *Conceiving Ada*, about a computer artist making a CD-ROM, which starred Tilda Swinton as Ada Lovelace and included appearances by John Perry Barlow, Bruce Sterling, and Timothy Leary. That same year—1997—Ellen Ullman's *Close to the Machine* (City Lights) was published, recounting her work as a computer engineer. I wrote about the camgirl art movement in the 2014 book *Art and the Internet* (Black Dog Publishing, 2014, 18–23). Jennifer Ringley reported that JenniCam received 100 million page views a week, but that was self-reported, and Theresa M. Senft quibbles with its likelihood in her book *Camgirls: Celebrity and Community in the Age of Social Networks* (Peter Lang, 2008, 24). There have been a few recent pieces looking back at Anacam, including Heather Saul in *The Independent* ("What Happened to One of the First Ever Internet Stars," January 29, 2016) and Ana Voog for *Vice* Broadly ("I Was One of the Most Famous People Online in 1998—Then I Disappeared," June 22, 2018). If one wishes to explore the "Universal Sleep Station," well, the Internet Archive has you covered (e.g., October 12, 1999, web.archive.org/web/19991012223749/http://www.voog.com/). Melissa Gira Grant's essay "She Was a Camera" appeared on *Rhizome* (October 26, 2011). Wafaa Bilal's anecdotes come from his book *Shoot an Iraqi: Art, Life and Resistance Under the Gun* (City Lights, 2008, 79–86). Nicole Carpenter wrote about "The Gentle Side of Twitch" for Gizmodo (April 23, 2019). "What is more beautiful than a road?" George Sand wrote in the 1845 novel *Consuelo* ("Qu'y a-t-il de plus beau qu'un chemin? pensait-elle; c'est le symbole et l'image d'une vie active et variée"). A *Wired* magazine style guide from the nineties said the term "Information Superhighway" covered the "whole digital enchilada," so I'm going with that definition. Anyone interested in more recent online communities of teenage girls, similar to my experiences, might wish to research Neopets and Laundromatic (Laundro), among other spaces. Some images and information about "DeadOnline" can be found at this website: http://14forums.blogspot.com/2013/05/deadonline_268.html. Leonsis's "Carnival Cruise Lines" quote comes from a *Wired* article (Mark Nollinger, "America, Online!," September 1, 1995). Leonsis's competition with two hundred thousand websites was discussed in *The New York Times* (Jesse Kornbluth, "Who Needs America Online?," December 24, 1995). Privatization of the internet backbone—principal data routes—allowed services like AOL to thrive, and background on that might be read on the website for the National Science Foundation ("A Brief History of NSF and the Internet," August 13, 2003). In response to a question on Quora, "How much did it cost AOL to distribute all those CDs back in the 1990s? Whose idea was it?," Reggie Fairchild, a former AOL employee, wrote, "When we launched AOL 4.0 in 1998, AOL used ALL of the world-wide CD production for several weeks. Think of that. Not a single music CD or Microsoft CD was produced during those weeks. I still remember hand delivering the Golden Master to Lisa in Marketing" (December 28, 2010). AOL issued a press release in February 2015 saying that it had 2.2 million subscribers in Q4 in 2014. Leonsis spoke with Kara Swisher on her podcast *Recode Decode* in 2016, and explained AOL's decline in tandem with the rise of Google ("I wake up one day and basically they took everything we did on AOL. Mail. Messaging. Maps. Streaming video. You just go down the list and they did it better, faster, cheaper. And it was free. They didn't have to be dependent on access"). Of course, the company did make AOL email accounts free in 2006 (Saul Hansell and Richard Siklos, "In a Shift, AOL Mail to Be Free," *The New York Times*, August 3, 2006). The company also attempted to pivot to surveillance capitalism with Oath, Verizon's bundle of AOL and Yahoo, which Nilay Patel and Ben Popper covered in the Verge ("Oath isn't just a terrible name—it's going to be a nightmare ad-tracking machine," April 5, 2017). Another quirky thing about the company is how many media and politics VIP types held on to their AOL addresses until as recently as the past ten years. Ben Smith, in a piece for *Politico* ("AOL Email as Status Symbol," September 9, 2011), listed a few AOL holdouts at the time, including David Axelrod, Arianna Huffington, Matt Drudge, and Tina Brown. He summarized that "part of the reason some never switched is that they were early adoptors of mobile devices, which don't care which service you're using. And if they've held on this long, there's really no reason to give up now on something that's cycled back to being a status symbol." The section about race on the internet largely draws from Lisa Nakamura's research in *Cybertypes: Race, Ethnicity, and Identity on the Internet* (Routledge, 2002). The founding of LatinoLink was reported in the *San Francisco Chronicle* (Jamie Beckett, "LatinoLink Founder's Vision for Hispanic Web Site Pays Off," June 22, 2012) and the New York *Daily News* (George Mannes, "Multi-cultural Web They Weave," October 27, 1996). Mikhel Proulx's studies of Skawennati Tricia Fragnito's CyberPowWow include a paper he published, "CyberPowWow: Digital Natives and the First Wave of Online Publication" (*Journal of Canadian Art History* 36, no. 1, Concordia University, Fall 2016). "When it comes to access to technology for persons of color," Jeffery Chester, the executive director of the Center for Digital Democracy (previously called the Center for Media Education), told *The Village Voice*, "The dividing line is income, not race. You have equal number of poor whites who have the same kind [of] tough odds of getting access as African Americans or Hispanics." Chester's quote comes from the story "Wired Like Me" (David Kushner, March 30, 1999), which profiles Benjamin Sun, the CEO of Asian Avenue, and addresses the challenges McLean Greaves and Lavonne Luquis faced raising capital. Cafe los Negroes came to life for me when I visited the old website courtesy of the Internet Archive's Wayback Machine. The note about the posters in Bed-Stuy comes from Charisse Jones's story in *The New York Times* ("Power Through Cyberspace," August 3, 1996). I interviewed Mendi and Keith Obadike over email in 2017. The earlier quote comes from Coco Fusco's interview with Keith Obadike in 2011, which is available to view on the Obadikes' website Blackness for Sale ("All Too Real: The Tale of an On-Line Black Sale: Coco Fusco Interviews Keith Townsend Obadike," September 24, 2001). The figure of 24,835 deaths due to AIDS complications in New York comes from a *New York* magazine feature ("AIDS in New York: A Biography," May 26, 2006). I had Sarah Schulman's *The Gentrification of the Mind: Witness to a Lost Imagination* (University of California Press, 2012) in mind when I was writing that section. But it is important not to forget, as the protesters at the Whitney Museum's 2018 David Wojnarowicz retrospective were there to remind us all, that "AIDS is not history." Phil Agre's paper was published in *The Information Society* 10, no. 2 ("Surveillance and Capture: Two Models of Privacy," 1994). Acid Phreak's trolling of John Perry Barlow with the assistance of Phiber Optik, as Fred Turner recounted in *From Counterculture to Cyberculture*, has a happy-ish ending of sorts. Barlow said in an August 2013 Ask Me Anything on Reddit, "I got a phone call from Phiber Optik, who is now back to being Mark Abene. He now lives in San Jose, has one small child and another soon to arrive, a successful Infosec company and a life. It was so great to hear from him. We are very excited to get together again. Meanwhile, we're still fighting exactly the same war we were then. It's just a lot bigger and more complicated than it was in those halcyon days."

## 3. VISIBILITY

In 2003, Jennifer Egan wrote a feature for *The New York Times Magazine* that captured what was haunting and surreal about meeting people through websites like Friendster: "No context becomes, in effect, a context all its own—an avatar, if you will, of the city itself. This is how the Internet was supposed to work, and it suggests that the deep impulse behind the success of online dating could reach well beyond dating itself" ("Love in the Time of No Time," November 23, 2003). The Mark Hamill quote comes from an interview in *Rolling Stone* (Brian Hiatt, "Skywalker Speaks: Mark Hamill on Returning to 'Star Wars,'" December 18, 2015). On the *Internet History* podcast, Jonathan Abrams insisted the website delays had more to do with Friendster's loss of users to Myspace. A number of his accounts in that interview contradict my research. Abrams said on the podcast that he created the platform for "friends," and the media misstated his intentions. But contrast these recent statements with what was written in a 2003 *New York Times* profile of danah boyd: "Friendster is trying to cut off any behavior that is not in line with their marketing perspective and the idea that this is a dating site," boyd told the *Times*. "He didn't want to know anything that would help user experiences unless it has to do with dating . . . At another point he told me that it was my type of people who were ruining the system, meaning the Burning Man, freak, San Francisco crowd" (Jonathan Abrams, *Internet History* podcast, September 19, 2016; Michael Erard, "Decoding the New Cues in Online Society," *The New York Times*, November 27, 2003). The quote about Friendster as a "way to surf through [Abrams's] friends' address books for good-looking girls" comes from another *New York Times* story (Gary Rivlin, "Wallflower at the Web Party," October 15, 2006). Abrams's "cute single friends" quote comes from the *SF Weekly* (Lessley Anderson, "Attack of the Smartasses," August 13, 2003). Abrams's denial comes from an interview with Mashable (Seth Fiegerman, "Friendster Founder Tells His Side of the Story, 10 Years After Facebook," February 3, 2014). Alice Marwick created a useful list of texts called the LiveJournal Academic Research Bibliography (https://archive.fo/kEr7T), and has written extensively about the platform as a transition from old internet habits to emerging blog culture and social media. My source for the information on Indymedia was C. W. Anderson's paper "From Indymedia to Demand Media: Journalism's Visions of Its Audience and the Horizons of Democracy" (in *The Social Media Reader*, edited by Michael Mandiberg, NYU Press, 2012, 77–96) and a CNN report on the Seattle Indymedia Center and WTO Protests (Don

Knapp, "Seattle Protests Seen Through Other Eyes," December 2, 1999). Danyl Strype wrote a more recent consideration of Indymedia's influence and decline, including its unique software ("What we would now call a CMS didn't exist in 1999. There was no Drupal [2000], no WordPress [2003], and no Joomla [2005]"). Strype's May 12, 2017, post "Indymedia in Hindsight" is available to read on the website CoActivate. For context on bloggers getting fired, it is worth reading Leon Neyfakh's report "Online Weblog Leads to Firing" (*The Harvard Crimson*, May 26, 2004). I was pleased to see that the blogger mentioned in the *Crimson* piece later went on to create another blog, just as sarcastic as before, with an "about" section that now reads, "This is a lame personal blog. It's mostly me whining!" It was last updated in the winter of 2018. (Other references for this section: Evan Hansen, "Google Blogger: 'I Was Terminated,'" CNET, February 11, 2005; Miles Klee, "A Very Personal History of Being Fired over Blogs," *The Daily Dot*, March 8, 2017; Stefanie Olsen, "Friendster Fires Developer for Blog," CNET, August 31, 2004.) "Almost 60 percent of all adults in America experienced the internet in 2002" comes from the Pew Research Center's August 2003 report "Internet Use by Region in the U.S." Second Life's average user age was thirty-seven, according to Rosa Mikeal Martey and Mia Consalvo's study "Performing the Looking-Glass Self: Avatar Appearance and Group Identity in Second Life," which appeared in *Popular Communication* 9, no. 3 (2011). The Roy Batty manifesto is discussed in Julia Angwin's *Stealing MySpace: The Battle to Control the Most Popular Website in America* (Random House, 2009, 55) and in a blog post by danah boyd, "The Fakester Manifesto" (*Apophenia*, July 30, 2003). The *SF Weekly* quote about the Lexington Club fakester comes from Lessley Anderson's "Attack of the Smartasses," a story that also covered the fakester parodies of Abrams. "Suddenly having access to people different than them, some users used the network to attack. On Friendster, the Neo-Nazis went wild, going after people of visible color. They used the power of the network to connect to large groups of people, pseudo-anonymously. For many, this was the ideal case. But for those being attacked, this was horrifying," said danah boyd in a presentation for the 2004 conference Etech. While there were multiple reports of white supremacists and neo-Nazis visible on Friendster, I could not corroborate this, or find examples of neo-Nazis ganging up and sending threatening messages to people of color telling them to get off the platform. Not that these users had teams to turn to when they were experiencing abuse. In a paper co-written with Jeffrey Heer ("Profiles as Conversation: Networked Identity Performance on Friendster," in *Proceedings of the Hawai'i International Conference on System Sciences* [HICSS-39], Persistent Conversation Track, Kauai, HI: IEEE Computer Society, January 4–7, 2006), boyd wrote, "A group of Neo-Nazis used the service to track down people of color." I was unable to confirm this independently and emailed boyd, who told me she no longer has the source for this anecdote. However, a 2003 blog post on HackWriters, "Confessions of a FRIENDSTER addict," indicates how visible these hostile users were to the Friendster community ("Apparently, a group of Neo Nazis were using the site to recruit members and spread information about upcoming hate mongering events. Many of these racial supremacists posted their dogs [usually pit bulls] online and linked them to other Petsters. They even had their dogs write gracious testimonials about other pets. Once this was discovered, lines were drawn in the Petster community whether to oust the Neo Nazis by reporting them to Friendster staff or to keep quiet about the matter as Petsters were risking their own expulsion at this time"). The section on Myspace draws from Julia Angwin's research in *Stealing MySpace*, including the detail on the name coming from a former online storage company (22). The quote about "trailer-park aesthetics" comes from Janet Maslin ("A Web Beast with a Rough Back Story," *The New York Times*, March 16, 2009). More than five times as many users visited Myspace as Friendster in 2005, according to Nielsen/NetRatings. The Spyspace "Frequently Asked Questions" page is archived at web.archive.org/web/20070708061856/http://spyspace.cc:80/faq.php. Spyspace was largely ignored in the media, with the exception of Reyhan Harmanci's story in the *San Francisco Chronicle* ("Online, No One Knows You. Really?," April 6, 2007). More recently, "Spyspace" was the name of a Government Communications Headquarters social networking site, according to "ALL OF THE SIGNALS ALL OF THE TIME," in Luke Harding's

*The Snowden Files: The Inside Story of the World's Most Wanted Man* (Vintage, 2016). I emailed the founder of Spyspace, who still checks the email account listed on its archived page. He told me, "whatta time to be alive!" but was unavailable for further questions. The danah boyd quote on Myspace and Facebook comes from "White Flight in Networked Publics? How Race and Class Shaped American Teen Engagement with MySpace and Facebook," which appeared in *Race After the Internet* (ed. Lisa Nakamura and Peter A. Chow-White, Routledge, 2012, 207). The Facebook cofounder Dustin Moskovitz attributes the moral panic around Myspace to Facebook's success. On Twitter, he wrote that "the 'tech was good and now it's bad' narrative is misrepresenting the past. There have always been quite negative stories about tech. Facebook was successful in part due to rampant 2004 fears about child predators on Myspace. Tech is/was good AND bad" (twitter.com/moskov/status/942470488017850369, December 17, 2017). Matt Richtel addressed the issue in "Myspace.com Moves to Keep Sex Offenders Off of Its Site" (*The New York Times*, December 6, 2006), and Alice E. Marwick further considered it in *First Monday* ("To Catch a Predator? The Myspace Moral Panic," June 2, 2008). Both men and women were ranked on Facemash before it became Facebook, but the ranking was arguably more insidious when applied to women at Harvard (Katharine Kaplan, "Facemash Creator Survives Ad Board," *The Harvard Crimson*, November 19, 2003). In 2007, a Harvard engineer created a secret app called both Judgebook and Prettyorwitty to rank random Facebook users. It was released internally with the launch of the Facebook Platform for third-party developers. It reminded Kate Losse of a comment Zuckerberg made about "having to choose between a girl who looks like a model or is smart . . . only in web application form" (*The Boy Kings*, 127). I learned about "babe ticker" in Angwin's *Stealing MySpace* (221). Annie Karni's *Politico* story "In Jared Kushner, Trump Finds a Kindred Spirit" (November 18, 2016) details, "At *The New York Observer*, which he bought when he was 25, Kushner pushed for the newspaper to launch a standalone website called 'Socialite Slapdown.' It was fully his idea: to rate Manhattan's 64 reigning socialites by 'birth, brains, beauty and brio' to see 'who comes out on top.'" See also reports about Jeff Bezos's "women flow," which wasn't an actual app but an approach to dating inspired by "deal flow" on Wall Street. The updates on Myspace Tom drew from Business Insider (Nicholas Carlson, "Myspace Tom: I Am 'The Guy Who Sold Myspace for $580 Million While You Slave Away Hoping for a Half-Day Off,'" December 20, 2012). Kyunchi's "Myspace is the new Woodstock" comment comes from a *Paper* magazine interview (Katherine Gillespie, "Kyunchi Is Making MySpace Music for 2019," January 28, 2019). Information about LiveJournal's transition comes from Steven T. Wright's reporting in Ars Technica ("'The Linux of Social Media': How LiveJournal Pioneered [Then Lost] Blogging," January 22, 2019; also see David Lumb, "George R. R. Martin, the Last Great LiveJournal User, Leaves the Platform," Engadget, April 16, 2018). Eva Giraud's 2014 paper for Convergence, "Has Radical Participatory Online Media Really 'Failed'? Indymedia and Its Legacies" provides context for the Independent Media Center decline. Josh Millard, in a MetaFilter Metatalk thread ("MetaFilter revenue update: holy cow, y'all!") dated June 28, 2018, says, "Recurring contributions supporting the site are up by almost $10,000 a month and growing, erasing our current shortfall and helping move MetaFilter toward a more sustainable, independent revenue model." The Art Spiegelman quote is a paraphrase—sort of—of Marshall McLuhan, and comes from a *Chicago Tribune* profile (Christopher Borrelli, "Art Spiegelman's Art Obliterates Category," May 25, 2013). Current ownership of Friendster is woolly: it's owned by MOL Global, but that company was acquired by Razer Inc.

## 4. SHARING

Something I was thinking about that didn't quite fit in this chapter, but nevertheless speaks of the period of transition, is that before *Lincoln* began filming in 2011, Daniel Day-Lewis sent old limericks to his costar Sally Field, signing off "Yours, A." The legendary Method actor stayed in character even over text message (Jessica Winter, "Daniel Day-Lewis: How the Greatest Living Actor Became Lincoln," *Time*, October 25, 2012). The figure "42 percent of American seniors" comes from a 2017 Pew Research report on technology use among seniors.

"Myspace users had been predominantly under the age of thirty-five," according to a 2010 Statista poll. Also relevant here is "Balk's Law," coined by the editor of the Awl, Alex Balk: "Everything you hate about The Internet is actually everything you hate about people." Aaron Sorkin's Golden Globes speech is widely available on video-sharing sites. "In 2010, Apple sold 39.9 million. By 2014 there were 169.2 million" comes from Statista polling, as well as "two hundred million new Apple phones, including the billion and a half iPhones already in someone's possession." The founders of both Airbnb and Uber were in Washington, D.C., for Obama's inauguration, according to Walter Isaacson in *The New York Times* ("How Uber and Airbnb Became Poster Children for the Disruption Economy," June 19, 2017). I wrote about the transition from flip phones to iPhones earlier in a piece for Medium ("iPhone Dreams," April 24, 2014). For more on the topic of sharing and context collapse, see the "Twitter is public" debate on Gawker and elsewhere circa 2013. One of the origins of Weird Twitter humor was Something Awful's FYAD (Fuck You And Die) forum, memorialized recently in *Vice* Motherboard (Taylor Wofford, "Fuck You And Die: An Oral History of Something Awful," April 5, 2017). Google "twitter 'what you had for breakfast'" and you'll find examples of this knee-jerk reaction to it circa 2009. Alan Rusbridger, the then editor in chief of *The Guardian*, said in a 2010 lecture in Sydney, "I've lost count of the times people—including a surprising number of colleagues in media companies—roll their eyes at the mention of Twitter. 'No time for it,' they say. 'Inane stuff about what twits are having for breakfast.'" A transcript of his lecture is available on *The Guardian*'s website ("The Splintering of the Fourth Estate," November 19, 2010). Instagram's iPhone exclusivity felt similar to Apple's subtle stigma of text messages in green bubbles—those that were sent from non-iPhone devices, often less expensive devices—versus the inter-iPhone text message exchanges sent in blue. Instagram is currently experimenting with features that hide metrics including the number of likes a post receives. Ben Grosser's art project *Facebook Demetricator* (2012–present), which removes metrics like number of shares or likes, might have been an inspiration for this move. The Lady Gaga quote comes from Ann Powers's profile in the *Los Angeles Times* ("Lady Gaga: 'I find that men get away with saying a lot in this business, and that women get away with saying very little,'" December 10, 2009). Nicholas Confessore, Gabriel J. X. Dance, Richard Harris, and Mark Hansen reported on the practice of buying and selling followers in *The New York Times* ("The Follower Factory," January 27, 2018). Another *New York Times* report touched on fake traffic to YouTube videos (Michael H. Keller, "The Flourishing Business of Fake YouTube Views," August 11, 2018). Gaby Dunn wrote a great piece, "Get Rich or Die Vlogging: The Sad Economics of Internet Fame," for Fusion (December 14, 2015). There is a physical world equivalent, too, as a Bloomberg story revealed (Sarah Frier, "Silicon Valley Is Sneaking Models into This Year's Holiday Parties," December 7, 2017). Sometimes the influencers themselves are fake. According to John Kelly, the founder and CEO of data analytics company Graphika, testifying in a Senate Intelligence Committee hearing, "far-right and far-left bot accounts produce 25 to 30 times more posts and messages per day than standard, authentic user accounts." This quote is summarized in a story in The Verge (Makena Kelly, "Lawmakers warn 'time is running out' in fight against online election interference," August 1, 2018). The Sally Mann quote comes from "The Munger System," in *Hold Still* (Little, Brown, 2015). For background on reaction images and appropriation, I recommend reading Lauren Michele Jackson's "We Need to Talk About Digital Blackface in GIFs" (*Teen Vogue*, August 3, 2017). Tumblr created a platform for an existing practice. Jason Kottke, on kottke.org—"one of the oldest blogs on the web"—has a post, "Tumblelogs," from October 19, 2005, that explains where the "quick and dirty stream of consciousness" style departs from typical blogging (https://kottke.org/05/10/tumblelogs). In 2013, nearly half of all Tumblr users were between the ages of sixteen and twenty-four, according to a GlobalWebIndex study. The Kate Zambreno quote comes from *Heroines* (Semiotext(e), 2012, 278). Richard Ford's comment about "some guy sitting in his basement in Terre Haute" comes from Motoko Rich reporting in *The New York Times* ("Are Book Reviewers Out of Print?" May 2, 2007). John R. MacArthur's comments come from a column, "I Won't Hug This File—I Won't Even Call It My Friend," which first appeared in *Providence Journal* and was later republished on the *Harper's Magazine* blog on December 17, 2010. Michael Dirda, a critic for *The Washington Post*, made a similar point: "If you were an author, would you want your book reviewed in *The Washington Post* and *The New York Review of Books*—or on a website written by someone who uses the moniker NovelGobbler or Biografiend? The book review section, whether of a newspaper or a magazine, remains the forum where new titles are taken seriously as works of art and argument, and not merely as opportunities for shallow grandstanding and overblown ranting, all too often by kids hoping to be noticed for their sass and vulgarity. Should we allow our culture to descend to this playground level of discourse?" The National Book Critics Circle blog, where his comment appeared, can be accessed through the Wayback Machine (https://web.archive.org/web/20070504052340/http://bookcriticscircle.blogspot.com/2007/04/marie-arana-book-editor-washington-post.html). Several websites have covered Tumblr's decline (Gita Jackson, "In 2018, Tumblr Is a Joyless Black Hole," Kotaku, July 2, 2018; Brian Feldman, "Tumblr's Unclear Future Shows That There's No Money in Internet Culture," *New York*, June 28, 2017; Seth Fiegerman, "How Yahoo Derailed Tumblr," Mashable, June 15, 2016; Joe Porter, "Tumblr was removed from Apple's App Store over child pornography issues," The Verge, November 20, 2018), but, as I write this, WordPress is set to buy it, so there's some hope for a turnaround. The EFF quote comes from an explainer on its website, "Section 230 of the Communications Decency Act." Sara M. Watson's report "Toward a Constructive Technology Criticism" is available to read on the *Columbia Journalism Review* website (October 4, 2016). Winona Ryder appeared on *Late Night with Jimmy Fallon* on January 10, 2011.

## 5. CLASH

A Twitter service known as Topsy indicated there were 75,465 #SolidarityIsForWhiteWomen tweets, according to Susana Loza's "Hashtag Feminism, #SolidarityIsForWhiteWomen, and the Other #FemFuture," which appeared in issue no. 5 of *Ada: Journal of Gender, New Media, and Technology*. Mikki Kendall wrote about her experience for

*The Guardian*, "#SolidarityIsForWhiteWomen: Women of Color's Issue with Digital Feminism" (August 14, 2013). For context, read Julia Carrie Wong, "Who's Afraid of Suey Park?" (*The Nation*, June 29, 2015), for her point that hashtags gave users the "power to direct thousands of people on social media and drive a narrative without permission from any editor, publication or other form of traditional media gatekeeper." The hashtag #BlackLivesMatter first appeared on Twitter in July 2013 in response to the acquittal of George Zimmerman. A Pew Research Center analysis of public tweets using Crimson Hexagon software found the hashtag had been used nearly thirty million times on Twitter, an average of 17,002 times per day from July 2013 through May 1, 2018 ("An Analysis of #BlackLivesMatter and Other Twitter Hashtags Related to Political or Social Issues," Pew, July 11, 2018). The code for scores that were part of *Slate*'s 2014 "The Year in Outrage" no longer works, so I referred to screenshots taken shortly after it was published. Kartina Richardson wrote about a similar project that took place on Gawker ("Gawker's 'Privilege Tournament' Is All About White Anger," *Salon*, September 30, 2013). Four years after the Outrage meters, *Slate*'s then editor in chief Julia Turner indicated a change in vision when she told the *Columbia Journalism Review*, "Broadly the internet has been good at elevating the voices of people whose voices were not necessarily sufficiently represented in traditional pre-internet news coverage. I think that's true about gender, I think it's true about race, I think it's true about sexuality" ("Slate's 'Pivot to Words,'" *The Kicker* podcast, January 25, 2018). The Sara Ahmed quote comes from a post on her blog, *Feministkilljoys*, entitled "Pushy Feminists" (November 17, 2014). Jon Ronson made the comment about users being worse than the NSA in interviews with Jon Stewart, *Boing Boing*, and others. Melissa Gira Grant first wrote about *Lean In* for *The Washington Post* ("Sheryl Sandberg's 'Lean In' Campaign Holds Little for Most Women," February 25, 2013). Anna Holmes confirmed the dinner party in a defense of Sheryl Sandberg for *The New Yorker*, arguing that "many of the most full-throated defenses of Sandberg came from women who had actually met her. Last autumn, Sandberg's P.R. team invited a group of about twenty writers—including this one—to a dinner at Estancia 460, a restaurant in lower Manhattan" ("Maybe You Should Read the Book: The Sheryl Sandberg Backlash," June 18, 2017). Other comments about the dinner party appeared on Twitter. Responses to Grant include Michelle Goldberg ("The Absurd Backlash Against Sheryl Sandberg's 'Lean In,'" *Daily Beast*, March 1, 2013), Jessica Valenti ("Sheryl Sandberg Isn't the Perfect Feminist. So What?," *The Washington Post*, March 1, 2013), and Katha Pollitt ("Who's Afraid of Sheryl Sandberg?," *The Nation*, June 29, 2015). The *Harvard Business Review* report "Research: Women Ask for Raises as Often as Men, but Are Less Likely to Get Them" was authored by Benjamin Artz, Amanda Goodall, and Andrew J. Oswald (June 25, 2018). Michelle Goldberg updated her views in the book review "Ivanka Trump's Book Celebrates the Unlimited Possibilities Open to Women with Full-Time Help" (*Slate*, May 2, 2017). "What If Trayvon Martin Was Wearing Google Glasses?" was posted to Medium by Eric Kuhn (July 15, 2013). The first issue of *Model View Culture*, which was published in January 2014, is available online. For more context, in 2014, Astra Taylor and I co-wrote an essay for *The Baffler* on sexism and Silicon Valley, "The Dads of Tech." The TechCrunch report "Julie Ann Horvath Describes Sexism and Intimidation Behind Her GitHub Exit" was authored by Alex Wilhelm and Alexia Tsotsis (March 18, 2014). GitHub hired a third-party investigator to look into Horvath's allegations. Chris Wanstrath published the findings on the company blog on April 28, 2014 ("Follow up to the investigation results"). The investigator found that "Tom Preston-Werner in his capacity as GitHub's CEO acted inappropriately, including confrontational conduct, disregard of workplace complaints, insensitivity to the impact of his spouse's presence in the workplace, and failure to enforce an agreement that his spouse should not work in the office." However, the "investigation found no information to support misconduct or opportunistic behavior by the engineer against Julie or any other female employees in the workplace. Furthermore, there was no information found to support Julie's allegation that the engineer maliciously deleted her code." There have been, unfortunately, many high-profile cases of harassment on- and offline even earlier, including Ariel Waldman's experiences on Twitter in 2008 and Adria Richards's experience at PyCon in 2013, but I chose to focus on Horvath's case because it was among the first to receive major media coverage. *Slate* published a piece looking back on #EndFathersDay and the women who unraveled the 4chan plot ("The Black Feminists Who Saw the Alt-Right Threat Coming," April 23, 2019). The tweets that I cited were saved in Storify, which is no longer in operation; however, the threads have been archived (archive.is/s4Bsy). I'Nasah Crockett wrote about her experiences in *Model View Culture* ("'Raving Amazons': Antiblackness and Misogynoir in Social Media," June 30, 2014). Sydette Harry also wrote about #YourSlipIsShowing for *Model View Culture* ("Everyone Watches, Nobody Sees: How Black Women Disrupt Surveillance Theory," October 6, 2014). "Men's rights activist" watchdog blog *We Hunted the Mammoth* includes links and quotes from some of the #EndFathersDay instigators ("#EndFathersDay: Trolls Being Trolls, or 'Black Propaganda' Designed to Tear Apart Feminism?," June 15, 2014). The Sydette Harry quote comes from a tweet dated June 17, 2014 (https://twitter.com/Blackamazon/status/478915430095265794). The Sarah Jeong quote comes from her book *The Internet of Garbage* (Forbes Media, 2015). Kathy Sierra looked back on her harassment in a piece for *Wired*, "Why the Trolls Will Always Win" (October 8, 2014). Greg Sandoval profiled Sierra for The Verge ("The End of Kindness: Weev and the Cult of the Angry Young Man," September 12, 2013). Sarah Nyberg's essay was posted to Medium ("I'm Sarah Nyberg, and I Was a Teenage Edgelord," September 14, 2015). Gabrielle Union had a piece about the celebrity photo hack in *Cosmopolitan* magazine ("My Nude Photos Were Stolen, and I'm Fighting Back," November 5, 2014). The case is ongoing as I write this, but Casey Viner and Tyler Barriss have pled guilty to the 2017 Wichita, Kansas, swatting, in which the victim was fatally shot ("Ohio Gamer Who Recruited 'Swatter' Tyler Barriss in Hoax That Turned Deadly Pleads Guilty," Associated Press, April 3, 2019). The Shiichan Anonymous BBS manifesto is available to view online (https://archive.fo/Ullmq). David Kushner wrote the *Rolling Stone* profile of moot ("4chan's Overlord Christopher

Poole Reveals Why He Walked Away," March 13, 2015). For more on the sale of 4chan, see Klint Finley, "4chan Just Sold to the Founder of the Original 'Chan,'" *Wired*, September 21, 2015). Poole's blog post dated March 7, 2016, "My next chapter," on his personal blog, *Chris Hates Writing*, discusses his move to Google. An interview with Natacha Stolz appeared in *Rhizome* (Anonymous, "Blogrolls, Trolls, and Interior Scrolls: A Conversation with Natacha Stolz," November 24, 2010). Later, I interviewed Cole Stryker for *Rhizome* ("Cole Stryker, Author of 'Epic Win for Anonymous,' on Interior Semiotics, Context Collapse, and 'You Rage You Lose,'" September 12, 2011). In that interview, he summarized 4chan's indignation by saying that the "internet used to be full of geeks like us, but now it's being overrun by normals trying to be cool, just like the real world we rejected in favor of the internet. We need to put them in their place." Whitney Phillips, an assistant professor of communication and rhetorical studies at Syracuse University, argues that much of what was called "internet culture" from 2008 to 2012 included harmful "identity-based antagonisms." This humor "didn't just have its tentacles in trolling circles, but was pervasive within academic institutions and news and entertainment outlets as well. Its underlying message, beamed in from all the channels I was tuned to (and bad on me for not having a more diverse set of channels), was that there are no consequences, it's just the internet, nothing is real. Lol" ("It Wasn't Just the Trolls: Early Internet Culture, 'Fun,' and the Fires of Exclusionary Laughter," *Social Media + Society*, July–September 2019). Mattathias Schwartz's story "Malwebolence—The World of Web Trolling" appeared in *The New York Times Magazine* (August 3, 2008). Jessica Bennett wrote about Nikki Catsouras in *Newsweek* ("One Family's Fight Against Grisly Web Photos," April 18, 2011). For context on white supremacy in music subcultures, see David Stubbs in *The Quietus* ("Eric Clapton & Enoch Powell to Morrissey: Race in British Music Since '76," August 9, 2016), Stephen Rodrick in the *Chicago Reader* ("Ska Story: The Sound of Angry Young England," March 22, 1990), and a reported piece in *The New York Times* (Wayne King, "Violent Racism Attracts New Breed: Skinheads," January 1, 1989). For more on early internet white supremacists, see David Lazarus, "AOL Lets Klan Site Remain," *Wired*, March 27, 1997, and further discussion in two books (Vron Ware and Les Back, *Out of Whiteness: Color, Politics, and Culture*, University of Chicago Press, 2002; and Jessie Daniels, *Cyber Racism: White Supremacy Online and the New Attack on Civil Rights*, Rowman & Littlefield, 2009). It's worth noting that AOL left the Texas Ku Klux Klan alone at the same time it deleted a page that glamorized serial killers, as Davis Cassel reported in *Salon* ("A Killer Site," October 3, 1997). Whitney Phillips has written widely on trolling and online hate groups, including "The Oxygen of Amplification," a paper for Data & Society (May 22, 2018). Cernovich said he received "seven figures" in a divorce settlement in *The New Yorker* (Andrew Marantz, "Trolls for Trump," October 24, 2016). Immolations's post "How Class Produced Milo, and How Class May Absolve Him" is available to read on Medium (February 26, 2017). It is also archived at https://archive.fo/6321j. Joseph Bernstein's reporting on Lane Davis for BuzzFeed ("Alt-Right Troll to Father Killer: The Unraveling of Lane Davis," July 18, 2018) also addresses the alt-right and its financial incentives, including fund-raising online. Twitter's longtime resistance to antiharassment protection was, in the end, an ill-advised business decision. In the fall of 2016, when the platform aimed to be acquired, companies like Google and Salesforce withdrew their bids, citing its problems with online harassment as a motivating factor. Lee Carter's Twitter thread from September 7, 2018, is available to read at https://archive.fo/cmCgE.

## 6. COMMUNITY

I interviewed Anna Leach on December 27, 2016. The comments cited may be viewed on the *Shiny Shiny* post "Has Facebook Finally Introduced 'Who's Looking at Your Profile'? + UPDATE: Facebook Respond" (December 8, 2010). The JavaScript bookmarklet "Stalker List," which scraped Facebook's JSON file that calculated the "affinity scores," was available on Thekeesh.com ("Who Does Facebook Think You Are Searching For?," March 28, 2013). The podcast and transcript of Mark Zuckerberg's interview with Kara Swisher is available on Recode ("Full Transcript: Facebook CEO Mark Zuckerberg on Recode Decode," July 18, 2018). I interviewed Kate Losse on March 31, 2018. Her comment "this person looks at another person's page a lot" comes from a previous interview with Losse that took place in 2013. On the subject of Facebook-branded relationships, I was inspired by Anna Lauren Hoffmann's observation that "information gathered on Facebook is, in fundamental ways, produced not by users, but by Facebook itself. Users are constrained by the categories and options Facebook offers; their activities are filtered through the site's biases and framed by Facebook's myopic view of sharing" ("Reckoning with a Decade of Breaking Things," *Model View Culture*, June 30, 2014). Kashmir Hill's reporting on the People You May Know feature appears in Gizmodo, including her stories "How Facebook Schemed Against Its Users" (December 12, 2018), "'People You May Know': A Controversial Facebook Feature's 10-Year History" (August 8, 2018), and "How Facebook Figures Out Everyone You've Ever Met" (November 7, 2017). The patent to detect when two phones are in the same location, using accelerometer and gyroscope data, was filed by Ben Chen on behalf of Facebook on July 10, 2014 (USPTO application number 20160014677, "Systems And Methods For Utilizing Wireless Communications To Suggest Connections For A User"). The tweet from user @dylanmckaynz, dated March 21, 2018, reads "Downloaded my facebook data as a ZIP file Somehow it has my entire call history with my partner's mum," and it includes a screenshot of the findings. Heather A. McDonald's essay "People You May Know" was published on *The Rumpus* on September 24, 2018. Zuckerberg's exchange with Stephen Hawking on Facebook in October 2014 has been widely quoted elsewhere, and I have screenshots of the exchange. There was a Chrome extension to harvest the names of users in private patient communities according to reporting in CNBC and elsewhere. A "members-only group for women that have a gene mutation associated with a higher-risk breast cancer, called BRCA"—and a BRCA Sisterhood Facebook group—brought attention to this privacy loophole. See Kate Fazzini and Christina Farr reporting for CNBC, "Facebook Recently Closed a Loophole That Allowed Third Parties to Discover the

Names of People in Private, 'Closed' Facebook Groups," July 11, 2018. The response to Zuckerberg at SXSW Interactive in 2008 was written up in *Wired* (Megan McCarthy and Michael Calore, "SXSW: Zuckerberg Keynote Descends into Chaos as Audience Takes Over," March 9, 2008). Zuckerberg's 2018 keynote was at the F8 Facebook Developer Conference at the McEnery Convention Center in San Jose, California. The note about his samurai sword comes from Business Insider (Alyson Shontell, "Young Mark Zuckerberg Allegedly Threw Water on an Engineer's Computer and Threatened Employees with a Samurai Sword," August 6, 2014), the publication that also published his old chat messages in which he called Facebook users "dumb fucks" (Nicolas Carlson, "Well, These New Zuckerberg IMs Won't Help Facebook's Privacy Problems," May 13, 2010). Dr. Edward Zuckerberg's "initial working capital" is noted in a 2012 SEC filing that explains that in December 2009, the Facebook board "issued an aggregate of 2,000,000 shares of our Class B common stock to Glate LLC, an entity owned by Mr. Zuckerberg's father." The September 13, 2010, *New Yorker* profile, "The Face of Facebook," in which Zuckerberg confirms the "dumb fucks" message, was written by Jose Antonio Vargas. Facebook rewarded its partners with user data, according to Olivia Solon and Cyrus Farivar, reporting for NBC News ("Mark Zuckerberg leveraged Facebook user data to fight rivals and help friends, leaked documents show," April 16, 2019). The emotional contagion experiment on 689,003 Facebook users, and the paper presenting its findings (Adam D. I. Kramer et al., "Experimental Evidence of Massive-Scale Emotional Contagion through Social Networks," *PNAS*, National Academy of Sciences, June 17, 2014), has been widely cited elsewhere. For an example of law enforcement creating actual fake profiles, see George Joseph's report "Meet 'Bob Smith,' the Fake Facebook Profile Memphis Police Allegedly Used to Spy on Black Activists" (The Appeal, August 2, 2018). Aura Bogado's report "How White Separatists Disable Native American Facebook Accounts" appeared on Colorlines (July 31, 2015). Dana Lone Hill also reported on this with the story "Facebook Don't Believe in Indian Names" for the website Last Real Indians (February 6, 2015). The Chris Cox quote comes from his

Facebook post on October 1, 2014, "I Want to Apologize to the Affected Community of Drag Queens, Drag Kings, Transgender . . ." Ello was a "Facebook killer," according to an October 23, 2014, headline on *Wired*, "'Facebook Killer' Ello Hatches Plan to Stay Ad-free Forever." The *Guardian* quote that Ello was "positioning itself as a network with a social conscience" comes from Ruby J. Murray, in a piece dated September 26, 2014, "Ello Might or Might Not Replace Facebook, but the Giant Social Network Won't Last Forever." Its "idealism might be the real deal" is a quote from Nathaniel Mott in "Why Ello's Idealism Might Be the Real Deal" (Pando, October 23, 2014). The "thirty thousand sign-up requests an hour" figure comes from Mike Butcher writing for TechCrunch ("Ello, Ello? New 'No Ads' Social Network Ello Is Blowing Up Right Now," September 25, 2014). The scandal involving the Ello cofounder Paul Budnitz began with a Facebook post by Colorado-based Black Sheep Bikes, dated July 11, 2013, which explained that Budnitz, in his previous venture, Budnitz Bicycles, "wanted us to make him replicas of the bikes we had already made with the potential to go over seas and have them massed produced. As you can imagine we felt like this wasn't the best idea for our company and went against why we build these bikes with our own hands here in Colorado in the first place . . . So we told him we weren't interested. Mr. B however is a man with money and the means to do as he pleases so he took our bikes had them replicated (kind of) at another American bike company and now has some being produced over seas." The post was further discussed on the blog *Bike Snob NYC* ("Your Monday Inspiration: The More Things Change, the More They Get Brittle, Old, and Crumbly," July 13, 2013) and in the comments on the blog *The Radavist* on July 22, 2014, regarding a post entitled, "Budnitz Bicycles: The Gift." For context on the "If You're Not Paying, You're the Product" idiom, see Mike Masnick, posting on the blog *Techdirt*, "Stop Saying 'If You're Not Paying, You're the Product'" (December 20, 2012). Nathan Jurgenson forwarded to me the emails he received from Justin Gitlin (Cacheflowe). Tweets from Gitlin to Jurgenson have been archived: https://archive.fo/4WKqM and https://

archive.fo/N0Jt8. Nick Srnicek's piece "We Need to Nationalise Google, Facebook and Amazon. Here's Why" ran in *The Guardian* (August 30, 2017). Daniel Roberts reported "Ello Running Facebook Ads About Creepy Facebook Ads" (*Time,* June 24, 2015). The "nonregistered users" even came up in Facebook, Inc.'s, responses to questions from the U.S. Senate Select Committee on Intelligence. The document is available on the website Intelligence.senate.gov ("Questions for the Record Senate Select Committee on Intelligence Hearing on Foreign Influence Operations Using Social Media," October 26, 2018). The story about the boy and dog with vitiligo appeared in the *Daily Mail* ("Heart-warming moment boy, 8, with vitiligo meets a dog with the SAME skin condition—and now the pair are inseparable," March 22, 2017). The Axios Harris Poll of the 100 Most Visible Companies, in which Facebook was ranked ninety-fourth in reputation, was published March 6, 2019.

### 7. ACCOUNTABILITY

I interviewed Kyra Gaunt in May 2018. She wrote about her ancestor for TED Ideas ("A Powerful Letter from My Great-Great-Grandfather, Who Escaped Slavery in 1855," December 30, 2015). Wikipedia sources were last accessed in 2018. It is notable that many of those like Barlow, speaking of grand utopia internet experiments, had more than just willpower—they had capital. As Audrey Watters has remarked about the place where Barlow wrote his groundbreaking manifesto—Davos, Switzerland, at the World Economic Forum—"that's neither a site nor an institution I've ever really associated with utopia" ("Invisible Labor and Digital Utopias," Hack Education, May 4, 2018). An early profile of Wikipedia in *The Atlantic*, written by Marshall Poe, provided context ("The Hive," September 1, 2006). "Jimmy Wales Is Not an Internet Billionaire," according to a story by Amy Chozick in *The New York Times* (June 27, 2013). On her personal website, Sue Gardner's blog post "Why Wikimedia's New Revenue Strategy Makes Me Happy" explains the revenue model (July 25, 2010). According to *The Boy Kings,* Mark Zuckerberg first imagined building a Wikipedia for all people when he was at Harvard; except for-profit, probably, and—just as crucially—without Wikipedia's editing and culling, for notability or otherwise (88). Brian Feldman, in *New York* magazine, makes an interesting point that Wikipedia can't really do micro-celebrity: there is no YouTube-style star system ("Why Wikipedia Works," March 16, 2018). Another good piece is by Ellen Airhart in *Wired* ("How Wikipedia Portrayed Humanity in a Single Photo," March 12, 2018). Charlie Warzel addressed how user-review sites can be gamed in "Sites Like Yelp and Twitter Are Just Pawns in the Culture War" (BuzzFeed, June 25, 2018). The Wikipedia user's quote about Zoë Quinn was told to Lauren C. Williams ("The 'Five Horsemen' of Wikipedia Paid the Price for Getting Between Trolls and Their Victims," ThinkProgress, March 6, 2015). Michael Mandiberg's text "The Affective Labor of Wikipedia: GamerGate, Harassment, and Peer Production" appeared in *Social Text Journal* (February 1, 2015). For background on Wikipedia, ANI, and harassment issues, I interviewed Caroline Sinders on July 25, 2018. Another problem with Wikipedia is that the "notability" distinction is often used against marginalized groups. Michelle Moravec wrote about this in *Boundary 2* ("The Endless Night of Wikipedia's Notable Woman Problem," July 31, 2018). Carolina A. Miranda reported on the demise of *Vermonica* for the *Los Angeles Times* ("After 24 Years at an L.A. Strip Mall, Sheila Klein's Beloved 'Vermonica' Light Sculpture Is Moved without Notice," November 30, 2017). Thanks to Kim Cooper at Esotouric tours for bringing it to public attention. I interviewed P. Tomi Austin on July 7, 2018. I interviewed Kat Lo in July 2018. Karl Popper's Paradox of Tolerance is often invoked as a counter to the policy of content free-for-all. He defined this in his 1945 book, *The Open Society and Its Enemies* (2nd ed., Routledge, 1952, 265): "Unlimited tolerance must lead to the disappearance of tolerance. If we extend unlimited tolerance even to those who are intolerant, if we are not prepared to defend a tolerant society against the onslaught of the intolerant, then the tolerant will be destroyed, and tolerance with them." Michelle Castillo reported on Reddit's transition from an ad-free platform to a company that began showing up at Cannes Lions in 2017, after raising

$200 million from investors that same year ("Reddit—One of the World's Most Popular Websites—Is Trying to Cash in Through Advertising," July 5, 2018). The BBC reported that Yishan Wong, in a private post to Reddit moderators, said that anything legal should remain on the platform even if "we find it odious or if we personally condemn it" ("Reddit Will Not Ban 'Distasteful' Content, Chief Executive Says," October 17, 2012). Reporting on Alex Jones is widely available online (Julia Carrie Wong and Olivia Solon, "Does the Banning of Alex Jones Signal a New Era of Big Tech Responsibility?," *The Guardian*, August 10, 2018; John Paczkowski and Charlie Warzel, "Apple Kicked Alex Jones Off Its Platform, Then YouTube and Facebook Rushed to Do The Same," BuzzFeed, August 7, 2018; Avie Schneider, "Twitter Bans Alex Jones and InfoWars; Cites Abusive Behavior," NPR, September 6, 2018). Josh Begley wrote about his rejections from the Apple store in *The Intercept* ("After 12 Rejections, Apple Accepts App That Tracks U.S. Drone Strikes," March 28, 2017). Rhett Jones wrote about the ban on Elon Musk parody accounts for Gizmodo ("Twitter Will Lock Your Account If You Try to Impersonate Elon Musk," July 25, 2018). Stephanie M. Lee reported on pro-ana content bans in BuzzFeed ("Why Eating Disorders Are So Hard for Instagram and Tumblr to Combat," April 14, 2016). Benjamin Plackett reported on Reddit moderators for Engadget ("Unpaid and abused: Moderators speak out against Reddit," August 31, 2018), and Casey Newton reported on contract workers moderating Facebook ("The Trauma Floor," The Verge, February 25, 2019). For an even earlier account of this practice, check out Rita Ferrandino's essay "Terms of Service" (*The Village Voice*, March 20, 2001), about her experiences in Albuquerque, New Mexico, where she worked as a moderator with AOL's "Community Action Team" in 1997. I also referred to Sarah T. Roberts's book *Behind the Screen: Content Moderation in the Shadows of Social Media* (Yale University Press, 2019, 73–133) for background on this practice. The quote from Tim Berners-Lee comes from an interview with Katrina Brooker ("'I Was Devastated': The Man Who Created the World Wide Web Has Some Regrets," The Hive, *Vanity Fair*, July 9, 2018). His 1999 statement,

"Happily, the Web is so huge that there's no way any one company can dominate it," comes from his book *Weaving the Web: The Original Design and Ultimate Destiny of the World Wide Web* (HarperOne, 1999, 133). I first came across the quote in Nathan Schneider's "Decentralization: An Incomplete Ambition" (OSF Preprints, March 5, 2019), which is a helpful primer on why decentralization alone is not enough. The "more than 70 percent of the internet" figure I first came across in a blog post by André Staltz on his personal website ("The Web Began Dying in 2014, Here's How," October 30, 2017). Sarah Jaffe wrote the op-ed "Nationalize Amazon" for The Outline (November 15, 2018). I feel it is too early for me to comment on whether the GDPR has been successful. If you search around you'll find pieces in *The Wall Street Journal* that report on how it is anti-competitive and hurts start-ups more than Facebook or Google—but that seems like something *The Wall Street Journal* is already inclined to believe. David Dayen wrote a compelling argument in *The New Republic* on why the best place to begin is to "Ban Targeted Advertising" (April 10, 2018). Darius Kazemi, writing for the Dat Foundation's blog, has explained how internet architecture continues to make decentralization possible ("Three protocols and a future of the decentralized internet," March 22, 2019). The piece "pandora's vox: on community in cyberspace," by Carmen Hermosillo, was included in the anthology *High Noon on the Electronic Frontier* (ed. Peter Ludlow, MIT Press, 1996). It is also widely available online. Adam Curtis appeared on *Jarvis Cocker's Sunday Service* on May 22, 2011, to discuss his documentary program *All Watched Over by Machines with Loving Grace*, which quotes humdog's manifesto. Kim Stanley Robinson defined utopia in an interview with *Amazing Stories* (R. K. Troughton, "Interview with Award-Winning Author Kim Stanley Robinson," September 25, 2013): "One point I've been making all along is that even in a utopian situation, there will still be death and lost love, so there will be no shortage of tragedy in utopia. It will just be the necessary or unavoidable tragedies; which perhaps makes them even worse, or more tragic. They won't be just brutal stupidities, in other words, but reality itself." He said something similar at an event with McKenzie Wark on October 21, 2013, at Eugene Lang College, which is available on YouTube. Utopia, he said, "still has death and still has lost love . . . Just because you're in a utopia doesn't mean you're going to be happy. Only the necessary tragedies."

### CLOSING: END USER

James Vincent reported the story "Transgender YouTubers Had Their Videos Grabbed to Train Facial Recognition Software" for The Verge (August 22, 2017). Samantha Cole reported on old Myspace data for Motherboard, and Olivia Solon reported on IBM scraping data for NBC News ("Actually, Myspace Sold Your Data Too," Motherboard, April 12, 2018; "Facial recognition's 'dirty little secret': Millions of online photos scraped without consent," NBC News, March 12, 2019). Jack Dorsey once compared Twitter, the platform he founded, to Washington Square Park. "There's tourists, students, filmmakers, musicians, street hustlers, weed dealers, chess players. And there's people talking out in the open," he said in an interview with *Rolling Stone.* "The park itself is completely neutral to whatever happens on top of it" (Brian Hiatt, "Twitter CEO Jack Dorsey: The Rolling Stone Interview," January 23, 2019). For more information on racism and public parks, I recommend the scholarship of Kangjae Jerry Lee and David Scott ("Bourdieu and African Americans' Park Visitation: The Case of Cedar Hill State Park in Texas," *Leisure Sciences,* 2016). Blue Origin and Amazon are structured as independent companies, but Jeff Bezos uses his Amazon stock to fund his aerospace company. He is constantly making comments like "Every time you buy shoes, you're helping fund Blue Origin," as he did at the Yale Club in New York in 2019; the transcript of this conversation is available at Business Insider ("Jeff Bezos Just Gave a Private Talk in New York. From Utopian Space Colonies to Dissing Elon Musk's Martian Dream, Here Are the Most Notable Things He Said," February 23, 2019). Tim Cook's announcement about the Apple Carnegie Library comes from a post to his Twitter account on May 1, 2019. The library held ninety-five thousand volumes according to *The Washington Post* (Judith Valente, "UDC Opens $4.2 Million Library, But Its Campus Not Likely to Be Built," December 11, 1980). Andrew Carnegie's philanthropy "was certainly not unimpeachable—it was often warped by his own ego and eccentricity—but we don't need to idealize it in order to admire elements of it, especially his library campaign," Benjamin Soskis wrote in a piece about the complicated history of the library for *Boston Review* ("Apple's Newest Store and the Perverse Logic of Philanthro-Capitalism," May 21, 2019). "Nothing about us without us" is a recommendation in a 2018 report, "#MoreThanCode: Practitioners Reimagine the Landscape of Technology for Justice and Equity," produced by the Research Action Design and the Open Technology Institute (Sasha Costanza-Chock, Maya Wagoner, Berhan Taye, Caroline Rivas, Chris Schweidler, Georgia Bullen, and the T4SJ Project, 2018. Available online at https://morethancode.cc). The closest the internet has to a central library is the Internet Archive. I am deeply appreciative of their hard work archiving websites and digital material, which largely made research for this book possible.

# ACKNOWLEDGMENTS

This book was made possible with time, space, and privacy provided by the Writer's Block and Plympton's Writing Downtown residency and the Logan Nonfiction Program at the Carey Institute. Thanks to Sean McDonald for thoughtful and keen edits. Additional thanks to Danny Vazquez, Naomi Huffman, and the wonderful staff at MCD and FSG, including the production, publicity, and design teams. Melissa Gira Grant believed in this project from the very beginning and offered advice on some of the earliest drafts. Divya Manian and JP LeBreton were also kind enough to provide early feedback on the manuscript. Another early reader (and a Friendster friendship that lasted), Heather McDonald, told me just what my book was actually about, when all I knew was that it was finished. The Carl & Marilynn Thoma Art Foundation, Eyebeam, and the School for Poetic Computation have been tremendous supporters of my work. Eyebeam provided space for the New Topics event series that served as inspiration early on in my research. Thank you to the speakers, including Bina Ahmad, Ingrid Burrington, Kade Crockford, Katherine Cross, Karen Gregory, Seda Gürses, Sydette Harry, Sarah Jeong, Erin Kissane, Karen Levy, Sabrina Majeed, Alice Marwick, Lauren McCarthy, Tressie McMillan Cottom, Sandra Ordonez, Raven Rakia, and sava saheli singh. Thank you, Stacey Allan, Stine An, Nicole Antebi, Dennison Bertram, Farrah Bostic, Allison Burtch, Brendan Byrne, Jace Clayton, Samantha Culp, Betty Devoe, Dan Fox, Chris Habib, Conner Habib, Sara Hendren, Robin Jacks, Sarah Jaffe, Darius Kazemi, Alix Lambert, Jonathan Lethem, Tim Maughan, An Xiao Mina, Richard Nash, Annie Nocenti, John Powers, Courtney Stanton, Astra Taylor, Sara Watson, Sarah Weinman, Jessamyn West, and Lydia Wills, for advice, support, and encouragement. Thank you, old friends from AOL, new friends on Mastodon, and all other friends—I have been very lucky in that regard. Greatest thanks to my family for their love and patience. And in memory of Michael Seidenberg, who cherished authors from the past with as much lively enthusiasm as he extended to people from his present. His boundless care for others is greatly missed. I am forever grateful to have found the eclectic sanctuary that Brazenhead Books once provided.

## A NOTE ABOUT THE AUTHOR

Joanne McNeil was the inaugural winner of the Carl & Marilynn Thoma Art Foundation's Arts Writing Award for an emerging writer. She has been a resident at Eyebeam, a Logan Nonfiction Program fellow, and an instructor at the School for Poetic Computation.